Sustainable Home Refurbishment

Sustainable Home Refurbishment

The Earthscan Expert Guide to Retrofitting Homes for Efficiency

David Thorpe

SERIES EDITOR:
FRANK JACKSON

earthscan
from Routledge

First published 2010 by Earthscan

2 Park Square, Milton Park, Abingdon, Oxon, OX14 4RN
605 Third Avenue, New York, NY 10017

Routledge is an imprint of the Taylor & Francis Group, an informa business

First issued in paperback 2020

ISBN: 978-1-84407-876-9 (hbk)
ISBN: 978-0-367-78753-0 (pbk)

Typeset by Domex e-Data Pvt. Ltd.
Cover design by Yvonne Booth

A catalogue record for this book is available from the British Library

Library of Congress Cataloging-in-Publication Data

Thorpe, Dave, 1954–
    Sustainable home refurbishment : the Earthscan expert guide to retrofitting homes for efficiency / David Thorpe.
        p. cm.
    Includes bibliographical references and index.
    ISBN 978-1-84407-876-9 (hardback)
1. Dwellings–Energy conservation. I Title.
    TJ163.5.D86T49 2010
    696–dc22
                                                        2010000824

Contents

List of Figures and Tables

Figures

Tables

Acknowledgements

Many people and sources provided help during the research for this book. I'd particularly like to thank the following, and apologize to any left out:

For invaluable feedback on early drafts:
Frank Jackson (Green Dragon Energy)
John Williamson (JPW Construction)
Nick Grant (Elemental Solutions)
Stephen Passmore (Housing Development Manager, Energy Saving Trust)
Tom Woolley (especially)

For letting me poke around their homes, quiz them and take pictures:
Alan Simpson
Andy Warren
Anna Jenkins
Chris Lord-Smith
Chris Twinn (Arup)
Dave Baines
Fran and Kevin Blockley
George Marshall
George Monbiot
Hyde Housing (Susie Ward)
John Doggart (chairman of the Sustainable Energy Academy and the Superhomes network)
John Newson
Jon Peck
Julie Grant
Linda Lime
Mark Gillott (Nottingham University Department of the Built Environment)
Penney Poyzer and Gil Schalom
Peter Harper (Centre for Alternative Technology)
Russell Smith (Parity Eco Solutions)

For information and advice:
Andy Rowland (Ecodyfi)
Association of Energy Conscious Builders
Bruce Heagerty
Building Research Establishment
Cath Hassell (Ech2o)
Charles Couzens (Ecos Trust)
Chris Laughton (Very Efficient Heating Company)
Colin Pearson (BSRIA)
Diana Berriman (Llanidloes Resource Centre)
Doug Clarke (SevernTrent)
Energy Saving Trust
Environment Agency

Environment Agency Ireland
Erik Alsema (Copernicus Institute/Utrecht University, the Netherlands)
Gavin Killip and Brenda Boardman (Environmental Change Institute, Oxford University)
Guy Forman (Marsh:Grochowski LLP)
Henrietta Lynch (C.A.T. and the Good Homes Alliance)
Ian Hunter and Dave Woods (Liverpool City Council, Municipal Housing)
John Cantor (John Cantor Heat Pumps Ltd)
Jon Lissimore (Environment Manager, Lambeth Council)
Judith Thornton (Elemental Solutions)
Leonie Onslow (Insulated Render & Cladding Association Ltd)
Lori Tokunaga (Silicon Valley Toxics Coalition)
Mark Cyril (Dewjoc Architects)
Martin Kemp
Paul Davies (Sustainability Technology Manager, Wates)
Phil Horton (Centre for Alternative Technology)
Phil Rigby (Knauf Insulation)
Sara Turnbull (Arup)
Sean Cahill and Daniel Johncock (United House)
Sue Curtis
Thore Oltersdorf and Marek Miara (Franhofer Institute, Germany).

List of Acronyms and Abbreviations

ACH	Air Changes per Hour
AECB	Association of Energy Conscious Builders
ASHP	Air Source Heat Pump
BFRC	British Fenestration Rating Council
BRE	Building Research Establishment
BSHF	Building and Social Housing Foundation
BSI	British Standards Institution
BSRIA	Building Services Research and Information Association
C.A.T.	Centre for Alternative Technology
CEPHEUS	Cost Efficient Passive Houses as European Standards
CFL	Compact Fluorescent Lamp
CHP	Combined Heat and Power
CIBSE	Chartered Institute of Building Services Engineers
CLP	CarbonLite Programme
CO2	carbon dioxide
CoP	Coefficient of Performance
CSH	Code for Sustainable Homes
DEC	Display Energy Certificate
Defra	Department for Environment, Food and Rural Affairs
DHW	Domestic Hot Water
DM	Demand Management
DPC	Damp-proof Course
DTC	Differential Thermostatic Control
EC	European Commission
ECD	Enhanced Construction Details
ELA	Effective Leakage Area
EnEV	German energy saving regulation
EPC	Energy Performance Certificate
EPDM	ethylene propylene diene momomer
EPS	Expanded Polystyrene
FSC	Forest Stewardship Council
GLS	General Lighting Service
GSHP	Ground Source Heat Pump
GWP	Global Warming Potential
HCFCs	hydrochlorofluorocarbons
HFCs	hydrofluorocarbons
ICE	Inventory of Energy and Carbon
IGSHPA	International Ground Source Heat Pump Association
INCA	The Insulated Render and Cladding Association
IPCC	Intergovernmental Panel on Climate Change
KfW	German, government owned development bank
kW	kiloWatt
kWe	kW electrical power
kWh	kWatt-hour

kWp	kW-peak
LBNL	Lawrence Berkeley National Laboratory
LED	Light-emitting Diode
LEED	Leadership in Energy and Environmental Design
lm	lumen
low-e	low-emittance
lx	lux
MDI	methylene diphenyl diisocyanate
Mt	megatonne
MVHR	mechanical Ventilation with Heat Recovery
NF3	nitrogen trifluoride
NO2	nitrogen dioxide
NOx	nitrogen oxide
OLED	organic LED
Ops	organophosphates
ORC	Organic Rankine Cycle
OSB	Oriented Strand Board
PBB	polybrominated biphenyl
PBDE	polybrominated diphenyl ether
PC	personal computer
PCM	Phase Change Materials
PEFC	Programme for the Endorsement of Forest Certification
PEMFCs	Proton Exchange Membrane Fuel Cells
PET	polyethylene terephthalate
PHPP	Passive House Planning (Design) Package
PI/PU	polyisoprene/polyurethane
PIR	polyisocyanurate
PM	Particulate Matter
PMCR	Polymer-modified Cementitious render
PU	polyurethane
PVA	polyvinyl acetate
PVC	polyvinyl chloride
PVC-U	PVC-unplasticized
PV	photovoltaics
RoHS	Restriction on the Use of Certain Hazardous Substances
SAP	Standard Assessment Procedure
SEDBUK	Seasonal Efficiency of Domestic Boilers in the UK
SF_6	sulphur hexafluoride
SHGC	Solar Heat Gain Coefficient
SIPs	Structural Insulated Panels
SO_2	sulphur dioxide
SOFCs	Solid Oxide Fuel Cells
SPF	German equivalent of coefficient of performance
SRHRV	Single Room Intermittent Heat Recovery Ventilation
SUDS	Sustainable Urban Drainage Systems
SWH	Solar Water Heating
THERM	Two-dimensional Building Heat Transfer Modelling program
TRV	Thermostatic Radiator Valve

USGBC	US Green Building Council
VCL	Vapour Control Layer
VOC	Volatile Organic Compound
W	Watt
Wh	Watt-hour
WUFI	Wärme und Feuchte Instationär
WWF	World Wide Fund for Nature
XPS	Extruded Polystyrene Foam
ZOZP	Zero Ozone Depletion Potential

Introduction

Domestic buildings are responsible for 60 per cent of EU building energy use, about 40–60 per cent of which is heating energy (DG TREN). Of the homes we will inhabit in 2050, around four out of five will be ones we inhabit now (Environmental Change Institute, Oxford). Germany, Ireland, Italy, Netherlands, Spain and the UK together hold 100 million dwellings of which about 50 million are uninsulated. The proportion in North America is similar. With a need in developed countries to make cuts in greenhouse gas emissions of 80 per cent by 2050, low-carbon retrofitting has a long but absolutely necessary way to go.

Retrofitting insulation and glazing can easily reduce heating/cooling energy use by 30–40 per cent in many buildings. With more effort, savings as high as 80 per cent can be achieved. Contrary to some arguments (e.g. XCO2, 2003), retrofitting is generally a better option than demolish-and-rebuild to higher standards because of the embodied energy in the existing building, compared to the energy cost of demolishing and replacing it (see Palmer et al, 2006; Livingstone, 2008).

There are three basic priority criteria that might be taken as a starting point for environmental refurbishment:

1   lowering current and future carbon use;
2   energy efficiency for heating and cooling;
3   wider issues of environmental sustainability.

They will each lead to prioritizing different types of measures. Different countries take different approaches according to their circumstances – housing type, ownership pattern, energy mix and climate.

In countries like the UK where the energy supply mix has a high level of built-in carbon, low carbon criteria are taking precedence in building regulations. This explains why the Standard Assessment Procedure (SAP) and Code for Sustainable Homes (CSH) include requirements for on-site renewable electricity. In a country like Sweden, where the energy supply mix is already low carbon, features like photovoltaic (PV) panels are absent on sustainable homes. There, the emphasis is on cutting heating bills. Finally, other criteria besides saving carbon or energy might be desirable but not included in specifications or building regulations – these are commonly to do with choices over the environmental impacts and internal air quality associated with certain building materials. In the absence of mandatory requirements, the cheapest materials will be chosen – for example, PVC (polyvinyl chloride) window frames over timber.

What I try to do with this book is to address all of these criteria, by presenting options, and letting you, the project manager, decide what weight you want to give to each.

Figure I.1 *Newly built 1930s-style semi-detached house at Nottingham University being used to monitor the effects of various efficiency measures*

What works?

It has never been compulsory for the building industry to monitor their constructions to see if they are effective. Post-Occupation Evaluation is a brand new discipline finding its feet. There is a strong argument that the need to do this should be included in future building regulations – it's the only way to find out what works and what doesn't. Meanwhile, my research for this book has revealed a lamentable shortage of documented, monitored or evaluated refurbishments. In other words, we are largely operating in the dark. What we do know is that of the environmental renovations that have been evaluated, on average they perform thermally only half as well as predicted. This could be because of poor installation, occupant behaviour or failure of the materials.

There are several monitored projects in progress as this book is being written. Retrofit for the Future is a UK government-sponsored programme tackling just this, and several other programmes are being conducted by social housing authorities and academics. Until these results are in, we are dealing with probabilities only.

Paul Davies is Sustainability Technology Manager for the building company Wates with a great deal of experience of refurbishment under real-world conditions, from blocks of flats to Victorian tenements and individual homes, with or without cavity walls. His opinion sums up the general feeling amongst those I spoke to. He feels that in the absence of a government-sponsored roll out of mass refurbishment, housing owners need to develop a strategy for refurbishment of properties based on housing types that might span 10–15 years into the future. Each housing type will have its own matrix of refurbishment priorities. The achievable and best quick wins should be implemented first and these will be chosen based on heating/cooling energy demand reduction. The best metric for this for him in the UK, especially with solid walled properties, is cost per tonne of carbon dioxide saved. Other measures will be implemented later as budget and opportunities permit. For example, when a home becomes vacant, when a boiler is due to be repaired, when windows are to be replaced, all of these are ideal opportunities or triggers for implementing the best available technology. In the case of a suspended ground floor that needs insulating underneath, or internal installation, this is labour-intensive and disruptive and best done when the property is empty. In the case of a home in a conservation area, can external insulation be applied at the rear? When a boiler needs replacing, it's time to consider solar water heating. If the tank needs replacing, install one that can accommodate solar water heating later. In general, insulation levels should be specified to the maximum possible level as it is likely that further upgrades to the building will prove rare, expensive and difficult.

All of these measures can be part of a long-term asset management plan.

To refurbish homes up to an 80 per cent CO_2 reduction will cost £30,000 to £100,000 depending on the property, and clearly the money may not be available immediately. If a property is vacant it can be gutted and a whole house refurbishment completed. If it is not, only piecemeal work can be done, but any work done now should not preclude further work in the future and should keep the plan in mind so that it doesn't have to be ripped out to do that further work. For example Gavin Killip, in his Victorian end-of-terrace house, could not afford to install solar water heating panels when he refurbished his roof, but did insert the pipes so that he would not have to rip out the insulation he had just put in when the time came to install the panels. Improvements will then be done over a period of time.

This is the approach adopted in this book – cheap wins first in Chapter 1, looking at the pros and cons of different insulation materials in Chapter 2, element by element installation in Chapter 3, and making the best of it with whole home renovation in Chapter 4.

Towards which standard?

Davies is among those who believe that the Passivhaus standard is the one we should be aiming for (see Chapter 4), because overall demand reduction is the overriding priority. 'It's not the job of the construction industry to think about energy supply mix: it's more efficient for government and utilities to decarbonize the grid', he says. But Passivhaus is only an aim, and unlikely to be reached in many cases. One strong argument for Passivhaus is that it is an absolute standard rather than a relative one. The target of an 80 per cent reduction in carbon use is relative and from an unknown baseline that will vary from property to property. The Passivhaus standard is for an absolute and measurable quantity of energy used per square metre of the property. Wherever practical, pragmatic measures should be taken that approach this target. Where Passivhaus reaches its limit is on consideration of materials and contextual criteria (see the last chapter).

Homes with cavities in the walls present particular problems. Usually the cavity is not wide enough to accommodate sufficient installation to reach the required target. If it already has been filled, and external wall insulation is applied to meet the target, there is a danger of condensation in the cavity due to cold bridging. There is therefore an argument for not filling the remaining cavities but applying sufficient external or internal wall insulation to meet the target. Currently, homes classed as 'hard to heat' are old, solid wall properties, of which there are 6.6 million in the UK. In May 2009 there were just 18,000 of these with external wall insulation – of which 13,000 were retrofits, and 16,000 with internal wall insulation – of which half were retrofits (Energy Saving Trust and the Energy Efficiency Partnership for Homes, 2009). These are nevertheless relatively easy to bring up to high standards. In the future it is possible that those with cavities will be the problematic ones. For this reason perhaps new-build homes should have solid walls with external insulation rendered in hemp or lime to help them breathe.

The challenge of climate change

Any solution to the problem of environmental refurbishment must be durable, reliable and holistic in its approach. The science of climate change is not exact, but we can be reasonably sure that the future climate is uncertain. Human settlements need to adapt not only to reducing their carbon impact, but to protecting themselves against future extremes of climate, whether it is flooding, extreme weather events, hotter weather, or even cold. The last IPCC (Intergovernmental Panel on Climate Change) report (AR4) said:

> *Robust and reliable physical infrastructures are especially important to climate-related risk management.*

The total energy used through the lifetime of a building comprises:

- energy used in construction, sometimes called embodied energy;
- energy used to refurbish and maintain a building;
- energy used to run and live in the building;
- energy used to dispose of the building at the end of its useful life.

We need to minimize the use of fossil fuels in all of these. Equally it is important that the low-income households especially benefit from refurbishment programmes as a priority.

> *In many areas, climate change is likely to raise social equity concerns and increase pressures on governmental infrastructures and institutional capacities.* (IPCC, 2007)

Priorities

1 draughtproof – remove leaks;
2 insulate to as high a standard as possible;
3 double or triple glaze;
4 eliminate thermal bridges;
5 make as airtight as possible;
6 install passive stack ventilation with night cooling or, if not possible, mechanical ventilation with heat recovery;
7 supply the remaining energy renewably only where appropriate.

The economic argument

One of the barriers to low carbon refurbishment is its perceived cost. But a 2008 study by The Building and Social Housing Foundation (BSHF, 2008) found that, measured over a 50-year period, there would be almost no difference in the average emissions of new and refurbished housing (using a sample of six dwellings). Renovation rather than rebuild could make an initial saving of 35 tonnes of CO_2 per property by removing the need for the energy locked into new build materials and construction. This compared new homes built to 2006 standards, and the same level for renovation. The new homes each were responsible for 50 tonnes of embodied CO_2 and the refurbished ones for 15 tonnes. The new homes eventually make up for their high embodied energy costs through lower operational CO_2 but it can take decades – often over 50 years.

In the near future carbon-saving standards will be much higher for new build; yet it is not clear how good standards will be for renovations, unless strong incentives are given. Pay-as-you-save loans, a new idea which aims to repay the loan to the home from the resulting energy savings, runs the risk of not meeting the cost of all the necessary modifications. But what if we alter the method of calculating the benefit of thermal insulation? 'Economic' levels of insulation are usually judged on simple payback, but the relationship is not linear; increasing insulation gradually reduces running costs but increases capital costs; but once a certain standard is achieved, lifetime costs jump down as the central heating system is no longer required, argues Cost Efficient Passive Houses as European Standards (CEPHEUS), an EU-funded Passivhaus demonstration project (www.cepheus.de). This standard includes the following minimum specifications (the U-value is a measure of insulation value, with a lower value being better):

Envelope: Well insulated: U-value: $0.2W/m^2K$. Airtightness: < 0.6 air changes per hour @ 50 Pascals (meaning hardly any air leakage). Low thermal bridging.

Glazing: Orientation and area optimized; approximately 25–30 per cent of floor area. Double glazing with low-e coating and insulated shutters or blinds, average U-value: $1.3W/m^2K$

Ventilation: Mechanical ventilation with heat recovery 70 per cent efficient. Supplementary heating via booster coil within air supply.

This standard approaches Passivhaus. Some buildings cannot be upgraded to this extent. There is therefore an argument for a programme of accelerated replacement of these remaining dwellings with new-build to the same standard or Passivhaus as far as possible, while the others are upgraded to this standard.

Sometimes, after a low energy refurbishment has been carried out, the expected lower energy consumption is not found. This is because residents continue to turn the heating up and enjoy higher levels of thermal comfort. Not surprisingly this is a source of great frustration to policy-makers. But, if the heating system is removed because there is so much insulation and airtightness that it isn't necessary, then this is less likely to happen! This process is analogous to removing inefficient appliances from the market as is happening with, for example, light bulbs and fridges.

A lack of research

There are plenty of unknowns, where more research needs to be done. One example of this is in the hygroscopicity of materials – their ability to absorb and release moisture, which is an important issue for addressing damp. Chris Morgan (2008) observes that:

We know that thermally massive construction can absorb and store heat, letting it out when the surrounding air is colder. Designed correctly, this can reduce heating costs and buffer both uncomfortable highs and lows of temperature. But hygroscopic materials do the same, partly through the movement of moisture in and out of them. The science is not widely understood, and the applicability of this not widely appreciated. There is [also] the issue of decrement delay and the ability of denser insulants, like woodfibre to help with cooling of lightweight structures where lighter and non-hygroscopic insulants like mineral wool cannot.

A quantum leap is required in our understanding of the way that heat moves through buildings and materials, how energy is used and how people live in their homes so they can be designed better to save energy.

Power and energy

To understand a little about energy efficiency in buildings we need to know a few basic definitions.

Power: the rate at which energy is consumed by an appliance or produced by a generator
Unit: the watt (W). 1000 watts is a kilowatt (kW).
Energy: the amount of power consumed by an appliance or produced by a generator over a period of time
Unit: the watt-hour (Wh). 1000 watt-hours is a kilowatt-hour (kWh), commonly a unit of electricity on a bill.

Examples:
*   One 80W light bulb on for two hours, or two 80W bulbs on for one hour would consume 2×80 = 160Wh.
*   Three 80W light bulbs on for six hours will consume 3×80×6 = 1440Wh or 1.44kWh.

Energy efficiency and lighting

For the same amount of luminescence over four hours:

*   An 80W incandescent bulb will consume 80×4 = 320Wh.
*   A low energy 18W compact fluorescent bulb will consume 18×4 = 72Wh.

From this we can see that an incandescent bulb (370Wh) uses 4.4 times as much energy as a compact fluorescent bulb (72Wh) while producing the same amount of light (320/72 = 4.4)

Fans and air conditioning

Fans consume less energy than air conditioners. A typical fan of 30W on for six hours will consume 30×6 = 180Wh. Conversely a typical air conditioning unit of 2kW or 2000W on for the same period will consume 2000×6 = 12,000Wh. That is 67 times more energy.

Calculating CO_2 emissions from buildings

To calculate the carbon load of an existing building, you have to multiply the power it uses by an efficiency factor to find the primary energy used to deliver your power, and multiply that by the figure for kilograms of carbon dioxide-equivalent per kilowatt-hour of delivered energy:

Table I.1 *Multipliers used to find the carbon load of a dwelling by fuel type*

Fuel	Efficiency factor	$kgCO_{2e}$/kWh
Coal	1.07	0.382
Oil	1.19	0.284
LPG	1.15	0.25
Wood	1.10	0.05
Natural gas	1.15	0.20
Grid electricity (UK)	2.50	0.591

Source: SAP, 2009 and AECB CarbonLite

For example if a building uses 50,000 kWh of delivered mains gas per year – found from the bills – the corresponding CO_2-equivalent emissions are 50,000 × 1.15 × 0.20 = 11,500kg or 11.5 tonnes. If it uses 36,000kWh of electricity, the CO_2-equivalent emissions are 36,000 × 2.5 × 0.591 = 53,190kg = 53.2 tonnes.

The figure is then divided by the area of the dwelling to find the per square metre usage that can then be entered into design software. For instance for the CarbonLite standards the following are required:

Table I.2 *Targets for CarbonLite standards*

Standard	Useful space heating energy (kWh/m²yr)	Primary energy consumption (kWh/m²yr)	CO_2 emissions (kg/m²yr)
Silver	40	120	22
Passivhaus	15	120	No explicit limit
Passivhaus in a UK context	15	78	15
Gold	15	58	4

These figures represent a reduction in CO_2 emissions compared to average UK dwellings of 70 per cent, 80 per cent and 95 per cent respectively.

Different methodologies are used for assessing compliance with different standards for low carbon building. For example, in the UK, the Code for Sustainable Homes (CSH) Level 5 method for achieving compliance with zero carbon housing is different from that for Level 6; the former only includes operational heating and ventilation energy. The Energy Performance Certificate (EPC) rules are also different from those in the Display Energy Certificate (DEC). The EPC is needed on construction, sale or rent/let of a property and counts the carbon emissions associated with heating, cooling, ventilation and lighting, whereas the DEC (used for larger public buildings), like CSH6, looks at the energy consumption carbon emissions of the whole building, including catering, computing and all small power plug loads. The Standard Assessment Procedure (SAP) calculations in certain circumstances will also give different results. The Passive House Planning (Design) Package (PHPP) is different again and, of all of the above (except DEC/CSH6, which comes close) is likely to be the most accurate, as it is the system most grounded in actual, real world figures rather than assumptions.

Eco-minimalism

And it's the real world that matters. There is a strong argument that less is more in sustainable refurbishment. A great deal of savings are to be had in prior modelling of refurbishment plans in the various thermal and energy modelling software packages available. The planning stage is where a good investment of time should be made in order to minimize mistakes and maximize savings in terms of value for money and value for carbon. This may help avoid the kind of 'eco-clichés' (such as thoughtlessly applied micro-wind turbines, photovoltaic panels on buildings with inefficient electrical appliances and heat pumps in badly insulated buildings) described by the architect Howard Liddell when he coined the phrase eco-minimalism (Liddell and Grant, 2002).

Nick Grant has developed this idea in subsequent writings. He quotes Emerson writing about Henry David Thoreau as he sought for simplicity at the height of the coal boom after 1854: 'He chose to be rich by making his wants few.' Elegance in building design involves making the best possible use of the fewest resources and results in different kinds of beauty according to the eye of the designer. It involves arranging the building elements so that they minimize energy use and make the best use of these resources. Grant gives many examples, such as 'arranging the services to minimize hot water pipelines and subsequent energy and water wastage, or ordering rooms to maximize useful living area, perceived space or solar gain'. Some of these options are not available in renovation, but a particularly appropriate one is 'avoiding the structure penetrating the thermal envelope'. He says 'ignoring this apparently simple rule will lead to thermal bridges and tricky airtightness details which increases cost and can more than double heat load' (Grant, 2008).

Throughout this book you will hopefully find many tips on how to apply this philosophy. I urge in particular that in all three areas of heating and cooling energy, electricity use and water use, the prime directive is to reduce demand as much as possible first and only then look to meet the demand from sustainable sources. Hopefully then there won't be unnecessary and expensive bolting-on of so-called 'green' technology to an inefficient structure, especially where the technology doesn't work.

The low carbon renovation challenge

A government report notes that the CO_2 savings from insulating Britain's homes has the potential to save 17.4Mt of CO_2 per year (BRE, 2007). Installation of energy efficient heating systems, the use of energy efficient lighting and appliances, glazing to 'C-rated' standard and other measures could save a further 45.3Mt.

But we must beware of apparent solutions that are offered by particular manufacturers, which may solve one problem but do not address all of the issues posed by the concept of low impact housing. I saw a house with no less than six different and expensive sources of renewable energy, but with a complete absence of draughtproofing. I saw a cutting edge passive house design which employed an oversized wood pellet boiler intended for heating both space and water that made the home too hot and meant that the householder resorted regularly to mains electricity for showers as a result. There are risks of fatal fires as a result of flammable insulation and breathing problems associated with mineral wool. Petrochemical-derived insulants emit carbon dioxide in their manufacture, whereas natural fibre ones such as cellulose 'lock up' atmospheric carbon in the fabric of a building and enable a structure to 'breathe'.

It is a huge challenge for housing renovation to help meet a target of reducing global emissions by 80 per cent by 2050, given the scale of action required. We can achieve a lot with currently available technology, but only if we act with absolute urgency. Meanwhile a huge amount of research is required and, inevitably, some behaviour change. We also need a massive training programme of designers and contractors, the roll-out of appropriate supply chains and not least the sensitization of building control to the issues, so that implementation of the detailing is scrupulously monitored and improved.

Hopefully this book will help to facilitate the process.

It almost goes without saying that this book is not a replacement for proper training in building regulations or building work; and all building-related regulations, health and safely codes and manufacturer's product instructions should be followed. But not quite.

References

BRE (2007) 'Delivering cost effective carbon saving measures to existing homes 2007', prepared by BRE for Defra

CEPHEUS available at www.cepheus.de, last accessed October 2009

BSHF (2008) 'New tricks with old bricks: How reusing old buildings can cut carbon emissions', BSHF, Coalville, www.emptyhomes.com/documents/publications/reports/New%20Tricks%20With%20Old%20Bricks%20-%20final%2012-03-081.pdf, last accessed March 2010

Energy Saving Trust and the Energy Efficiency Partnership for Homes (2009) 'Solid wall insulation supply chain review', report prepared for the Energy Saving Trust and the Energy Efficiency Partnership for Homes, April

Grant, N. (2008) *Green Building Magazine*, Winter

IPCC (2007) 'Fourth assessment report (AR4) – Climate change 2007: Impacts, adaptation and vulnerability: Technical summary', IPCC, Geneva

Liddell, H. and Grant, N. (2002) 'Eco-minimalism: getting the priorities right', *Building for a Future*, Winter

Livingstone, J. (2008) 'UK residential tower blocks demolish or refurbish: The energy perspective', MSc thesis for University of East London/Centre for Alternative Technology

Morgan, C. (2008) 'Breathing buildings', *SelfBuild*, www.locatearchitects.co.uk/download/moisture-in-buildings.pdf, last accessed February 2010

Palmer, J., Boardman, B., Bottrill, C., Darby, S., Hinnells, M., Killip, G., Layberry, R. and Lovell, H. (2006) 'Reducing the environmental impact of housing: Final report', Environmental Change Institute, University of Oxford

XCO2 (2003) 'Insulation for sustainability: A guide', study by XCO2 for BING, London

1

Airtightness: Reducing Energy Demand for Heating and Cooling

The core aim of sustainable refurbishment is to reduce the demand for energy for heating and cooling while improving the health and comfort of occupants. The first step to achieving this is to reduce unwanted draughts or air infiltration and leakage. Uncontrolled airflow in and out isn't what we need. Instead, homes must breathe in a controlled way that permits the occupiers to regulate air quality – humidity, cleanliness, temperature and so forth. This will ensure huge savings over the building's lifetime.

> *If I'm wearing a wool jumper on a windy day, the wind will blow right through it. If I put on a wind or rain jacket and zip it up, then the wool insulation can do its job properly. It's the same with a building. You might have insulation in your house, but you'll still be cold if the wind is penetrating. The idea is to keep all the warm air inside the building and all the cold air outside, to prevent draughts and high heating bills.*
> Andreas Schmidt, SIGA

The aim of airtightness is to 'build tight, ventilate right'. This means that there are no breaks or gaps in the envelope of the building fabric, to maintain a controllable interior temperature at low operating cost regardless of the conditions outside – a climate-controlled home can keep out hot air during hot spells, as well as banish cold air streams in wintry weather. Airtightness can be measured with pressure testing. All openings and ventilation systems are sealed and a fan is used to put the building under a standard pressure difference of 50 Pascals. You can then measure how much air is leaking out.

Where does air come in?

Air finds its way in through all kinds of cracks and gaps. The following non-exhaustive list will not apply to every single dwelling – for example flats do not have lofts – but some will apply to all.

Airtightness

Airtightness is measured in air changes per hour (ACH) – the number of times the home's air is replaced by outside air in an hour. In a typical unrefurbished UK home air change rates average between one and two volumes per hour but can be much higher. Newer construction tends to be tighter – below one. Tightly constructed homes may reach an ACH of 0.6 to 0.5 or less.

Airtightness is also described in terms of building envelope permeability – in cubic metres of air leakage per square metre of external area of the building per hour – m^3/m^2 h at 50 Pascals. It is defined in BS EN 13829. Minimum targets apply as follows:

Target	m^3/m^2h
Part L of the UK Building Regulations	10[a]
Energy Saving Trust Best Practice	5[b]
Code for Sustainable Homes (CSH) level 3–5	3[c]
Higher CSH levels (they go up to 6)	1
Passivhaus	0.6

Notes:

[a] *Source:* Amendments to SAP 2005 (version 9.81) April 2008.

[b] Upper limit under Part L Source: 'Proposed Building Regulations Part L1a 2010': NHER Summary of the Consultation, National Energy Services Ltd, June 2009; Source: EST CE83.GPG155 'Energy-efficient refurbishment of existing housing' (Nov 2007 edition).

[c] The Code itself stipulates no figures for airtightness or permeability. Instead it discusses the building fabric in terms of heat loss parameters. But the Energy Saving Trust has produced helpful documents to show strategies for achieving the targets, which take for granted a target of 3m³/h m² at 50 Pascals. Sources: 'Energy efficiency and the Code for Sustainable Homes Level 3 EST CE290' (June 2008 edition); 'Energy efficiency and the Code for Sustainable Homes Level 4 EST CE291' (May 2008 edition); 'Energy efficiency and the Code for Sustainable Homes – Levels 5 and 6 EST CE292' (May 2008 edition).

In other words, the lower the figure, the better the performance of the building.

The way you go about dealing with these gaps depends on whether the home is being renovated piecemeal fashion, room by room, whether an extension like a loft or conservatory is being added, or if it is a whole building refurbishment. If it is any of the last three options it's much better to install interior or exterior insulation with a vapour-permeable membrane (see Chapter 3).

This chapter deals with measures to take if you are draughtproofing on a less comprehensive scale. Proceed methodically from room to room applying the measures below in each category. When you've fixed all the obvious gaps, check whether you've been successful by using the smoke from a candle or burning incense held near a suspect area on a windy day, or a day when there is a temperature contrast between inside and outside, to see whether the smoke direction reveals a draught. After attending to any further leaks found, a pressure test could be conducted as a final check.

Depending on where you are starting from, some of these measures will be zero net cost and quick wins (highlighted below by a 'Q' next to the measures).

Figure 1.1 *Brush seals on the inside of a letterbox*

Letterboxes (Q)

If the flap doesn't close properly a brisk draught can invade. Fit a good quality outside flap with a strong sprung return mechanism to ensure that it closes properly. Fit a second flap or a brush unit inside.

Key holes (Q)

A mortice lock is a hole. Fit a flap over the outside hole that pivots out of the way when the lock is used. Fit a second one on the inside.

Cat flaps (Q)

Cat flaps are a bad idea, but if one is essential, choose an airtight, insulated one with a close-fitting flap and strong return mechanism. (Some even come with a coded transponder that is fitted to your cat's collar so only yours can come in!)

Doorframes and doors (Q)

Badly fitting doors are major sources of draughts. Draughtstripping is inexpensive, simple to install and can greatly improve comfort as well as reducing fuel bills. Exterior doors should be fixed first, then (unless you're installing whole house ventilation) the interior doors, to stop air travelling from unheated (or uncooled) areas of the building to others. Typical payback for doors and windows is three to four years.

Various types of seals are available depending on the door and the side to be sealed:

- **Compression seals:** for external doors. Draughtstrips with a range of 6mm and a compression allowance of 3mm will allow for a seasonal variation in gap size of up to 3mm. The seal is maintained if the gap expands and when it shrinks the door will still close. Synthetic rubbers (including EPDM and silicone seals), sheathed foam or nylon brush, all perform well, with rigid PVC-U or aluminium carriers nailed or screwed to the frame of the door. Don't over-paint them.
- **Low-friction or wiper seals:** suitable for most doors and window types. Commonly made of nylon brush pile, they are self-adhesive and available in a variety of heights for different gaps; especially good on sliding windows and doors. Rubber blade types are good for wooden doors and casement windows and sliding applications.
- **Gun-applied sealants and fillers:** larger gaps, including those at the heads of windows, can be filled using silicone or polyurethane sealants. These expand, set and harden to fill the gap permanently. Do not apply to dusty or wet surfaces and check that the filler has fully filled the gap and bonded.

Figure 1.2 *Brush strip*

Source: © Energy Saving Trust

Figure 1.3 *Wiper seal*

Source: © Energy Saving Trust

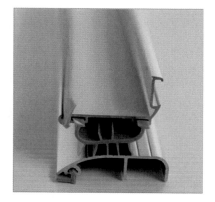

Figure 1.4 *Compression seal*

Source: © Energy Saving Trust

Figure 1.5 *Screw fastenings on attic hatch*

Source: © Energy Saving Trust

Heat loss paths around a typical window opening – traditional construction

Figure 1.6 *Air paths around a typical window*

Source: © Energy Saving Trust

Door replacement

Some doors may need to be replaced. Replacement doors and windows should have insulated cores, in other words, insulation between the two outer surfaces, to prevent cold-bridging. You can get ones with U-values as low as $0.6W/m^2K$, commonly using an insulating core of polyurethane sandwiched between an outer skin, preferably of hardwood timber. Windows should be double or triple glazed. Apply an external mastic seal to all door frames and a bead of mastic to seal any internal gaps between the reveals and frames.

Attic hatches

Use compression seals all round, with catches so that when fastened they pull the hatch down to make a tight fit and it can't be blown up by a gust of wind. On the upper side of the hatch fix at least 25cm of insulation, matching that in the rest of the loft.

Window frames and openings (Q)

A typical UK home loses 10 per cent of its heat through the windows. Many of the same seals used for doors can be used for most casement windows and can be fitted to the frame. Repair any damage and ensure the casements, sashes and top-lights close firmly. Replace any ineffective closing mechanisms with tight-fitting ones.

Apply draughtproofing to gaps around window opening casements, sashes and top-lights. Outside, use a sealant to fill the gaps around frames to prevent air leakage from the reveals. Inside, apply a bead of mastic to any gaps between the wall reveals/window boards and units.

Fitting draughtstrips can be difficult because of varying gap sizes around the edges of the frame. Strips are meant for specific gap ranges, for example, 3–5mm or 1–2mm. Choose the right one for your gap size. Tiny gaps along the length of a door or window may be tackled by enlarging the gap so it can take a strip, or one can be fitted outside the gap (face fixed).

Face-fixed seals have two parts: a seal which moves against the door or window to close the gap and a carrier fixed to the frame which holds it firmly in place. These are adapted to the variable gaps of warped frames and doors by adjusting the position of the carrier. For historic buildings, specialist companies cut grooves into the frames to hide the draughtstrips. Hidden brushes or seals can be fitted to the bottom sections of wooden doors which retract automatically upon opening.

Sash windows present a particular problem. The gaps around the average one can equate to an aperture measuring up to 10 square inches ($25cm^2$). Various brush or plastic/rubber beads are available. Some can be push-slotted in without damaging the timber, also preventing rattle and improving sound insulation. Compression seals are also good. A compression of 3mm is usually fine.

Louvre windows are the worst for draughts. Tiered panes of glass open outwards by pushing a control lever in the frame. It's impossible to ensure an airtight gap when these are closed. Replace them, or add secondary glazing.

Secondary glazing is an improvement on draughtstripping, if the windows cannot be replaced. These are removable glazed frames constructed to fit snugly in the window recess to prevent draughts and be easy to remove for window cleaning, painting or opening. They can also really help in cutting noise from outside. Both new windows and secondary glazing are covered in Chapter 5.

Vented skylights: make sure they are well draught-proofed or sealed and not left open unnecessarily. In airtight homes that rely on controlled ventilation they should never be opened except in emergencies.

Shutters

Being made of wood, shutters have a higher insulating value than glass and can be fitted externally and internally. Interior shutters are hinged – sometimes double-hinged so they can fold open – and provide a better draught-reducing effect than curtains, while reducing the radiative effect of cold from a single-glazed window at night. All shutters must be well-fitting and draught-proofed as for windows.

Mediterranean climates use internal and external shutters and thick curtains on the inside of the internal shutters. These are all closed in the day during the hot season and opened in the evenings as required. They are thus as highly effective at keeping both direct solar heat and indirect warm draughts out of the building as they are at keeping cold air out. Whatever the outside temperature, the interior temperature can be relatively unaffected.

Curtains, over windows and doors, can be a simple, cheap draught-preventer. They should be lined. However, they can never make a building airtight! Roll-down inflatable or expanding blinds, including translucent varieties, are very effective. Even net curtains help, by restricting the air-flow across the glass.

Frames

Poorly fitting window frames can also be a source of draughts. Check particularly underneath the window sill, where it penetrates the wall.

Gunned-in compatible sealant is ideal for small joints, but first clean joints and prime surfaces to ensure a good bond. For larger openings use a pre-compressed flexible expanding foam strip. Ensure that where present the airtight membrane meets and overlaps the seal to maintain the airtight layer overall.

Figure 1.7 *Secondary glazing on a sash window (Machynlleth, Powys)*

Figure 1.8 *Interior shutter and curtains (Lacemaker's House, Nottingham)*

Figure 1.9 *Interior shutters and curtains (Barcelona)*

Figure 1.10 *Exterior shutters on a block of flats (Barcelona)*

If the windows are not to be refitted, sometimes it is necessary to hack away old plaster or mortar to access the gap. On the outside, for small gaps, use gunned-in sealant to seal joints between frames and the surrounding wall. Inside, apply it to gaps between the wall reveals or window boards and the window or door units. In the case of larger gaps it may be necessary to fill them with polyurethane foam and re-plaster. This is one situation where spray foam, despite its contrary ecological effects, may have the advantage over other materials, because of its ability to be pumped into small areas, form a vapour barrier and be highly insulating, but it has been known to shrink and break the seal later.

Foams are spray applied as a semi-viscous liquid. They then expand by 20–30 per cent to fill every crack and gap, so make sure that you don't overfill a space that might yield under pressure (for example plasterboard). An important issue related to choosing foam insulation is the environmental impact of any blowing agents used during manufacture. Check that they have been blown with pentane rather than ozone depleting or greenhouse gases (HCFCs or HFCs). Foam comes in two types:

- Open-cell foam is porous, allowing water vapour and liquid water to penetrate.
- Closed-cell foam is non-porous, and not moisture-penetrable, thereby effectively forming a vapour barrier.

Vapour barriers are usually required by the Building Codes, regardless of the type of insulation used. Closed-cell foam should therefore be used, as it can also attain a thermal conductivity k value of 0.020W/m/K, or R-values of 5 to 8 per inch (RSI-0.88 to RSI-1.41 per inch). (For comparison, glass and mortar are 0.9, brick 0.8 and plasterboard 0.25). See the next chapter for more information.

Cap the foam sealant with an airtight finish.

Cavity walls (Q)

If there is a cavity in the wall of the building, there is a debate about whether this should be filled or whether external or internal insulation should be applied instead. See Chapter 3 for this discussion.

Figure 1.11 *Air leakage path hidden behind skirting board*

Source: Energy Saving Trust GPG 224, reproduced with permission

Holes in the building fabric

The external wall can have cracks or tiny holes, particularly where extensions have been bolted on to the original dwelling. Inspect and repair mortar joints and fill any holes.

Gaps between floorboards (Q)

Draughts from gaps between floorboards are ideally plugged where the air first gets into the building. But this is often hard without a more complete refurbishment, especially in old buildings or those with cavity walls. Beam-and-block floors may be riddled with cracks, particularly if the screed is poor. Gaps can be filled with several materials:

- papier maché or sawdust mixed with dye that matches the colour of the boards, and PVA or resin;
- thin slices of cork from a cork board;
- oakum – loose hemp or jute fibre obtained by unravelling old ropes;
- rolls from DIY stores, usually made from plastic (not as sustainable or effective).

Large area boards with tongue-and-groove edges fixed on to floorboards can reduce air leakage, but you must plug all the gaps in the floorboards before laying them.

If a cavity wall is filled and the problem persists, take the floorboards up, insulate between the joists and lay an airtight permeable layer above the joists before relaying the boards, taking care not to puncture the membrane except where the screws are.

As a stop gap, the boards can be covered with linoleum or well-fitted wall-to-wall carpet, taking care to seal the edges – but this will not be airtight. Don't cover timber floors with plastic sheeting as this may cause the unventilated timber to rot.

Other gaps: Between walls, floors, ceilings, skirting boards and cornices (Q)

Suspended timber floors will almost certainly have gaps at the junctions with walls (inside and out), ceilings, cornices and around service entry points (water pipes behind baths, sinks and WCs). Air can slip to and from the unheated floor void. Often it's because blocks were left out somewhere or large holes cut through them to let pipes pass through.

First, seal around the edges of rooms. With solid ground floors, junctions between the ground floor slab and the external walls are usually hidden by the skirting board; air can leak through the small gap underneath. In the absence of a damp-proof membrane, gaps and cracks in the ground floor can allow air and ground gases (e.g. radon and landfill gas) to be drawn into the home. Cracks may develop in solid floors as the concrete cures and shrinks away from the walls. All of these should be filled, with concrete, mastic or DIY solutions, as for floorboard gaps.

Gaps around pipes and cables (Q)

Seal gaps around service pipes and cables that pass through external walls, ceilings and ground floors. You may have to move baths, sinks, kitchen units, boxing around service pipes, washing machines, and so on, to get at them. Check for holes behind baths and under shower trays and where heating pipes penetrate floorboards and walls, or subfloor air supplies come in to solid fuel heaters – even room thermostats and heating controllers.

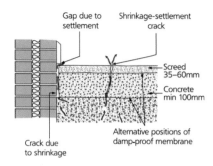

Figure 1.12 *Air leakage paths through solid floors*

Source: Energy Saving Trust GPG 224, reproduced with permission

Figure 1.13 *Air leakage through gaps around service pipes in suspended timber floors*

Source: Energy Saving Trust GPG 224, reproduced with permission

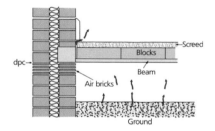

Figure 1.14 *Air leakage around perimeter of beam-and-block floors*

Source: Energy Saving Trust GPG 224, reproduced with permission

Figure 1.15 *Sealing gaps around the skirting board*

Source: © Chris Twinn

Figure 1.16 *Sealing gaps around pipes to preserve the airtightness*

Source: © Chris Twinn

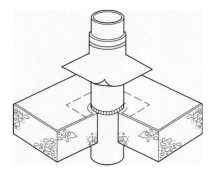

Figure 1.17 *Pre-formed collar to seal around service pipe that penetrates through the floor*

Source: Energy Saving Trust GPG 224, reproduced with permission

Loose fill insulation can be stuffed into the gap behind where a pipe comes through a floor. If possible, a fitted vapour membrane should reach up to the edge of the pipe around the outside of a pre-formed collar – sometimes called a 'top hat'. This is then stuck and double taped to the membrane and around the throat of the pipe to make an airtight seal. Mend any tears in the fabric using the most durable tape. Where there is no membrane gun-apply sealant around the pipe/cable on the outside and inside, before plastering.

Ensure there's a good seal around boiler flue pipes where they pass through the external wall/ceiling. It must not of course be affected by heat.

Light fittings often recess into ceilings. Always buy airtight light fittings. Any airtight membrane should then continue smoothly without a break around the top of the fitting. Seal any holes around the fittings, switches and pull cords. If the fitting isn't airtight install an airtight box over it in the ceiling void.

Outside, seal holes around services coming out of the walls, including water, drainage, gas pipes, boiler flues and cables.

Chimneys

Fit chimney balloons into empty chimneys (Q)

If chimneys are used only some of the year, insert chimney balloons when not in use. These inflate into whatever shape is required to fill the gap; the air inside the balloon acts as an insulant. They are cheap and easy to install. They can be used in combination with dampers.

Seal gaps (Q)

Gaps should be checked and sealed around:

- any flexible flue liner sealed into a chimney;
- the seal in a chimney fitted with an open-flue gas fire where the flue outlet is sealed to the chimney;
- flues for room-sealed boilers or room heaters;
- air-conditioning or mechanical ventilation intakes and outlets.

Fit dampers to chimneys and flues

A damper seals the fireplace shut when it's not in use so that heated air won't vanish up the chimney. An open or leaky damper can seriously increase heating costs. Some dampers are located in the throat of a masonry chimney just above the firebox. Others may be mounted on top of the chimney; these will also keep rain, birds, other animals and cold air out, so, if the lower part of the chimney structure is within the living spaces, those will also stay warmer. The damper seals should consist of silicone rubber gaskets to form an airtight join. The damper should be adjustable to help control combustion rate.

Block unused chimneys

If a chimney is completely unused, block the fireplace off at the bottom with insulated plasterboard; a closable vent might be left in if it's felt necessary to fight damp in the chimney with ventilation. If the top of the chimney is also blocked off, this will not be necessary except in old properties. For cost-effectiveness only do this if other jobs require scaffolding and access to the roof, e.g. repairs, solar panels.

Fitted air-conditioners, heaters, boilers' exhaust fans (Q)

Intermittent-running extract fans which extract air (from the kitchen, bathroom, and so on), including cooker hoods, should have well-fitting self-closing

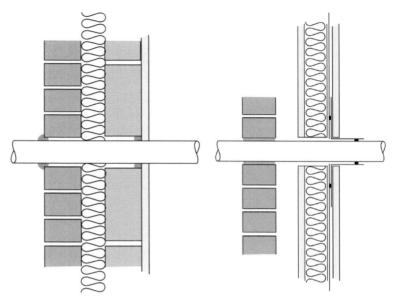

Figure 1.18 *Gun-applied sealant around a service pipe through an external wall, prior to the application of plasterboard*

Source: Energy Saving Trust GPG 224, reproduced with permission

Figure 1.19 *Pre-formed collar around service pipes, sealing the air barrier in timber frame construction*

Source: Energy Saving Trust GPG 224, reproduced with permission

covers which securely close when not in use. Fit or repair where appropriate. Check for gaps round the vents and apply sealant inside and out – heat resistant around boiler flues.

Trickle vents and air bricks

These should be inspected and either blocked, unblocked or replaced depending on whether you think they're necessary and effective. Make sure any fires or boilers – and people – aren't starved of air. Trickle vents help. Many older windows won't have them, in which case either fit them or leave off two metres of draught-stripping per room. In kitchens, bathrooms and other wet rooms consider including extractor fans or, where possible, passive stack ventilation (see Chapter 6).

Construction joints between materials

Gaps between slats in timber construction, around the ends of floor joists or joist hangers and between solid insulation and rafters, struts or floorboards are all your enemy – sources of draughts which can ruin your best attempts to be airtight. Apply the same logic here as described above under window and door frames: ensure the joints between boards are sealed. If there are many large gaps consider fitting an airtightness membrane.

Figure 1.20 *Draught cover for exhaust fans*

Source: Advantec Ltd

Drylining is also notoriously air leaky. Parge-coat the interior surface of the wall for airtightness. See Chapter 3 for more on this.

Ceiling to wall joints at the eaves

This topic is also dealt with more fully in Chapter 3. If you're draughtproofing, but not insulating, remember that to prevent condensation and timber rot, air must enter the roofspace of a pitched roof from under the eaves on the outside of the insulation and not enter the heated areas of the building. Seal any holes around services that enter the loft space from inhabited areas, especially those from kitchens, bathrooms and airing cupboards and the edges of ceilings.

Conclusion

Draughtproofing is an essential first step for creating a low carbon dwelling. Depending on the original energy efficiency of the building, it is possible to reduce carbon emissions by up to 50 per cent by draughtproofing alone. Most of the above measures can be carried out by the occupant or owner themselves as fairly simple DIY jobs. But generally, except for loft insulation, most of the remaining activities detailed in this book are likely to be the preserve of professionals. Insulation and taking airtightness to high levels (which make it possible to reach approximately an 80 per cent reduction in energy use for heating and cooling) are the subjects of the next three chapters.

2
Insulation Materials

Insulation materials come in many different forms, shapes and sizes. How do we choose between them? If we are modelling our refurbishment plans, we need technical information about their performance and characteristics. This chapter will examine some of the criteria before moving on to evaluate most common insulation materials according to their characteristics, origins and life cycles. In the following chapter, we look at how to use them.

How insulation is described

Firstly, what is the relationship between thermal conductivity, thermal resistance (the R-value) and heat transfer (the U-value)? How do these relate to the standard of insulation we want for a low carbon building?

Thermal conductivity (k)

Thermal conductivity, k (also known as psi), tells us how well a material conducts heat. It is:

$$k = Q/t \text{ times } 1/A \text{ times } x/T$$

or the quantity of heat, Q, transmitted over time t through a thickness x, in a direction perpendicular to a surface of area A, due to a temperature difference T. The units used are either SI: W/mK or in the US: Btu/(h/ft/°F). To convert, use the formula 1.730735Btu/(h/ft/°F) = 1W/mK.

R-value

The R-value is a measure of how well a material resists heat travelling through it. It is the ratio of the temperature difference across an insulator and the heat flow per unit area through it. The bigger the number the better the insulator. It is the depth or thickness of a material divided by its thermal conductance, in other words, R = d/k.

To compare two insulants with different thickness and thermal conductivity, you have to calculate the value of R for each.

R-values are given in metric units: square-metre Kelvin per watt or m^2K/W (equivalent to $m^2°C/W$); or, in the United States, in $ft^2°F/h/Btu$. It is easy to confuse them because R-values are frequently cited without units, e.g. R-3.5. One R-value (US) is equivalent to 0.1761 R-value (metric), or one R-value (metric) is equivalent to 5.67446 R-value (US). Usually, the appropriate units can be inferred from the context and their magnitudes.

Doubling the thickness of an insulating layer doubles its thermal resistance. R-values are often used when there are multiple materials through which heat can travel. The R-values of adjacent materials can be added together to calculate the overall value; e.g., R-value (brick) + R-value (insulation) + R-value (plasterboard) = R value (total).

U-value

R-value is the reciprocal of U-value (and vice versa of course). A lower U-value is better than a higher one, indicating greater insulation value. It is commonly used in Europe and is the overall heat transfer coefficient, describing the rate of heat transfer through a building element over a given area, under standardized conditions. The usual standard is at a temperature gradient of 24°C, at 50 per cent humidity with no wind.

It is described in watts per square metre Kelvin ($W/(m^2K)$) or the amount of energy lost in watts per square metre of material for a given temperature difference of 1°C or 1K from one side of the material to the other. Another way of understanding it is to see it as thermal conductivity divided by the depth of insulation, or $U = k/d$ where k is the thermal conductivity of a material, d the materials depth.

Building Regulations provide minimum standards of thermal insulation, typically expressed as a U value.

Thermal properties of some building materials

Table 2.1 lists the thermal properties of some building materials: their density, thermal conductivity (k) and specific heat capacity (a measure of how much heat energy is required to increase its temperature by a specific amount).

Using U-values

U-values have to be calculated for building elements in order to work out the carbon load of the dwelling. For example, in the UK and many other countries, a submission of Building Notice or full plans to a local authority is now mandatory for most refurbishment work. For the UK:

- full replacement of roofs requires U-values of below 0.25;
- full replacement of walls requires U-values of below 0.35;
- renovation of existing roofs and walls requires the same, subject to technical feasibility and a payback of less than 15 years;
- dwelling extensions under Part L2B require roof and wall U-values of 0.2 and 0.3 respectively (large extensions come under Part L2A);
- for Passivhaus Standard, all components of the exterior shell must achieve a U-value equal to or less than 0.15.

How much can you save?

Table 2.2 illustrates increases in energy efficiency – as well as by how much annual CO_2 emissions and costs can be reduced – as a result of implementing

Table 2.1 *Thermal properties of some building materials*

Material	Density specific (kg/m³)	Thermal (k) conductivity (W/mK)	Heat capacity (J/kgK)
WALLS			
Brickwork (outer leaf)	1700	0.84	800
Brickwork (inner leaf)	1700	0.62	800
Cast concrete (dense)	2100	1.40	840
Cast concrete (lightweight)	1200	0.38	1000
Concrete block (heavyweight)	2300	1.63	1000
Concrete block (mediumweight)	1400	0.51	1000
Concrete block (lightweight)	600	0.19	1000
Fibreboard	300	0.06	1000
Plasterboard	950	0.16	840
Stone (artificial)	1750	1.3	1000
Stone (limestone)	2180	1.5	910
Tile hanging	1900	0.84	800
SURFACE FINISHES			
External rendering	1300	0.50	1000
Plaster (dense)	1300	0.05	1000
Plaster (lightweight)	600	0.16	1000
ROOFS			
Aerated concrete slab	500	0.16	840
Asphalt	1700	0.50	1000
Felt/bitumen layers	1700	0.50	1000
Screed	1200	0.41	840
Stone chippings	1800	0.96	1000
Tile	1900	0.84	800
Wood wool slab	500	0.10	1000
FLOORS			
Cast concrete	2000	1.13	1000
Metal tray	7800	50.00	480
Screed	1200	0.41	840
Timber flooring	650	0.14	1200
Wood blocks	650	0.14	1200
INSULATION			
Expanded polystyrene slab	25	0.035	1400
Glass fibre quilt	12	0.040	840
Glass fibre slab	25	0.035	1000
Mineral fibre slab	30	0.035	1000

Table 2.1 *Thermal properties of some building materials* (Cont'd)

Material	Density specific (kg/m³)	Thermal (k) conductivity (W/mK)	Heat capacity (J/kgK)
Phenolic foam	30	0.040	1400
Polyurethane board	30	0.025	1400
Urea formaldehyde foam	10	0.040	1400

Source: Bath University Civil Engineering Department, www.bath.ac.uk/mech-eng/sert/embodied

Table 2.2 *Typical improvements in a mid-terrace, solid-wall property refurbished to best practice standards*

Specification	SAP 2005	Energy rating band	Annual CO_2 emissions (kg/yr)	Annual space and water heating costs (£)
Base house	56	D	3250	263
Base house plus best practice roof only	58	D	3090	250
Base house plus best practice floor only	58	D	3060	248
Base house plus best practice windows, doors and draught stripping only	61	D	2850	231
Base house plus best practice heating system (CHeSS – Year 2005) specification only	64	D	2440	197
Base house plus best practice walls only	69	D	2070	167
Base house plus all of the above best practice refurbishment specifications	81	B	960	78

Note: Assumptions for SAP calculations: typical two-storey mid-terrace, solid-wall property.
Original specification prior to refurbishment:
- floor (uninsulated): U-value = 0.48W/m²K;
- wall (solid): U-value = 2.10W/m²K;
- window (poor double glazing): U-value = 3.50W/m²K;
- roof (100mm insulation): U-value = 0.44W/m²K;
- heating system = gas boiler (72% efficiency), room thermostat only;

Best practice refurbishment specification:
- Solid concrete floor: U-value = approx 0.17W/m²K;
- wall: U-value = 0.30W/m²K;
- window BFRC Rating in band C or better (U-value taken as 1.50W/m²K for calculation);
- door: U-value = 1.0W/m²K;
- roof: U-value = 0.16W/m²K.

Source: EST (2006)

various refurbishment options. U-values quoted are only for particular constructions. It's important to calculate the exact U-value achievable and assess the risk of condensation within the structure. SAP (Standard Assessment Procedure) values refer to a British standard requirement for building regulations and the Energy Performance of Buildings Directive. The higher the number, the better the theoretical performance.

Calculating U-values

The U-values should be calculated for the whole floor, walls and roof. They are worked out by totalling the U-values of each of the elements multiplied by the net internal area. Using software can save a huge amount of money and time, avoiding costly mistakes. It is a learning process which allows you to anticipate problems before they are encountered in reality and devise solutions for them.

SAP

One methodology of doing this is described for the UK in the 2009 UK SAP supporting document:

> The areas of building elements are based on the internal dimensions of surfaces bounding the dwelling. Window and door area refers to the total area of the openings, including frames. Wall area is the net area of walls after subtracting the area of windows and doors. Roof area is also net of any rooflights or windows set in the roof. Losses or gains through party walls and floors to spaces in other dwellings or premises that are normally expected to be heated to the same extent and duration as the dwelling concerned are assumed to be zero (and these elements are therefore omitted from the calculation of heat losses).

The document then goes on to refer to the relevant British Standards. For example:

> U-values for walls and roofs containing repeating thermal bridges, such as timber joists between insulation, etc, should be calculated using methods based on the upper and lower resistance of elements, given in BS EN ISO 6946.

At the time of writing, the UK is still relying for calculations for renovation purposes on the 2005 SAP methodology which, amongst other things, gives average U-values for most types of construction elements in all parts of the UK. These can be found in Appendix S (at http://projects.bre.co.uk/sap2005/pdf/SAP2005_9-82.pdf). Similar resources are available in most other developed countries. These values can be input into software to calculate a baseline from which the proposed improvements can be made. Calculations for the proposed improvements are then inputted into software to see what effect they will have.

PHPP

But SAP will give different results to calculations used for Passivhaus construction and, indeed, for the requirements of the Energy Performance of Buildings Directive. One reason is that they give different emphases to thermal bridges and heating sources. SAP has been criticized for not allowing 'for detailed analysis of solar and incidental gains, the effects of thermal mass and efficient electrical use' (AECB and Jim Parker, CSH Assessor and consultant, 1st Base Projects, 2009). Because it represents the foremost thinking in this area, the software produced by the Passivhaus Institute – The Passive House Planning (Design) Package (PHPP) – is more accurate. It consists of a calculation workbook and a handbook and includes:

- energy calculations (incl. R- or U-values);
- design of window specifications;
- design of the indoor air quality ventilation system;
- sizing of the heating load;
- sizing of the cooling load;
- forecasting for summer comfort;
- sizing of the heating and domestic hot water (DHW) systems;
- calculations of auxiliary electricity, primary energy requirements of such (circulation pumps, etc.), as well as projection of CO_2 emissions;
- verifying calculation proofs of KfW and EnEV (Europe);
- Climate Data Sheet: climate regions may be selected from over 200 locations in Europe and North America. User-defined data can also be used;
- . . . and a lot more, e.g. a calculation tool to determine internal heat loads, data tables for primary energy factors, etc.

Although more complicated, this software has an advantage over others in that whereas others may be accurate on particular technical areas, they don't take enough account of site-specific factors (like angle-dependent radiation transmission through glazing; the shading of solar radiation by balconies, lintels, angles and depths of reveals and so on). The software has been refined since its introduction in 1998 based on cross-checking results with measurements at actual installations and has been developed specifically around the Passivhaus principle of only a 15kWh/m²/annum energy requirement.

PHPP is available from:

- BRE in the UK at www.passivhaus.org.uk;
- the Passivhaus Institute at www.passiv.de in German or English.

The BRE website www.bre.co.uk holds details of suppliers of appropriate technology and materials for achieving the necessary levels of airtightness and insulation.

Insulation materials

How to choose

There is a wide variety of materials, ranging from the conventional – polystyrene and mineral wool – to the traditional and novel, such as sheep's wool and hemp. How should we choose between them?

Embodied energy

The net climatic effect of building insulation is the sum of the greenhouse gas emissions associated with the energy used in manufacturing plus the leakage into the atmosphere during use of any (halocarbon: significant; pentane: less so) expanding agents that have a greenhouse effect, minus the emissions saved due to energy saved as a result of the insulation (which is zero if renewable energy is used for heating/cooling that would not been used elsewhere). There are two schools of thought.

The first argues that at present we don't really know how much embodied energy or embodied carbon there is in buildings. Most current assessments are based on partial evidence and partially understood science. One of the foremost analyses of building materials is the Inventory of Energy and Carbon (ICE) produced by Professor Geoff Hammond and Craig Jones of Bath University (Version 1.6a 2008). Its introduction confesses that there are many limitations to the data, particularly about embodied carbon, which, it says, has proved useful only in about 20 per cent of sources. The range of values (from least to most) in embodied energy per kg in the raw data can vary by a factor of several hundred. Overall the Inventory is a terrific source (at www.bath.ac.uk/mech-eng/sert/embodied) but it should be used with care – bear in mind that it's derived from secondary sources, using varying methodologies.

The theory is that we shouldn't worry because the embodied energy of the insulants will probably typically be around 1–3 per cent of the energy they save over 100 years (based on calculations for 100m² of wall insulated to U = 0.2 W/m²K). For this reason, producers of fossil carbon-based insulation argue that their products are better, as they are longer lasting, being less prone to damage by water or pests than more natural materials with a lower embodied energy.

The second school of thought is based partly on as yet unpublished research commissioned by a major London-based building company wishing to build zero or low carbon buildings. This information is reportedly rigorous and comes to the conclusion that over the lifetime of a building the embodied energy of fossil insulants may be as high as 50 per cent of the total energy used. One argument against carbon offsetting by planting trees is that the activity you are offsetting has already sent global warming gases into the atmosphere, but it will be many years before the trees that you have planted will recapture the equivalent amount of carbon dioxide from the atmosphere. Meanwhile those molecules are contributing to global warming. A similar argument can be applied to the use of fossil fuel-derived insulation. The global warming cost of their manufacture is already present in the atmosphere. The energy saved by their insulation value in a building is only potential and only realized over the 100-odd years of the building's life. Given that there is an overriding need to fight climate change urgently by immediately slowing down the release of global warming gases, shouldn't we try to avoid using these insulation materials – and instead use materials which lock up carbon in the fabric of the building?

The latest published study on the subject, confirms this, concluding:

Cellulose and other natural materials have a negligible embodied energy and negligible marginal payback times, while fibreglass or rock wool have a significantly lower embodied energy than foam insulations, and so would be preferred whenever this is possible. (Harvey, 2007)

The organic insulants like cellulose, fibreboard and hemcrete are listed below.

However, it is important to compare like with like. 'The Green Guide to Specification' published online by BRE, while disagreeing with this thesis, does compare insulants on the criteria of '1m² insulation with sufficient thickness to provide a thermal resistance value of 3m²K/W'. On this basis for example it calculates that mineral fibre (embodied energy 16.8MJ/kg) has a higher embodied energy than PIR (embodied energy 110MJ/kg) to achieve the same level of insulation, because the former is five times denser. That's why we give below, where possible, the K-value, embodied energy and density, so you can work it out for yourself once you know the U-value you want to obtain.

Carbon storage

The organic insulants (which incorporate biomass) are also taking carbon that has been absorbed from the atmosphere while the plant is growing and keeping it in the structure of the building. They are therefore a form of carbon storage, keeping that carbon out of the atmosphere, at least in the building's lifetime, from the moment they are harvested. Using them creates a market for this type of carbon storage and discourages the market for more polluting fossil-based insulants. In general, these materials also enhance the breathability of your structure and hence its ability to withstand fluctuations in internal humidity.

Other criteria

The general priorities for selecting materials are:

- thermal performance;
- longevity and durability;
- environmental issues.

But there are other more job-specific ones.

Suitability

Very few can be used in all contexts: sheep's wool suits ventilated wall construction but not unventilated cavities. Excepting spray foam and loose-fill insulation, all loft insulating materials need to be fixed into place with supports, or cut accurately into a tight fit to hold themselves in place. Rolls of material, like fibreglass & Rockwool, are not meant for pitched roof or vertical walls, but for placing above ceilings or below floors. Batts, slabs and boards are instead designed for these places.

Ease of installation

Installation time varies considerably. Sheets and batts are perfect for large areas, where the distances between joists are standard sizes or where shapes are rectangular. Loose-fill cellulose (e.g. Warmcel) can easily be blown into a horizontal space and unusual shapes.

Cost

This should be compared on the basis of total installed cost per unit of area, per unit of U- or R-value, bearing in mind that different thicknesses will be required for different materials to achieve the same value. Costs should also include:

- transport cost: the compressible types of insulant are generally cheaper to deliver than rigid forms (except foils);
- installation cost: the so-called 'blow in' insulants (loose fill) are cheap and easy to install;
- environmental considerations – external costs, perhaps suffered by the building's inhabitants, such as off-gassing, and some by the environment in general, such as ozone-depletion, pollution from manufacture or disposal, or mining.

Fire resistance

Most insulants are either not flammable, or treated to resist fire. In some cases this may deteriorate over time. Materials generally are evaluated under criteria of ignitability, spread of flame, heat released and smoke released. Fossil-based insulants like polyurethane used for cladding apartment blocks have possibly been a factor in fatal fires. A government report has published caution about their use in certain circumstances: 'Potential risk of fire spread in buildings via external cladding systems' (EFRA, 2000).

Many materials are discussed below, grouped into the following categories:

1 organic;
2 mined non-carbon minerals;
3 'multi-foil' insulation;
4 fossil carbon.

In some cases the life cycle information below is independently sourced, in others it comes from the manufacturer; newer products have not all had their claims objectively verified. Always specify foams that use no ozone-depleting blowing agents.

Materials in each section are listed in order of performance, with the best ones first. The mention of any brand names is not to be taken as a recommendation

Figure 2.1 *Sheep's wool batt*

'Risk assessment for acute toxicity from sheep ectoparasite treatments, including organophosphates (Ops) used in plunge dipping'

Source: Crown Copyright 2002, Health and Safety Laboratory HSL/2002./26

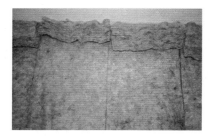

Figure 2.2 *Sheep's wool batts in situ*

Source: © Dave Baines

Figure 2.3 *Cotton and hemp batt internal wall insulation*

Source: © Russell Smith

for a particular product but as an example of a product type based on the material described. All embodied energy values are from ICE.

1 Organic sources

Sheep's wool batts and rolls (BBA certified available)

K-value: *0.038–0.043W/mK* (CIBSE, 2006). A recyclable, renewable resource with a low embodied energy (more if imported). Safe to install. Can absorb some moisture whilst remaining efficient, but when very wet assumes the U-value of water – high. Naturally resistant to decay and fungus, borate-treated to enhance pest and fire resistance but excessive wetness can leach out the borax. Expensive. Will eventually biodegrade in landfill. Sheep do produce the greenhouse gas methane! Organophosphates are used as a pesticide in sheep dips and are linked to illness in farmers (see www.hse.gov.uk/research/hsl_pdf/2002/hsl02-26.pdf); and can damage fish stocks when released into watercourses.

Wood fibre batts

K-value: *0.038–0.043W/mK*. Hygroscopic up to 20 per cent. Cut to shape using sharp blade – easy and safe to install, no irritating fibres. Good dimensional stability. Fire-resistant and uses no glue (formed under high pressure). Recyclable, renewable, biodegradable in landfill, non-hazardous. Use FSC (Forest Stewardship Council) approved sources or recycled cellulose. Good for most walls, ceilings, roofs, timber joisted floors. Embodied energy: 20MJ/kg or 2800MJ/m³ at 140kg/m³.

Cotton-based batts and rolls (e.g. Inno-therm)

K-value: *0.038–0.043W/mK*. Recyclable, recycled and renewable, a natural, non-hazardous fibre that's safe to install. Cotton mill scraps or recycled cotton is mixed with a bulking fibre such as hemp and a thermoplastic binder like polyester. The low-melt polyester gives structural integrity to make it self-supporting in stud wall applications, therefore it contains fossil-carbon-based elements. Comes as slabs or rolls. Good acoustic insulation and hydrophobic properties, it is biodegradable. Borate additives for pest, fungal and fire control pose none of the health concerns associated with some synthetic pesticides. Well-suited for breathable construction; good sound insulation; stable, durable and rot-proof.

Cellulose (loose, batt or board) (e.g. Warmcel, Homatherm)

K-value: *0.038–0.040W/mK*. Recyclable, renewable, made from finely shredded newspaper, safe to install. Loose-fill is blown in dry, e.g. in lofts, or wet on non-horizontal spaces. Long-term research is needed to ascertain whether there is a significant degree of settling over time. Breeze can displace loose-fill uncovered in loft-spaces. In batt form it is comfortable to work with and is readily cut to fit. The board form includes recycled jute sacking and is supplied in various thicknesses with tongue and groove edges. Boards may be used for external walls, reveal coverings, over rafter insulation and as internal non-water-resistant insulating fibreboard for use in floor, roof and wall constructions. Easy to cut with a sharp knife. Treated with an additive to resist insects and fire (borax is preferable to aluminium sulphates) and sometimes a binder to reduce settling. Hygroscopic, so can absorb moisture and gently give it off again. However performance is lowered if it gets damp too often. Beware of mould in non-ventilated damp spaces. Biodegradable in landfill, low embodied energy: 0.94 to 3.3MJ/kg.

Figure 2.4 *Semi-rigid cellulose slabs made of wood chippings – over 90% recycled – and polyolefin fibres*

Source: © Homatherm GmbH

Flax batts, slabs and rolls (e.g. CR flax, Natili)

K-value: *approximately 0.042W/mK*. Made from a plant whose fibres are bound together with potato starch and treated with borax to make them fire and insect resistant. Recyclable, renewable, a natural, non-hazardous fibre, safe to install. Some products may use plastic binding agents. Biodegradable in landfill. Prolonged exposure to water will cause decay. Embodied energy: 39.5MJ/kg or 1185MJ/m³ at 30kg/m³.

Hemp batts

K-value: *0.043W/mK*. Recyclable, renewable, natural, non-hazardous. Like wool and cotton batts, contains 15 per cent polyester fibre to retain lift and stability and borax. Biodegradable in landfill. Relatively expensive; embodied energy unknown/variable. Prolonged exposure to water will cause decay.

Figure 2.5 *Spraying in cellulose loft insulation*

Source: © Excel Industries

Coconut fibre board

K-value: *0.045W/mK*. Made from the outer husk of coconuts with borax and minimal processing. Made into batts or used in screed or timber floor and ceiling constructions. Sustainable/renewable, with variable embodied energy; reclaimable/recyclable/biodegradable, stable, durable, non-toxic, naturally resistant to rot, bacteria and mildew; well suited to a breathable construction.

Cork board (e.g. Korktherm, Westco)

K-value: *0.042–0.050W/mK*. Renewable resource from largely sustainably managed cork forests (harvesting the outer bark of cork oak), may contain recycled cork. Commonly used as underlay under hardwood and ceramic floors. Cork is granulated, expanded

Figure 2.6 *Spraying in cellulose into sloping loft insulation. Holes to be filled afterwards*

Source: © Russell Smith

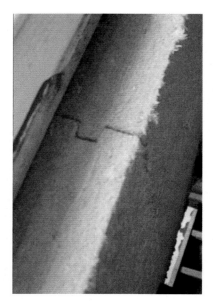

Figure 2.7 *Interlocking wood fibre board*

Source: © Gavin Killip

Figure 2.8 *Layered wood fibre board used for internal insulation of solid wall*

Source: © Dave Baines

and glued together under high pressures and temperatures. No binders need to be added as intrinsic resins do the job, but sometimes glue is used that can cause slight formaldehyde off-gassing. Inhibits sound and vibration. Contains suberin, a natural wax impermeable to gasses and liquid. Hygroscopic. Naturally resistant to rot, fire and termites. Retains its shape over time; its compression-resistance makes it ideal for flat roofing. Recyclable and bio-degradable. Embodied energy: 4MJ/kg or 640MJ/m³ at 160kg/m³.

Wood fibre board

K-value: *0.080W/mK*. The rigid insulation has a higher (worse) U-value than the batt form. Works due to sealed air cells within the fabric. Fire-resistant and uses no glue (formed under high pressure). Recyclable, renewable, biodegradable in landfill, non-hazardous. Some products are made from recycled cellulose. Good for wall and pitched roof construction. Embodied energy: 20MJ/kg or 2800MJ/m³ at 140kg/m³.

Strawboard (also used as internal partitioning)

K-value: *0.101W/mK*. Recycled, recyclable, renewable agricultural waste – 100 per cent straw. Produces its own binding resin (one product uses formaldehyde-free MDI resin as a binder). When used as partitioning, reduces timber requirements. Susceptible to fungal decay but can be treated with borax. Heavy. Need special skills to be installed. Must be kept dry to prevent swelling. Biodegradable. Embodied energy: unknown.

Hemcrete (e.g. Hemcrete, Canobiote, Canosmose, and Isochanvre)

K-value: *0.12–0.13W/mK*. Comprises hemp shiv with a lime matrix. High elasticity and vapour permeability. Long-lasting, doesn't shrink, is pest, water and fire resistant, flexible, low embodied energy. Easy to install (possible with dry-spray machinery), for roof, underfloor and wall insulation inside and out. Needs to be cast onto temporary shuttering. Typical compressive strength around 1MPa, >20 times lower than low grade concrete. Density: 15 per cent of traditional concrete.

2 Insulation derived from naturally occurring minerals

Aerogel (e.g. Spacetherm)

K-value: *0.013W/mK*. Aerogel has given rise to highly expensive new products such as flexible sheets and laminates, a type of glass and composite materials including plasterboard and sandwiched within PVC panels. Uneconomic but useful where width is limited as performance is so good. Made by extracting water from silica gel, replacing it in nano-sized pores with a gas such as carbon dioxide to comprise 99 per cent of volume. Very high compressive strength, high strength-to-weight ratio. Do not drill holes through to screw on wall, but fix on to battens. A type of insulating glass – 'Airglass', k-value: 0.021W/mK – looks like a normal windowpane, but is much lighter. Good electrical and sound insulating properties, stable and rigid, durable and rot-proof, impermeable to water-vapour, non-combustible, reclaimable. However, highly processed, non-renewable, high embodied energy and non-bio-degradable.

Fibreglass mineral wool batts and rolls (BSI kitemarked available) (e.g. British-Gypsum Isover, Knauf, Superglass) or Fibreglass board (e.g. Isowool, Dritherm)

K-value: 0.033–0.040W/mK. Made from molten glass, sometimes with 20 to 30 per cent recycled content. The most common residential insulant. Usually applied as batts, pressed between studs. Can be unfaced, paper-faced with a thin layer of asphalt (vapour retarding), or foil-faced (vapour barriers; the vapour barrier must face the proper direction). Long-lasting and rot-resistant. Moisture ingress and compression will reduce performance. Most mineral wools include a formaldehyde-based binder – exceptions are beginning to appear. Non-renewable, durable and rot-proof, non-flammable, except for the facing, non-biodegradable, reclaimable, not recyclable. Manufacturing can emit chlorides, fluorides, particulates, VOCs (volatile organic compounds) and solvents. Risks of cancer and breathing problems from exposure to glass fibres – use protective clothing when installing. Formaldehyde may off-gas from backing/resin. High embodied energy: 28MJ/kg at 30kg/m³ or 840MJ/m³ at 30kg/m³.

Mineral (rock & slag) wool batts and rolls (BSI kitemarked available) (e.g. Rockwool)

K-value: 0.033–0.040W/mK. Made of steel slag (over 75 per cent) with basalt rock (25 per cent or less). Energy-intensive: diabase rock and recycled briquettes are melted in a furnace and the result spun to form fibre. 3 per cent binder (often formaldehyde-based) and oil make it stable and water repellent. It is then heated again before final processing. Can be made from recycled steel slag. Used for loft and cavity wall insulation – blown in through a hose. Fireproof, recyclable, long-lasting, rot-resistant. Moisture ingress and compression will reduce performance. Installation may irritate skin, nose, eyes (wear a mask). Non-renewable, non-bio-degradable, highly reliant on fossil fuels. Embodied energy: 16.8MJ/kg (Rockwool) or 1008MJ/m³ at 60kg/m³.

Figure 2.9 *Rockwool made from stone wool waste and residue from other industries, used for external insulation of solid wall on Lacemaker's House, Nottingham*

Source: © Marsh-Grochowski

Foamed glass slab (e.g. Foamglas)

K-value: 0.042W/mK. Contains tiny sealed cells formed by reacting finely-ground oxidized glass (up to 60 per cent recycled) with carbon at high temperature. No additional foaming agents, CFCs,

Figure 2.10 *Mineral wool in loft insulation*

Source: © Chris Twinn

HCFCs, organic binders or other potentially harmful substances. Photochemical oxidants, SO_2 and NO_2 released in manufacture. High, durable compressive strength, non-permeable, high thermal mass, inherently resistant to fire and air movement. Needs bitumen or synthetic adhesives to install. Re-usable. High embodied energy: 27MJ/kg or 3240MJ/m³ at 120kg/m³.

Perlite

K-value: *0.045–0.05W/mK*. Naturally occurring volcanic glass that greatly expands and becomes porous when heated sufficiently. Loose-fill, granular, light weight. Poured into place, to fill concrete block cores, or mixed with cement to create a lighter, less heat-conductive concrete. Also made into boards of expanded perlite, cellulose binders and waterproofing agents. Top surface is treated to retain bitumen for tight bond with a membrane. Must be installed in sealed spaces. Reclaimable, safe to install, non-flammable, moisture resistant. Non-renewable, mined. High embodied energy.

Exfoliated vermiculite

K-value: *0.063W/mK*. Clay-based, otherwise like perlite with many of same properties, advantages and disadvantages.

Expanded clay aggregate (LECA or Hydroton)

K-value: *0.09–0.1W/mK*. Small, fired pellets like vermiculite; a structural, lightweight granular aggregate. Many of the same features.

3 Multi-foil insulation (or 'Radiant barriers')

K-value: *disputed*. Layers of polyethylene coated foils spaced with wadding and closed cell foams. Its thinness makes it ideal for places where little width is available. Made from non-renewable petrochemicals and aluminium. Can have poor airtightness. Expensive, vulnerable to being punctured, which will render it useless. Very effective in reducing radiant heat transfer. Opinion sharply divided over effectiveness. Tests by the National Physical Laboratory (who have United Kingdom Accreditation Service accreditation) using test methods in accordance with BS EN ISO 8990 have indicated an R-value of 1.69–1.71m²K/W. Manufacturers claiming R-values of 5–6m²K/W. A study by the Irish Sustainability Institute (2007) found the Tri-Iso 10 insulation performed worse than Rockwool, which itself performed worse than Holzflex flax board and sheepswool, under laboratory conditions. High embodied energy, non-biodegradable in landfill.

Figure 2.11 *Multi-foil insulation used for internal insulation*

Source: © Chris Twinn

4 Fossil carbon

All manufactured at high temperatures, derived from fossil fuels. Extremely high embodied energy. Vulnerable to sunlight and high temperatures – do not use near high temperatures, such as chimneys, steam pipes, electrical heaters. Flammable. Emit more toxic fumes when burnt, non-biodegradable in landfill, must be recycled at end of life. Reclaimable, hydrophobic. Long-lasting, resistant to moisture, air movement, rot and compression. Make sure the quoted conductivity is in accordance with European Standard BS EN 13166 giving the 'aged' or long-term value. Leakage of blowing agents will deplete effectiveness over time.

The expanding agent used in foam insulation can be a halocarbon, pentane, water, or CO_2 depending on the type of insulation and its use. Halocarbons harm the ozone layer and cause global warming. Pentane is a green house gas but has a much lower global warming potential (GWP) of 7 (CO_2 has 1). The least damaging options for blowing agents for each type of insulant are:

- polyisocyanurate and polyethylene terephthalate (PET) foam: pentane, cyclopentane;
- polyurethane (PU): pentane, CO_2, CO_2/H_2O (for spray foams); various isomers of pentane;
- Extruded polystyrene (XPS): pentane, CO_2; cyclopentane/isopentane blends (Ashford et al, 2005).

Figure 2.12 *Phenolic-backed plasterboard used for internal insulation of solid wall*

Source: © Penny Poyzer and Gil Schalom

Phenolic foam board (e.g. Kingspan Kooltherm)

K-value: *0.020–0.25W/mK*. Closed cell phenolic foam is designed for roofing, cavity board, external wall board, plaster board dry linings systems, floor insulation and as sarking board. Manufactured by sandwiching phenolic resin (petrochemical-derived), a catalyst and blowing agent within facings, one of which is usually reflective, passing it through ovens.

Expanded polystyrene board and beads (EPS)

K-value: *0.032–0.040W/mK* (beads are towards the high end of the scale). Thermoplastic, melts if heated (for moulding or extrusion), produced from 90–95 per cent polystyrene and 5–10 per cent gas – pentane or carbon dioxide. Expanded into foam using heat. Polystyrene beads are used primarily in masonry cavities. Can be recovered for re-use or recycled into new sheeting. Boards not recommended for older, breathable constructions, but their rigidity, lightweight, acoustic insulation, longevity and other properties listed above make them very popular. Embodied energy: 88.6MJ/kg or 1772MJ/m³ at 20kg/m³.

Figure 2.13 *Phenolic foam board*

Source: © Hyde Housing Association

Extruded polystyrene board (XPS) (e.g. Kingspan Styrozone)

K-value: *0.028–0.036W/mK*. Uniform closed-cell structure, smooth continuous skin. Some products use recycled polystyrene. Very high compressive strength.

Figure 2.14 *Polystyrene internal insulation round wall and window reveal*

Source: © Chris Twinn

Figure 2.15 *Foil-backed polyurethane board internal insulation round wall and window reveal*

Figure 2.16 *Foil-backed polyurethane board internal insulation in roof*

Polyurethane/polyisocyanurate board and foam (e.g. Kingspan Therma)

K-value: *0.02–0.033 W/mK*. Foam or rigid board. Foam is sprayed in at high temperatures; within seconds it will expand by over 30 times giving a seamless rigid covering. Stable, durable, ideal for plugging gaps or leaks. Any thickness can be achieved. High in compressive strength. Hydrophobic. The use of gastight foils such as aluminium can reduce the degradation. Embodied energy: 72.1MJ/kg or 2307MJ/m^3 at 32kg/m^3.

Spray foam

Convenient but highly controversial, more sustainable alternatives do exist.

Pros:

- expands while curing, filling gaps, providing resistance to air infiltration (unlike batts and blankets, which can leave gaps and air pockets, and better than some types of loose-fill. Wet-spray recycled cellulose (paper) is comparable;
- provides sound insulation;
- can be used in places where loose-fill cannot;
- can be applied in small quantities;
- highly insulating.

Cons:

- see the notes on blowing agents above;
- most, such as polyurethane and isocyanate, contain hazardous chemicals such as formaldehyde, benzene and toluene. Health effects of isocyanate exposure include irritation of skin and mucous membranes, chest tightness, and difficult breathing:
- many are made from petrochemicals but some are made from renewable or recycled sources;

- wear protective mask or goggles during installation;
- can crack or overfill, reducing airtightness or causing damage;
- leakage to the atmosphere of the blowing agent halocarbon – a greenhouse gas – which happens during the product's lifetime, reduces its effectiveness. The time required for the insulation-related emission savings to offset the manufacturing and leakage losses for differing thicknesses of insulation is called the marginal payback time. Harvey (2007) recommends taking this into account if it is used to top off pre-existing insulation in building up to very high insulation levels (RSI 6-10). He says 'it is worth adding insulation, from a climate point of view, up to the point where the marginal payback time equals the expected lifespan of the insulation (usually assumed to be 50 years)', but cautions: 'The small additional [climate] savings in heating energy emissions using halocarbon blowing agents is swamped by the larger impact of leakage of the blowing agent. Thus, non-halocarbon blowing agents are again better from a climate point of view.'

These products are more sustainable alternatives:

- Cementitious foam: U-value: 1.456. Fireproof. Air is the blowing agent. Will not smoke at all upon direct contact with flame and is a two-hour firewall at a 10cm (3.5 inch) application. Made from magnesium oxide cement. Relatively environmentally friendly and non-toxic, even during application. Gives off no VOC (volatile organic compound) emissions. Insect proof. Can be friable and fragile at low thicknesses, so may crack if there is movement in the building. Contains a lot of water and will need a drying period before wall can be closed up. Brand name: Air-krete.
- Vegetable oil foams: made from soybean oil and recycled plastic bottles, and from castor oil. Use zero ozone depletion substances as blowing agent (water) and also contain no VOCs or CFCs. Renewable product storing carbon in the building. Brand names: Icynene, BioBased, Pur and Polarfoam.

Eco-wool (e.g. non-itch) – batts

K-value: *0.039–0.042W/mK*. Recycled alternative to glass wool, made from 85 per cent recycled plastic. Comes in rolls or slabs of varying thicknesses. Suitable for loft and stud walls. Easy to install, reclaimable/recyclable, stable, durable, rot-proof, non-toxic, non-irritant. Good sound insulant, impermeable to water-vapour. No protective equipment required to install. High embodied energy, non-biodegradable.

Structural Insulated Panels (SIPs)

K-value: *variable approximately 0.040W/mK*. A building method using pre-cut expanded polystyrene (EPS) or extruded polystyrene foam (XPS) to erect an airtight structure quickly that eliminates thermal bridging. Pre-fabricated panels are shipped to sites where a shell of a building can be erected quickly, saving labour time and money. For renovation work they may be used for building

Figure 2.17 *Structural insulated panel*

Table 2.3 An alternative thermal insulation comparison table

Common form	Product	R-value m²K/w (R)	Conductivity 25°W/m²K (k)	Thickness mm (t)	Density kg/m³ (D)	Mass kg/100m² at R2.5 (M)	Decomp temp °C (Tdec)	Max. service temp (Tmax)	Thermal perform. ranking (Pi)	Fire perform. ranking[c] (Pf)	ALH toxicity ranking (Pt)	Normalized ranking overall (Po)
loose	Rockwool granulated	2.5	0.038	95	32	304	700	650	1	1	0	1
batt	Glasswool batts	2.5	0.038	95	10	95	400	350	5	1	0	2
loose	Vermiculite	2.5	0.08	200	230	4600	1200	1000	12	0	0	3
foam spray	Urea formaldehyde	2.5	0.049	123	10	123	250	100	3	2	3	4
board	Calcium silicate	2.5	0.044	110	200	2200	1050	950	17	0	0	5
board	Foamglas	2.5	0.05	125	136	1700	600	538	18	0	0	6
loose	Cellulose F/retarded	2.2	0.04	100[a]	32	320	200	60	2	6	2	7
'board'	Foil FR batts	1.4[b]	n/a	25	n/a	58	150	80	8	5	1	8
loose	Seagrass	2.5	0.04	100	40	400	200	60	3	6	3	9
blanket	Dacron (Polyester)	2.5	0.058	145	78	113	250	150	10	5	0	10
board	Phenolic foam	2.5	0.036	90	30	270	160	120	6	3	4	11
board	Melamine foams	2.5	0.028	70	25	175	250	120	11	4	3	12
board	Polyimide foam	2.5	0.042	106	7	74	300	260	21	2	0	13
blanket	Sheep's wool batts	2.5	0.057	143	8	114	200	60	7	7	3	14
blanket	Acoustifoam	2.5	0.03	75	25	187	150	110	13	7	2	15
blanket	Modacrylic	2.5	0.05	125	8	100	150	140	9	9	2	16
board	Rigid polyurethane	2.5	0.024	60	32	192	140	110	14	8	3	17
loose	Sheep's wool loose	2.5	0.048	120	32	384	200	60	3	6	10	18
board	Polyisocyanurate	2.5	0.026	65	32	208	150	140	15	8	3	19
board	Polystyrene extruded	2.5	0.029	73	29	210	140	74	16	10	2	20
board	Thermotec P/E foam	2.5	0.039	98	40	390	100	90	19	10	3	21
board	Nitrile foams	2.5	0.038	95	96	912	120	110	18	4	10	22

Notes: [a] Settling allowance for cellulose 15–20 per cent of installed thickness.

[b] R-Value is for single cell foil batt, winter-time, heat flow upwards, 'aged' dusty upper surface only, no leakage losses or bridging allowed for.

[c] Fire performance comparison based on best available data and is relative only since not all products tested by same test methods.

Source: Mr Roeland Ansems, Ansems Engineering and Management, for Australasian Insulation Supplies (www.ais-group.com.au/homeinsulation/comparative_survey.htm)

Table 2.4 *Further comparison of insulants*

Material	K-value	Renewable	Recyclable	Embodied energy	Pollution/toxic
Vacuum insulated panels	0.004	No	Reclaimable	HCFC free	Low
Phenolic foam board	0.018–0.025	No	Reclaimable	High	Low
Aerogel	0.021	No	Reclaimable	High	Low
Expanded polystyrene (EPS)	0.032	No	Yes	High	Low
Fibreglass	0.032	No	Reclaimable	High	Low
Extruded polystyrene (EXP)	0.032	No	Reclaimable	High	Low
Polystyrene (blown beads)	0.032–0.040	No	Yes	High	Low
Polyurethane	0.033	No	Yes	High	High
Mineral wool batts	0.035	No	Reusable	Low	High
Cellulose blown or loose	0.036	Yes	Yes	Low	High
Cotton polyester mix quilts	0.037	Yes	Yes	Low	No
Wool quilts	0.037	Yes	Yes	Low	HCFC free
Cellulose or wooden boards	0.038	Yes	Yes	Low[a]	High
Flax/hemp quilts	0.038	Yes	Yes	Low	High
Eco-wool	0.039–0.042	Yes	Yes	No	Low[a]
Mineral fibre blown	0.04	No	No, mined	High	HCFC free
Glass fibre blown	0.04	No, mined	No[b]	High	Low
Cork boards	0.041	Yes	Yes	Low	High
Foamed glass slab	0.042	No	Reusable	HCFC free	High
Coconut fibre board	0.045	Yes	Yes	Low	High
Straw	0.05	Yes	Yes	Low	High
Perlite beads	0.05	No	No, mined	High	High
Latex Foam	1.5	No	No	High	High

Notes: [a] depending on binder.
[b] recycled glass.

Source: www.sustainablebuildingresource.co.uk/products/natural_insulation/1485.
Derived from manufacturers' data, reports and the AECB

extensions or new walls or even external insulation. A typical construction consists of two 10–20cm thick boards sandwiched between two oriented strand boards (OSBs) or other structural facing materials. Same structural properties as I-beams or I-columns. Structural Insulated Panels (SIPs) replace components such as studs and joists, insulation, vapour barrier and air barrier. Many different applications such as exterior wall, roof, floor and foundation systems. R-value depends on density, typically R-3.8 to R-5.0 per inch. Share the disadvantages of EPS and XPS. Quality of installation is vital to performance. There are reports of insects and rodents tunnelling throughout the SIPs, so some installers suggest adding insecticide, which might have adverse side-effects.

Conclusion

Now that we have a better understanding of the palette of materials available to us, the next two chapters deal with how we can employ these materials to make our homes more comfortable, cheaper to run and more climate-friendly.

Websites

Irish Sustainability Institute, www.sustainability.ie
Scottish SelfBuild and Renovation Visitor Centre, www.buildstore.co.uk/ScottishSelfBuildCentre
Sustainable Energy Authority of Ireland, www.seai.ie

References

AECB and Jim Parker (2009) 'Projecting energy use and CO_2 emissions from low energy buildings: A comparison of the Passivhaus Planning Package (PHPP) and SAP', Report, September, AECB, Llandysull

Ashford, P., Wu, J., Jeffs, M., Kocchi, S., Vodianitskaia, P., Lee, S., et al (2005) 'Foams', Chapter 7 in 'IPCC/TEAP Special report on safeguarding the ozone layer and the global climate system: Issues related to hydrofluorocarbons and perfluorocarbons', Cambridge University Press, Cambridge

Bevan, R. and Woolley, T. (2008) *Hemp Line Construction: A Guide to Building with Hemp Line Composites*, BREPress, Bracknell

CIBSE (Chartered Institute of Building Services Engineers) (2006) *Guide A: Environmental Design*, CIBSE, London

EFRA (2000) 'Potential risk of fire spread in buildings via external cladding systems', EFRA select committee report, Her Majesty's Stationery Office, London

EST (Energy Saving Trust) (2006) 'CE184 – Practical refurbishment of solid-walled houses', EST, London

Hammond, G. and Jones, C. (2008) *Inventory of Energy and Carbon (ICE) Version 1.6a 2008*, Bath University, Bath, www.bath.ac.uk/mech-eng/sert/embodied, last accessed March 2010

Harvey, L. D. (2007) 'Net climatic impact of solid foam insulation produced with halocarbon and non-halocarbon blowing agents', *Building and Environment Journal*, vol 42, pp2860–2870

Irish Sustainability Institute (2007) 'Sustainable housing: The case for renovation', *Sustainability Magazine*, vol 1, Spring

3
Insulation Strategies

If at all possible it is generally easier and cheaper to insulate a whole structure – even a whole terrace or apartment block – at once. However, it is not always possible to do this, so this chapter, after looking at general principles, goes on to discuss how to insulate the building elements – walls, roofs, floors, etc. – one by one. We'll look at how 'tight' and 'warm' the standard aimed for should be and what this means for different property types, particularly older, solid wall homes. We'll also look at 'wind tightness'.

The whole dwelling approach

Making over a whole building is easier because access is easier, and there is no disruption to occupants – hopefully they will have moved out!

In the case of a single house a proper attempt can be made to secure airtightness by encasing the entire occupied area within an unbroken airtight barrier inside the insulation layer. You may need to redesign the way services enter the building and are accessed by occupants. In the case of a block of flats, each flat within the block should itself be treated as an airtight container with its own insulation and ventilation scheme, so that for instance the stack effect (for ventilation) can be managed and the heat from one occupied unit is not leaking into an unheated unit, or cold air being drawn into the heated area from an unheated one. The same principle applies to semi-detached houses and terraces, where, although the exterior walls and roofs and floors may have been taken care of, there can be significant leakage into adjacent properties through party walls, especially in attic spaces. In each case, designs should be thoroughly detailed, so that the airtightness membrane line is known with confidence throughout, comprehensive detailing is specified, the exact impact of all elements is known and a schedule of work has been drawn up.

Wind tightness is another concept, known from experience potentially to severely compromise the effectiveness of insulation. It's not yet catered for in building regulations in most countries and again, it is easier to address this issue on a whole building basis.

Figures 3.1 and 3.2 *Before and after a whole (council) house renovation, using Permarock mineral fibre external insulation with acrylic render and traditional brick slip finish, with new windows, doors and canopies. This upgraded the properties to 0.30W/m²K*

Source: © Permarock, an INCA member

External insulation is also more easily applied to an entire building, apartment block or terrace; once teams are on location and scaffolding in place, they can more cost-efficiently tackle a whole terrace or block. Terraced dwellings will feel the benefit as heat can otherwise be conducted from an insulated to an uninsulated exterior wall on an adjacent property if there is no overlap of insulation and there will be no irregular outer dimensions of adjacent properties.

Aiming for airtightness

An insulation layer is as effective as it is airtightly sealed. In one German experiment even a tiny leak of just 1mm meant that performance of the insulation was reduced 4.8 times. The study, at the Fraunhofer Institute of Building Physics, looked at 14cm thick insulation with a seamless vapour barrier/check with a measured U-value of $0.30W/m^2K$. Gaps of various widths were then made in the vapour barrier and it was tested at various pressures. The 1mm gap meant that the U-value was not $0.30W/m^2K$ but $1.44W/m^2K$.

So installers must strive for the total elimination of gaps – but the quality of design and specification is vital too and can bring significant financial and carbon savings. Over a 200-day heating period, a house with eight air changes per hour and a 100m² floor area, heated to 20°C, will cost three times more to heat than an equivalent house with three air changes per hour, according to an energy calculator (SIGA).

If you want to move beyond simple draught-proofing as described in Chapter 1 you should really first decide what standard of airtightness to aim for. Air changes per hour (ACH) of 0.6 at 50 Pascals (Pa) pressure, or $1m^3/h/m^2$ (one cubic metre of air changed per hour per square metre of floor space), is the goal for Passivhaus certification. For comparison, 'best practice' in the UK is currently a target of $3m^3/h/m^2$ for dwellings with whole house mechanical ventilation (with or without heat recovery) and for dwellings with other ventilation systems, while 'good practice' is considered to be $4m^3/h/m^2$ and $7m^3/h/m^2$ respectively. Thus, Passivhaus is a demanding target, frequently missed but worth striving for.

Measuring airtightness

As noted in Chapter 1, 'air changes per hour' at the artificially induced pressure of 50 Pa (ACH50 or n50) is the accepted metric for measuring airtightness in continental European countries. Another way of looking at the rate of air leakage is in terms of whole building permeability, or the volume of air leaking per hour per square metre $(m^3/h/m^2)$ of total surface area (ceiling area + wall area + floor area) at 50Pa (known as Q50). This is used in the UK, for example in Part L of the Building Regulations. It is defined in BS EN 13829.

How do the two relate? Q50 is the flow divided by the area of the envelope and n50 is the flow divided by the building volume. The shape of the building therefore affects how close these figures are to each other. Unless the building is an unusual shape, there is little difference between the two. A house achieving an air permeability of $20m^3/h/m^2$ at 50Pa could be assumed to have an ACH at 50Pa of say, 18.

Air leakage is driven by differences in pressure. Normal pressures are in the range of 1–4Pa so ACH is also calculated at 4Pa (ACH4) to estimate how much air movement is happening under normal air pressure conditions. You can estimate this figure by dividing the above figure by 20, which, in the above example, would yield 1 ($m^3/h/m^2$ or ACH).

It's important to realize that the stack effect (warm air rising) and mechanical heating/cooling/ventilating systems can create pressure differentials in the range of 5–10Pa, while wind can cause differences as great as 150–1500Pa.

It may help to visualize the size of the problem by converting the leakage rate to an 'effective leakage area' (ELA) or hole in the outer wall. Assuming the building was airtight, the size of this hole is relative to the rate at which the air is being pushed through the hole, which may be the pressure used in the blower door test, or in the real world, how windy it is. For example, if there were 30 air changes per hour at 50Pa (ACH50 or n50), this would equate to about 1.5 air changes per hour at normal pressures (ACH4 or n4), so the leakage rate (Q50) would be 25$m^3/h/m^2$ – the equivalent of having a 49cm square opening in the envelope at 4 Pa. Effective leakage area is calculated using specialist software.

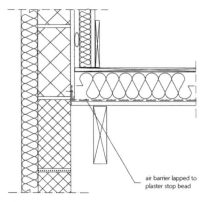

air barrier lapped to plaster stop bead

Figure 3.3 *Example of detailing showing the airtightness barrier marked in blue*

Note: Taken from the Energy Saving Trust's Enhanced Construction Details: suspended floor insulation.

Source: © EST

The airtightness barrier

The next stage lies in choosing where you're going to draw the line on draughts with your airtightness barrier. It must form a continuous envelope around the structure within the insulation. This is easier if you are renovating the whole building, but even if not, it is a good idea to plan for the future on the assumption that eventually the wrapping will be continuous, if there is not the budget or opportunity to do it now.

The devil is always in the detail and the most problematic details here are at the boundaries of the barrier with punctures of the walls such as windows, skylights, joists, doors and service entries. The simpler the geometry of the building, the fewer junctions there will be, so the less risk of leaks. Timber joists built into a block or brick wall can be dealt with using mastic and tape but this is a poor solution as gaps can develop. At least one company supplies polypropylene joist seals for these gaps. A better idea, if a building is to be gutted, is using joist hangars. Curved joins, as on bay windows, are a challenge. Careful attention must be paid to where services penetrate.

What is the airtight barrier made of? Any suitable impermeable material able to withstand pressures created by wind, stack effect or ventilation systems. In the case of masonry wall construction, it might be the internal plaster. For a concrete wall construction, concrete itself could be taken as the air barrier. In the case of timber frame construction, a polyethylene membrane, protected from the wind, could perform this function.

The National Building Code of Canada defines an air barrier as one with a maximum air permanence of 0.05$m^3/h/m^2$ @ 50Pa. The Association of Energy Conscious Builders (AECB) gives examples of materials which meet this definition: '0.15 and 0.25mm thick polyethylene membranes, in situ concrete walls, plastered masonry walls, and most practical thicknesses of foamed in situ polyisocyanurate foam. Variable-vapour-permeability polyethylene membranes of the above thicknesses usually comply also'. The AECB discounts certain materials which would normally be used for lower standards but which are not appropriate here: e.g., Nilvent, Monarperm and Tyvek, as well as boards such as OSB and foam such as EPS which are not intrinsically airtight. To meet the Canadian standard, sheet materials of adequate vapour resistance and thickness with permanently sealed joints between boards would be needed instead of a fully sealed airtight membrane.

The question of 'permanently sealed' is a difficult one, as insufficient years have elapsed since the standard came in for research to have been conducted on the optimum sealing method. With this in mind, it's best as a precaution to incorporate failsafe fallbacks; so, should one air barrier fail, another will challenge the air movement further on – requiring some thought about how vapour may move from one element or space to another.

In lightweight constructions, particularly timber elements of masonry and timber frame constructions, the airtightness layer typically acts a vapour control layer as well. It prevents warm humid air from inside coming into contact with cooler elements outside the insulation and causing interstitial condensation, which can lead to rot. We therefore have two reasons to beware of leaks in the vapour barrier. The same experiment by the Fraunhofer Institute of Building Physics described above also found that a 1mm gap in the layer increased the amount of moisture leaking out by 1600 times!

Breathable plasters like lime are airtight. For timber or steel framed structures, the barrier must be an elastomer membrane. These come in different thicknesses and some are self-adhesive. Tapes of maximum durability are supplied to fix and join them. In this instance breathability is important and using an intelligent airtight membrane (see below) greatly increases drying capacity. If the rate of moisture penetration into the wall or ceiling is greater than the evaporation rate then structural damage will inevitably set in. Usually, the vapour resistance of the building envelope's layers should increase towards the inside, but sometimes, as with a flat roof, the outer layer must have a very high vapour resistance. The appropriate vapour control layer is chosen by reference to internal humidity, temperature and pressure differences. For example, high performance layers will be needed on bathroom walls where humidity and temperature are higher.

Intelligent membranes

Airtight membranes with variable vapour resistance are known as intelligent membranes. These have the almost magical property of being able to resist vapour migrating into structural elements, particularly in timber frame constructions, to fight interstitial condensation over the lifetime of the building. They consist of a sheet with various layers that allow or obstruct moisture-laid air from passing through it according to the relative humidity, temperatures and pressures on either side. For example if a room has high temperature and humidity and it is cold on the outside it would prevent the moisture from travelling outwards and risk condensing on cold surfaces. Conversely, when it is cooler on the inside and there is less humidity, moisture can gradually return to help dry out the interstitial space.

If moisture is present inside and cannot dry towards the outside, in summer months it would tend to be pushed inwards as the sunshine warms the outside surface. When it reaches the intelligent membrane, humidity will increase, which triggers it to become up to 50 times more diffusion open, allowing moisture which may otherwise become trapped behind the vapour check to dry out as quickly as possible. Intelligent membranes can be used in combination with ventilation as a fallback in case the ventilation fails.

Interstitial condensation

The risk of interstitial condensation should be assessed by a calculation method (undertaken by the insulation manufacturer) to determine if and where it is likely to take place, whether it will be harmful and the optimum level of vapour control for that part of the structure. BS EN 15026 – a standard for calculating interstitial condensation – outlines this particular effect very clearly. Its variables include dew point assessment, the effect of driving rain, colour of external cladding, the hygroscopic behaviour of materials, heat and moisture storage, latent heat effects and liquid and convective transport under realistic boundary and initial conditions.

Using the WUFI (Wärme und Feuchte Instationär) calculation software (www.wufi.de) is another way of carrying out such assessments. It permits the accurate calculation of the moisture content of building elements after one, 10 or 20 years, as well as two-dimensional heat transport in multi-layer building components exposed to natural weather. It's based on the most recent findings regarding vapour diffusion and moisture transport in building materials and has been validated by comparison with measurements at the Fraunhofer Institute for Building Physics. (It does employ German units for vapour resistivity but supplies a formula for transferring Sd values to MNs/g.) You'll get detailed and accurate information on the risk of interstitial condensation and potential remedial treatments.

We shall return to this complex topic later, but one factor likely to be involved is the presence of thermal bridges.

Thermal bridges

A thermal bridge is created when materials with U-values higher than those demanded by the energy-efficiency requirements of the surrounding structure pass through the insulation or building envelope, conducting heat out, or conducting cold in. Examples include fixings, windows, joists, services, wall ties in cavities and concrete balconies that extend the floor slab through the building envelope. The loss of heat per unit length of thermal bridge is quantified by the k- or psi-value, whose unit is W/mK (see Chapter 2).

Condensation (e.g. in floor-wall connections, window reveals, etc.) as well as mould growth in humid environments is often down to a thermal bridge. As more and more insulation and draught-proofing is used in a building, thermal bridging becomes increasingly significant as a factor in heat transfer. Thermal bridges are classified as:

- repeating: where they follow a regular pattern, e.g., wall ties penetrating a cavity wall;
- non-repeating: e.g. a single lintel crossing a cavity wall;
- geometrical: at the junction of two planes, e.g., the corners of walls, or wall/ceiling junctions.

The solution is to break them – by inserting insulation. For example, timber window frames should have insulation sandwiched between the inside and outside to halt heat transfer through them.

Wind tightness

So, the vapour control membrane is situated on the warm side of the insulation. But how does wind affect the performance of the insulation itself? Thermal imaging of the same walls and roofs taken on calm and windy days can show completely different colour patterns – the cool blues and greens changing alarmingly to warm reds and oranges. This is because winds of surprisingly low speeds can draw heat out of insulated buildings, by 'wind washing', or cause convection inside insulation that compromises its theoretical effectiveness. Dubbed 'wind tightness' this is not catered for in building regulations in most countries, although campaigners are working towards this.

A study by Bednar and Deseyve (2005) in Austria showed that wind induced ventilation in non-ventilated compact roofs due to leaky eave or ridge details and unsealed underlay caused a tenfold increase of the heat flux near the eaves. The size of the effect depends on the wind direction relative to the roof, the quality of the workmanship and the construction detail of the eaves and the ridge. Furthermore, if cold air can penetrate through to the vapour control layer, it lowers its temperature, causing the warmer internal air to cool as it touches the membrane, which potentially also may lead to condensation, mould and damage.

To tackle this, a windtightness layer into spaces where this may be a problem must be designed, for example above insulation in a roof space, from the eaves and outside of insulation in exposed exterior walls. Softboard, ply, polythene and sarking are all examples of materials that may be used. Skylights should be airtight on the inside and windtight on the outside. If all movement of air around the outside of the insulation is minimized it performs much better.

Pitched lightweight roofs with thermal insulation should be fully insulated air- and windtight sandwich constructions, where the diffusion resistance of the sub-roof can never be too small.

Construction

Having fixed the design the next step is to choose properly trained contractors. Your installers must 'get' the principles of airtightness, and what they have to do to achieve it. Try to pick contractors who have been on an accredited course. Membrane sheeting should be chosen in the largest possible specification to

Figures 3.4 and 3.5
Thermographic images – warmer colours reveal the escape of heat. Right: a door with and without draught-proofing

Source: © BSRIA and Sto, an INCA member

Figure 3.6 *Blower test on a ventilation (MVHR) system*

Source: © JPW Construction

reduce joints. Special attention must be paid to how the edges of membranes are joined together. Suitable long-lasting tape must be applied, but there is in reality no guarantee of how many years it will last – especially if you consider the potential lifetime of the building versus the lifetime of the adhesive. So, it's best not to rely solely on the use of tape. Fit membranes vertically from top to bottom, so that the lap happens over a stud, floor joists, door and window frames, where the joint can be filled with mastic and then taped, after which a batten is nailed over it to maximize the longevity of this vital bond.

Each piece of detailing must be talked through with the contractors and responsibility allocated to somebody on the team to ensure that it has been carried out correctly before it is covered up. It may even be worth photographing details as they are completed and before they are covered to keep a record for later reference should problems arise at, say, the pressure testing stage. The system must last the life of the building without emitting any harmful levels of volatile organic compounds (VOCs) – which can come from some adhesives and solvents. Products with solvents and high boiling points dry out much faster but become more brittle over time and can therefore fail.

Testing for airtightness

Once the airtightness operation is complete it should be tested before plasterboard or other covering is put over the layer. This is done with a blower door – or pressure – test, by sealing up the chimneys and flues and placing a fan over an exit to pressurize the building to 50Pa, then measuring how quickly the pressure is reduced and calibrating it with the volume of the interior. Standards exist for calibrating this process; one recommended procedure is contained in ATTMA TS1 'Measuring air permeability of building envelopes' (ATTMA, 2007). This standard allows the results to be compared with each other.

Figure 3.7 *Whole house blower test*

Souce: © Russell Smith

The test should ideally be carried out while the vapour control layer is still visible, so that any faults can easily be repaired. It is essential that the person carrying out the pressure testing knows exactly what they are doing otherwise any results can be seriously inaccurate and invalid. Pressure testing is not cheap – the equipment and operator must be hired for a day – but it is a worthwhile investment considering all the trouble you're going to and the effect that it can have on bills over the lifetime of the building. Infrared thermography is also extremely helpful, with the building heated of course (see illustrations above).

Mechanical ventilation with heat recovery

Extreme airtightness is not favoured by all environmental builders and architects because it usually implies reliance upon the use of mechanical ventilation with heat recovery (MVHR) systems to maintain a healthy indoor atmosphere, unless passive stack ventilation can be employed (see Chapter 6). This equipment inevitably consumes electricity and so instead some advocate well-insulated structures that are naturally ventilated and fuelled by low or zero carbon sources. However, MVHR energy consumption is coming down as manufacturers adopt low wattage fans and motors and are improving the efficiency of their heat exchangers. MVHR and high levels of airtightness are usually partners, with the technology necessary for health and safety below a level of three ACH at 50Pa. We'll look at this more in Chapter 5.

How 'warm' should it get?

Table 3.1 below gives U-values for these basic building elements that are considered best practice by the UK's Energy Saving Trust. Passivhaus standard will strive to go beyond this and is discussed in the next chapter. For each building element, an approximate existing U-value is given, together with a strategy and then the approximate result of implementing that strategy.

How do you estimate the U-values of an existing building? Usually these are derived with reference to the structure's design, age and the standard of the building regulations in force at the time of its construction. In England and Wales this information can be obtained from the Energy Saving Trust, which publishes documents on how to assess the U-values of existing housing (Northern Ireland's is publication CE127, and Scotland's is publication CE84).

Insulation element by element

If you can't renovate the whole building the best priority for renovating the elements is in the order of roof/ceiling, walls, floor. External insulation makes it easier to avoid cold bridges and so achieve higher savings but maybe costlier upfront. (Radiant barriers can be useful where space is limited. However you have to maintain sealed air gaps between and around all layers.)

Cavity wall insulation

Cavity walls were originally introduced in windy, wet areas to stop wind-driven rain from penetrating a building. They spread to drier areas because someone noticed it made buildings a bit warmer. Since 1945 lightweight blocks, rather than

Table 3.1 *Summary of recommended insulation standards*

Existing construction element	Typical U-value W/m²K	Improvement measure	Target U-value W/m²K
Cavity walls	1.5	Fill cavity with insulation. It is highly recommended to consider adding additional external or internal insulation to achieve improved levels of performance.	0.5–0.6
Solid walls	2.1	Insulate internally using insulation backed dry-lining, insulation with studwork, or insulate externally using wet render, dry cladding or bespoke systems. Between 80 to 140mm of insulation will be required in all cases to achieve the target U-value (dependent upon insulation conductivity).	0.30
Floor	0.70	Insulate above and below concrete slab, or between joists of timber ground floor with 100 to 200mm of insulation (depending upon geometry).	0.20–0.25
Pitched roof (uninsulated)	1.9	Install 250 to 300mm mineral wool quilt (first layer between joists, second layer across joists).	0.16
		Insulate between rafters with insulation in addition to 40 to 100mm of insulation either above or below the rafters (dependant upon insulant conductivity).	0.20
Flat roof	1.5	Add 100 to 160mm of insulation above structural deck (dependant upon insulant conductivity). If replacing, a pitched roof should be considered.	0.25
Glazing	3.1	Replace with high performance windows that incorporate integral draughtstripping.	BFRC rating in B and C or better

Note: BFRC British Fenestration Rating Council.

Source: Energy Saving Trust CE83

bricks, have been used for the inner leaf and, since the 1980s, new houses have been built with insulation in the cavity – commonly waterproof rigid foam boards, semi-rigid mineral wool, or glassfibre 'batts' – fixed to the inner leaf, leaving a

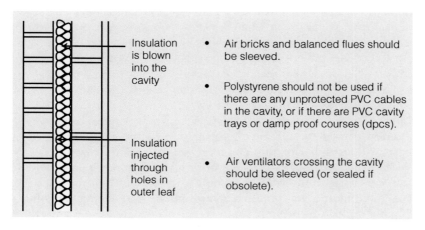

Insulation is blown into the cavity

Insulation injected through holes in outer leaf

- Air bricks and balanced flues should be sleeved.

- Polystyrene should not be used if there are any unprotected PVC cables in the cavity, or if there are PVC cavity trays or damp proof courses (dpcs).

- Air ventilators crossing the cavity should be sleeved (or sealed if obsolete).

Figure 3.8 *Insulation injected into cavity*

Note: For more detailed guidance on cavity wall insulation see EST (2007).

Source: © Russell Smith

Figure 3.9 *Insulation injected into cavity*

Source: © EST

narrow cavity to intercept any rainwater that penetrates the outer leaf. You can tell if a building has a cavity wall because it usually has the bricks placed lengthways (stretcher bond). The two 'leaves' are held together using metal or, more recently plastic, wall ties.

Remaining empty cavities, which range from 50–85mm in width, must be filled as a priority, unless internal or external insulation is being applied to a higher U-value. Cavities less than 50mm should not normally be filled. Insulation involves drilling holes in the outside and blowing in the insulatant – usually mineral wool but sometimes foam or polystyrene beads. It usually takes less than half a day and the occupants can remain in the dwelling. The result is a U-value of around 1.5W/m²K. The payback is short – around two years – and heat loss through the walls will be reduced by up to 60 per cent. Most cavity walls up to 12 metres high can be filled, even some over 25 metres following special assessments.

Almost all the approved systems assume that the outer leaf is constructed in accordance with the requirements for local exposure conditions – so that water penetration of the outer leaf is minimal. The exception is urea formaldehyde foam, which should not be used – it is subject to restrictions in places and in some forms of construction. Cavity walls not suitable for insulation can be treated as solid walls.

This is the procedure:

- installers should survey the cavity, and proceed only if the wall meets standards;
- injection holes are drilled through the mortar joints at 1m intervals;
- barriers are installed to prevent the fill entering next door's cavities;
- air ventilators that cross the cavity are sleeved (or sealed, if obsolete);
- the insulant is injected;
- quality checks are carried out;
- the holes are filled with colour-matched mortar/render.

There's often no choice of insulant and it's hard to avoid fossil fuel-dependent material. Try to avoid the use of ozone-depleting blowing agents; check that pentane is used. Polystyrene shouldn't be used if there are any unprotected PVC cables in the cavity, or PVC cavity trays or damp proof courses (dpcs). Water absorbing insulants like recycled cellulose should be avoided. Wool is the only natural material suitable for use in a potentially moist situation like this, and clearly there are installation and cost hurdles, and it won't work if it gets too wet or settles.

Problems with cavity wall insulation typically centre around internal condensation caused by gaps in the insulation, damp in geographical areas where the wall faces driving rain and increased corrosion of wall ties.

Typical two-storey cavity wall masonry houses contain joists, butted into the inner leaf of the cavity wall, that run across the width of the house. When they were built, mortar was buttered up around the joists, but many joints were probably not sealed up correctly so air free in the cavity can get into the floor void and cause draughts anywhere in the house underneath floorboards, completely ruining the effects of any insulation. The problem is acute in partial fill cavity walls. So it's essential that the insulation is packed tight; even a small gap can provide a route for warm air to escape. It may be possible to use joist

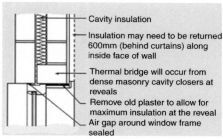

Insulating thermal bridge at reveal

- Cavity insulation
- Insulation may need to be returned 600mm (behind curtains) along inside face of wall
- Thermal bridge will occur from dense masonry cavity closers at reveals
- Remove old plaster to allow for maximum insulation at the reveal
- Air gap around window frame sealed

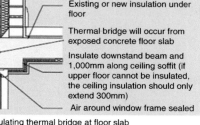

Insulating thermal bridge at floor slab

- Cavity insulation
- Existing or new insulation under floor
- Thermal bridge will occur from exposed concrete floor slab
- Insulate downstand beam and 1,000mm along ceiling soffit (if upper floor cannot be insulated, the ceiling insulation should only extend 300mm)
- Air around window frame sealed

Figure 3.10 *Insulating thermal bridges in wall cavities*

Source: © EST

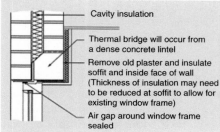

Insulating thermal bridge at lintel

- Cavity insulation
- Thermal bridge will occur from a dense concrete lintel
- Remove old plaster and insulate soffit and inside face of wall (Thickness of insulation may need to be reduced at soffit to allow for existing window frame)
- Air gap around window frame sealed

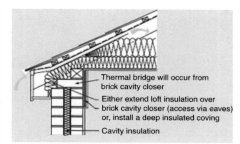

Insulating thermal bridge at eaves

- Thermal bridge will occur from brick cavity closer
- Either extend loft insulation over brick cavity closer (access via eaves) or, install a deep insulated coving
- Cavity insulation

seals. A thermal imaging photograph taken of a cavity wall will show up the gaps – which reportedly happens in many cases – as cold spots on the interior wall. They may be due to debris dropped down the cavity, the settling of the material over time and wall-ties covered with mortar droppings. Infrared thermography should be backed up by visual inspection before injection holes are filled. If it's not possible to eliminate gaps then an airtight layer or extra insulation must be installed on the inside of each room (including floors) or the outside of the building.

Increased internal condensation is another consequence of these gaps, which can happen when air bricks are inadvertently blocked up by the insulation installers. Problems can occur if rain penetrates the outer leaf because mineral wool can transmit water across the cavity. This typically occurs in walls which are poorly maintained and face driving rain, which lets the water in. If the mineral wool becomes damp, it begins to lose its insulating characteristics. BRE Good Building Guide 44: Part 2: 'Insulating masonry cavity walls – principal risks and guidance' (BRE, 2000) British Standard BS8104 (BSI, 1992) and Building Regulations Approved Document C (Her Majesty's Stationery Office, 2006) outline these risks and remedies. The best solution is protection from the rain by attention to pointing, exterior rendering or cladding.

This dampness can also corrode wall ties. Warm, moist air from inside will condense on the colder wall ties, even in the mortar of the outer leaf. BRE Digest 401 describes how to assess the condition of wall ties prior to cavity wall insulation by removing two bricks on each elevation at high and low levels.

Foam and bonded polystyrene beads are inherently waterproof and should not exacerbate the above problems but are more expensive. Beads have been known to escape through airbricks, into loft spaces, or through soffit vents into the gutters. Foam insulation can crack wall surfaces due to the expansive force of the foam as it cures.

Thermal bridges in cavity walls

Ties and bridging bricks across the cavity can cause thermal bridges which can also sometimes be identified by damp and mould on the inside. Apply internal insulation to the affected areas.

Condensation can also occur where concrete floor slabs pass through the external wall to support an upper-level wall. The ceiling can be protected with internal insulation taken back one metre from the wall. Ideally, the floor above should also be insulated. In top storeys, a thermal bridge may also occur if the cavity closer at the top of a wall is made of brick. This can be reduced by extending the loft insulation over the wall head, which you can get at via the fascia or soffit board. An alternative might be to fit deep insulated coving internally.

Cavity wall insulation is not enough

A better solution is to insulate a cavity wall on the outside or the inside. In each case it is more visible and controllable and any subsequent defects are easily spotted and rectified. Anyway, the U-value of about $1.5W/m^2K$ achieved by, say, 65mm cavity wall insulation alone is not high enough for a building that has any hope of reaching 60 or 80 per cent reductions in carbon emissions. Furthermore, cavity construction is never airtight; a gap anywhere in one leaf will lead into the cavity and thence to a gap anywhere in the other leaf. The only way of achieving a target U-value below $0.30W/m^2K$ is to add more insulation inside or out.

Hollow block walls

Also known as cavity block walls, these are not the same as cavity walls. They are single skinned with two faces of a hollow block, each about 40mm wide, linked by three cross members or webs of about 35mm thick concrete. When in situ, the hollows align vertically up the wall. They are also distinguished from terracotta cellular poroton blocks, which have naturally better insulating characteristics, each cell isolated from those in adjacent blocks by the thin-bed mortar.

Wind-driven moisture can penetrate the outer skin of a hollow block. Air movement in the passages encourages its evaporation, however it also reduces its thermal performance since any warmed air will rise, to be replaced by cooler air below through any gaps left by the construction process, reducing the energy efficiency of lower storey rooms. Hollow blocks are supposed to have a k-value of 0.21W/mK, but this has been seriously thrown into question, especially when they're wet.

Studies have shown (Kunzel 1998, Little 2009) that filling the hollows with insulation is the worst thing that can be done, as it can actually increase the amount of mould forming on the inside, as well as being the worst performing solution. By far the best solution is external wall insulation, as it keeps the wall warmer, enhances the wind-tightness, and gives its inner (plastered) surface the best chance to dry out. Any form of internal insulation is a second-best solution.

Figure 3.11 *The overhang on the front of this 1950s single-leaf brick walled home can accommodate external insulation but not that on the side without roof modification*

External wall insulation

External wall insulation involves applying an insulating layer and a decorative weatherproof finish to the outside wall of a building. The aim is to reach U-values of below 0.30W/m²K (half of this for Passivhaus standard). The external cladding or render is generally the major cost, so you want to maximize the amount of insulation to maximize the benefits.

Benefits

- allows the wall's thermal mass to moderate the internal temperature, reducing the need for heating and cooling;
- unlike cavity wall insulation (limited by cavity size) can achieve almost any thermal performance – used on 'zero carbon' buildings;
- can be installed without inconvenience to occupants and reduction in room sizes so can often be easier and quicker especially if a whole block or terrace is treated at once;
- interstitial and internal condensation (damp, mould) can be banished;
- any gaps and cracks in the wall are covered in one go;
- weather protection;
- a wide variety of decorative finishes;
- solves thermal bridging problems for example where there is an exposed concrete frame;
- protects the structure from external/internal temperature differentials;
- the dew point, where vapour from inside the building is likely to condense, is further towards the outside and away from critical structural or load-bearing wall elements.

Challenges

- how to treat, for example, down pipes, gutters, gas mains, phone lines, aerials, window sills, rainwater downpipes, eaves overhangs, gable ends, windows, doors and projections such as porches or conservatories. (For help, use the free robust details for junctions that are available for most typical construction types, available at www.est.org.uk/housingbuildings/calculators/robustdetails or www.carbonlite.org.uk). For example, insulation should be turned into window reveals to prevent condensation on uninsulated surfaces. Ideally, insulation with an R-value of below 0.50m²K/W should be specified. However, frame thickness may sometimes necessitate a reduced insulation depth;
- finishes might not be robust – damage could lead to damp ingress and weathering;
- joints must be sealed effectively;
- the damp proof course and window trickle vents must not be covered.

Figure 3.12 *140mm polystyrene external insulation with acrylic render on a Victorian house*

Note: The eaves of the roof were extended to accommodate the extra thickness. U-value: 0.23 and a 860 per cent improvement in insulation value according to the home owners and developers Penney Poyzer and Gil Schalom.

Source: © Penny Poyzer and Gil Schalom

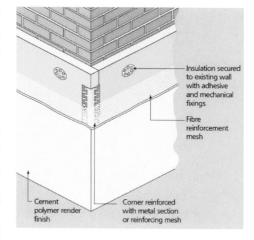

Figure 3.13 *Basics of external insulation*

Source: EST (2006)

Table 3.2 shows how to get the U-value with different insulation types and thicknesses, and the thickness needed at reveals to limit thermal bridging.

External insulation is frequently used on high-rise dwellings to protect their fabric and give a literal facelift as well as increase energy efficiency and comfort levels for those inside. They help eliminate problems of damp, condensation and

Table 3.2 *External wall insulation*

Insulation type	Typical thermal conductivity (W/mK)	External wall insulation						Reveal insulation thickness
		Insulation thickness (mm)						Thickness (mm) to achieve best practice R-value of 0.5m²K/W
		40	60	80	100	120	140	
		U-values achieved						
Phenolic	0.022	0.44	0.32	0.25	0.21	0.16	0.12	8
Polyisocyanurate and polyurethane	0.023	0.45	0.33	0.26	0.22	0.16	0.12	8
Expanded polystyrene and mineral wool (slab)	0.038	0.65	0.49	0.39	0.33	0.25	0.19	13
Cellular glass and woodfibre	0.040	0.67	0.51	0.41	0.34	0.26	0.20	14

☐ Worse than best practice in refurbishment   ▨ Achieves best practice in refurbishment

Note: Assumptions for Table 3.2:
- 20mm lightweight plaster, 220mm brick, insulation with 4 fixings per m² (fixings are 10mm² and 50W/mK), 20mm sand and cement render;
- U-values are only applicable to the exact construction described.

In these tables 'best practice' is as defined by the Energy Saving Trust in 2006 but the standard was under revision at the time of writing.

Source: EST (2006)

Table 3.3 *U-values for directly applied internal wall insulation*

Insulation type	Typical thermal conductivity (W/mK)	Internal wall insulation directly applied						Reveal insulation thickness
		Insulation thickness (mm)						Thickness (mm) to achieve best practice R-value of 0.34m²K/W
		40	60	80	100	120	140	
		U-values achieved						
Phenolic	0.022	0.42	0.31	0.25	0.21	0.18	0.16	8
Polyisocyanurate and polyurethane	0.023	0.43	0.32	0.26	0.21	0.18	0.16	8
Extruded polystyrene	0.030	0.52	0.39	0.31	0.26	0.23	0.20	11
Expanded polystyrene and mineral wool (slab)	0.038	0.60	0.46	0.38	0.32	0.28	0.24	13
Cellular glass	0.040	0.62	0.48	0.39	0.33	0.29	0.25	14

☐ Worse than best practice in refurbishment   ▨ Achieves best practice in refurbishment

Note: Assumptions for Table 3.3:

- 12.5mm plasterboard, insulation, plaster dabs/adhesive and 15mm airspace (bridging fraction = 0.20);
- insulation with two fixings per m² (fixings are 10mm² and 50W/mK), 220mm brick;
- the U-values quoted are only applicable to the exact construction described. Contact the manufacturer of the selected insulation to discuss the technical requirements and assess the potential for interstitial condensation. This should be done prior to commencing work.

Source: EST (2006)

mould (when accompanied by controlled ventilation). Terraces belonging to local authorities or housing associations are often tackled in one go, saving on costs.

It may not always be appropriate for a household with low daytime occupancy. Drylining, or internal insulation, means rooms will heat up quicker from cold which could suit a family of commuters, but they will also cool quicker. External insulation on a solid masonry wall that is exposed to the free heat of the sun all the year round would make it unable to conduct that heat inside. The designer ideally needs to check the insulation patterns, the building's orientation and windows and model a choice accordingly. Choosing external wall insulation for a thermally massive structure also implies that the best choice of heating is constant and low-level, such as underfloor heating or skirting radiators.

Systems available

Three generic types of external insulation are available:

1   wet render systems;
2   dry cladding systems;
3   bespoke systems.

The first two are often proprietary products for specific situations. Bespoke systems are designed for particular projects and combine elements of proprietary systems, often incorporating dry cladding.

Wet render systems

These eliminate the need for extensive re-pointing, saving money. In general they are cheaper than dry cladding. What distinguishes a high-performance from a low-performance system is the quality and thickness of the render. They consist of:

*   insulant;
*   adhesive mortar and/or mechanical fixings;
*   profiles and edgings used on corners, at damp-proof course (DPC) level, window reveals, verges and copings;
*   a base-coat render, incorporating a glass fibre, plastic or metal mesh;
*   a top-coat render, with or without a finish.

Traditional render and polymer-modified cementitious render can be used in low-rise and high-rise applications. Polymer helps make the render more workable on site and,

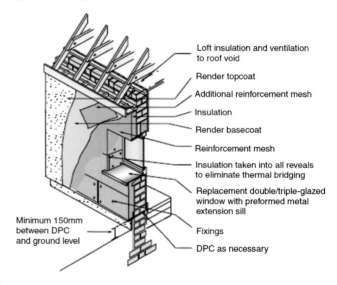

Figure 3.14 *Typical wet render system applied to an existing solid masonry wall*

Source: © EST

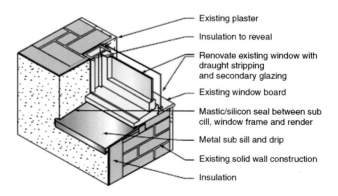

Figure 3.15 *Window reveal detail*

Source: © EST

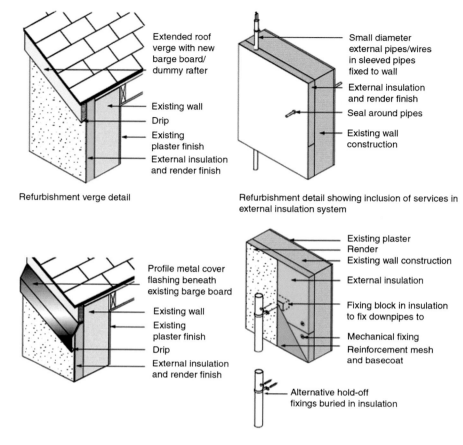

Refurbishment verge detail

Extended roof verge with new barge board/ dummy rafter

Existing wall

Drip

Existing plaster finish

External insulation and render finish

Refurbishment detail showing inclusion of services in external insulation system

Small diameter external pipes/wires in sleeved pipes fixed to wall

External insulation and render finish

Seal around pipes

Existing wall construction

Alternative refurbishment verge detail

Profile metal cover flashing beneath existing barge board

Existing wall

Existing plaster finish

Drip

External insulation and render finish

Detail showing a fixing through external insulation system

Existing plaster

Render

Existing wall construction

External insulation

Fixing block in insulation to fix downpipes to

Mechanical fixing

Reinforcement mesh and basecoat

Alternative hold-off fixings buried in insulation

Figure 3.16 *External insulation details*

Source: EST (2006)

in larger quantities, gives weather protection and flexibility. However its quality is variable – watch out for this; it can weather appallingly, especially on EPS, making maintenance a headache. The reduced weight may be advantageous in high-rise. These coatings do not need movement joints unless the building substrate has them.

Dry cladding systems

Useful where fixings have to be restricted to particular areas. Seldom used on low-rise as cost can be prohibitive. Access can be gained for periodic checks and maintenance, often necessary on high-rise buildings. Use a variety of supporting frameworks fixed to the substrate or building structure. The cladding is fixed to the framework using standard technologies. They consist of:

- the insulant, fixed to the substrate in a similar way to wet systems;
- a supporting framework or cladding fixing system;
- a ventilated cavity;
- cladding material and fixings.

The insulant may be independently fixed to the substrate with a mechanical or adhesive fixing, or partially retained by the framework. Supporting frameworks are made of treated timber, steel or aluminium. An adjustable framework enables a true plane to be constructed over an uneven substrate. With a stand-off framework or cross-battening, a continuous layer of insulation can be applied, minimising thermal bridging. Quilt material (rolls) can also reduce this risk by forming a tight fit around the framework. Insulation boards may be mineral fibre, expanded polystyrene, polyisocyanurate or phenolic. One brand is manufactured from recycled marine and industrial waste and used specifically on 'park homes' – mobile homes/bungalow-chalets.

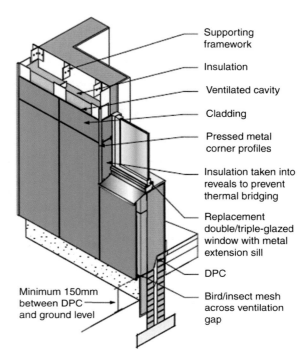

Figure 3.17 *Typical dry cladding system*

Source: © EST

These systems can span over substrate areas where fixings cannot be anchored. The size and frequency of framework members, as well as the strength of fixing to the substrate, must be designed to withstand wind-loadings in accordance with manufacturers' recommendations. Most systems incorporate a ventilation cavity between the cladding and the insulation to ensure that any penetrating moisture is carried away. Materials must not be flammable.

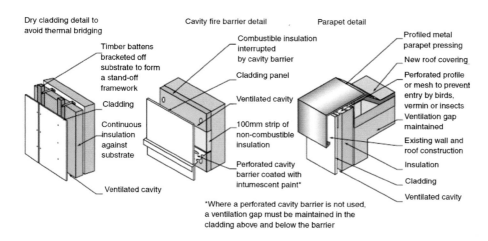

Figure 3.18 *Details for dry cladding systems*

Source: © EST

Figure 3.19 *Bespoke system using unseasoned oak cladding, by Gale and Snowden Architects*

Source: © Clive Boursnell

Common cladding materials include:

- resin-impregnated laminates;
- highly compressed mineral wool;
- fibre-reinforced calcium silicate aluminium panels;
- clay tiles;
- recycled glass granulate suitable for seamless thin coat render.

A rainscreen cladding will have open joints, while a fully sealed system will have sealed joints. A wide range of colours and textures are available. Pressed profiles, trims and cover/edge retention strips can be added to enhance the decorative effect.

Bespoke systems

Designed for individual projects and tend to have simple detailing, allowing a non-specialist to construct them. A typical design may consist of a rainscreen fastened onto a substrate such as single blockwork with timber framing.

Figure 3.19 illustrates the use of unseasoned oak weatherboard as an external cladding and blockwork providing internal thermal mass. Timber studwork and a sheathing material create a 250mm cavity filled with loose cellulose insulation.

Water ingress can be prevented by a ventilated cavity and/or dynamic suction. Designers also need to consider imposed loads, fire protection, maintenance and durability. If solid timber studwork is used, it can be bracketed off the blockwork to avoid thermal bridging. Alternatively, consider lightweight composite I-beams of low thermal conductivity. The whole construction is vapour permeable and airtight.

Base renders

Cementitious sand-cement renders are prone to cracking through temperature changes and moisture variations. Thinner, more flexible, acrylic-based renders are much less inclined to crack. Movement joints should be at no more than 5m intervals, horizontally and vertically, on areas not exceeding 42m².

Cement render

Consists of up to three coats, 16–25mm in depth, reinforced with stainless or galvanized steel mesh. Often supplied pre-mixed with additives to improve application and curing and used in harsher climatic or damage-prone conditions. Liable to crack, so movement joints should be used.

Polymer-modified cementitious render (PMCR)

Consists of up to two coats, 6–12mm, reinforced with mineral fibre or glass mesh. Lighter than cement and used in less harsh climatic or damage-free conditions. The polymer mix varies considerably.

Acrylic render

Consists of two coats, 4–6mm, reinforced with mineral fibre or glass mesh and uses acrylic to bind higher quality aggregates/sand. Lighter than PMCR and used in conditions exposed to light and no risk of damage. Highly elastic, weather resistant and breathable.

Hydraulic lime renders

Consists of Foamglas insulation rendered with a 10–12mm coat of hydraulic lime containing glass fibre mesh reinforcement topped with a 3mm decorative layer.

Insulating renders

Contain polystyrene balls, perlite or vermiculite. Offer no significant advantage in thermal efficiency but can be used to reduce thermal bridging and prevent mould growth in areas such as window and door reveals where other insulation materials won't fit. Old plaster is hacked off and replaced with a base mortar containing the granules.

Hemp-lime render

Combined with a lime plaster finishing coat, this uses more sustainable, natural materials. Using hemp stores atmospheric carbon in the building. Manufacturers claim a modest improvement in the performance of a solid brick wall – an increase in U-value from 1.71, for an uncoated 215mm brick wall, to 1.00 when coated with 50mm of hemp-lime render. Can take up to 90 days to dry out completely depending on weather conditions and thickness.

Table 3.4 shows the A, B or C environmental rating for different external insulation systems. Ratings are awarded against the issues described an A, B or C, indicating the best third, middle, or worst third of the list of systems examined. Any use of insulation that does not have ZODP (zero ozone depletion potential) rating has automatically received a 'C' summary rating. In summary:

- Group A: Expanded polystyrene, glass wool, mineral wool, recycled cellulose;
- Group B: Corkboard, foamed glass, polyurethane (ZODP);
- Group C: Extruded polystyrene (ZODP).

The criteria rated in Table 3.4 are:

- climate change: global warming gases;
- fossil fuel depletion: coal, oil and gas consumption;
- ozone depletion: gases which destroy the ozone layer;
- freight transport: distance and mass of freight moved;
- human toxicity: pollutants which are toxic to humans;
- waste disposal: material sent to landfill or incineration;

Table 3.4 *Environmental rating for different external insulation systems*

Element type	Element	Insulation groups ABC	Summary rating	Climate change	Fossil fuel depletion	Ozone depletion	Freight transport	Human toxicity	Waste disposal	Water extraction	Acid deposition	Ecotoxicity	Eutrophication	Summer smog	Minerals extraction	Typical replacement interval	Recycled input	Recyclability	Recycled currently	Recycling energy
Bespoke timber clad	Local timber cladding, timber framework	Any – A B or C	A	A	A	A	A	A	A	A	A	A	A	C	A	30	C	A	B	A
Dry cladding systems	Aluminium/plastic board, aluminium framework	Any – A B or C	B	B	A	A	A	C	A	B	A	A	A	A	A	40	A	B	A	B
	Aluminium/plastic board, steel framework	A rating	A	A	A	A	A	B	A	A	A	A	A	A	A	40	B	B	A	B
	Epoxy resin laminate board, aluminium framework	B or C rating	B	B	B	B	A	C	A	A	B	B	B	A	A	40	B	B	A	B
		Any – A B or C	C	C	C	A	A	B	B	B	C	A	A	C	A	30	C	C	B	C
	Fibre cement board, aluminium framework	A or B rating	A	A	A	A	A	B	A	C	A	A	A	A	A	40	A	B	A	A
		C rating	B	B	B	A	A	B	A	C	B	A	A	A	A	40	A	A	A	A
	Terracotta rainscreen cladding, aluminium framework	A rating	A	A	A	A	A	B	A	B	A	A	A	A	A	30	A	B	A	B
		B or C rating	B	B	A	C	A	C	A	B	A	B	C	A	A	30	B	B	A	B
Insulating render	Insulating lime render	n/a	C	B	A	A	C	A	C	A	A	A	A	A	C	30	C	A	A	A
Polymer-modified cementitious render	Polymer-modified render, render glass wool mesh	A or B rating	A	A	A	A	A	A	B	B	A	A	A	A	B	25	C	A	A	A
		C rating	B	B	B	A	A	A	A	B	B	A	A	A	B	25	C	A	A	A
Polymeric coating	Polymeric coating, glass wool mesh	A or B rating	B	B	B	A	A	B	A	A	B	A	A	B	A	20	C	C	C	C
		C rating	C	B	C	C	A	C	A	A	B	C	C	A	A	20	C	C	C	C
Traditional render	Sand/cement render, glass wool mesh	Any – A B or C	A	A	A	A	A	A	B	C	C	A	C	A	C	30	C	A	A	A

Source: BRE Centre for Sustainable Construction – Green Guide to Housing Specification (BR 390). Elements of this may be been superseded by *The Green Guide to Specification* (BRE, 2009), and it is regularly updated on www.thegreenguide.org.uk

- water extraction: mains, surface and ground water consumption;
- acid deposition: gases which cause acid rain, etc.;
- ecotoxicity: pollutants which are toxic to the ecosystem;
- eutrophication: water pollutants which promote algal blooms, etc.;
- summer smog: air pollutants which cause respiratory problems;
- minerals extraction: metal ores, minerals and aggregates mined.

Factors affecting the choice of insulant include:

- rigidity and workability (e.g. panel, quilt or loose beads/fibres);
- ease of forming or fitting around external features;
- degree of support required for the render or finish;
- fire resistance;
- chemical composition;
- embodied energy;
- cost.

Internal insulation

External insulation is usually the best solution but it can be more expensive and, for example with listed buildings in conservation areas, may not be possible. Internal insulation is therefore the way to go and is also used when the dwelling is being renovated piecemeal fashion.

A U-value of at least 0.30W/m²K is the aim. A major disadvantage, besides the loss of internal space, is the need to move electrical sockets and light switches and problems in a home with character features such as coving, panelling and picture rails. The condition of the wall must be assessed and repaired first. Then consider where any fixtures such as kitchen units, radiators and wash basins may be located afterwards and fit timber fixing battens within the insulation layer. However, the battens form thermal bridges and should be minimized.

Avoid covering cables in insulation – especially high load ones – it can cause them to overheat and create a fire hazard; if in doubt, consult an electrician, as with all work associated with electrical systems. PVC-sheathing on electrical cables may degrade in contact with polystyrene – use cover strips or place in ducts. Cables less than 50mm from the surface of the plasterboard should be enclosed in metal conduits.

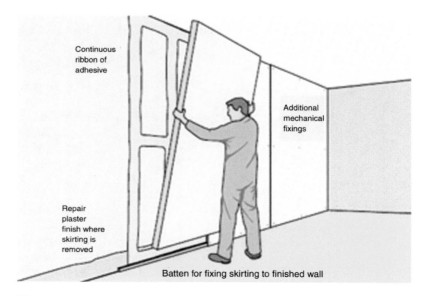

Figure 3.20 *Directly applied internal insulation using insulated plasterboard*

Source: © EST

Figure 3.21 *Spraying cellulose insulation into a stud wall*

Source: © Russell Smith

Where ceilings, floors and internal walls join the main outside walls there will be thermal bridges. Here – in kitchens and bathrooms especially – it's a good idea to return insulated dry-lining a short distance along these internal surfaces to avoid the risk of condensation.

This will, however, create a 'step' in level of the surface of the wall/floor/ceiling which will need to be designed for. Where the outside wall receives driving rain you'll need a small space (2–3cm) behind the dry lining to break any moisture transmission path and reduce damp risk.

Two techniques are available:

1   Insulated plasterboard: thermal boards glued directly on to the internal walls. Can be a plasterboard sheet laminated to an insulation board, or the board may be separate. Some have a built-in vapour control layer to stop moist internal air condensing on the cold brick behind the insulation. The thicker the board, the lower the U-value (higher R-values). There must be absolutely no gaps between the boards. If the brickwork is uneven (perhaps after the removal of existing plaster), render the wall first to provide an even surface. Apply thick continuous ridges of plaster adhesive round the edges of the wall and around all openings (such as sockets and plumbing) to preserve airtightness by plugging potential leaks. Leave a small cavity between the internal wall surface and the insulation. Some even recommend spreading adhesive over the entire surface area to eliminate the possibility of any air movement.

2   Studs: should be employed on a wall that has previously suffered from damp. This lets you create a cavity between the internal wall surface and the insulation. Studwork is also good where the wall is bowed or uneven and space is not at a premium. Three types of systems are available:

   • steel systems with thermally broken sections will give improved performance but higher embodied energy;
   • insulating studs made of extruded polystyrene laminated to oriented strand board (OSB), like timber studs but with an improved U-value;
   • traditional timber – treat with preservative, including exposed end grain.

A damp-proof membrane should be placed between the studs and wall. Studs are fixed to the walls at intervals relative to the thickness of the material that's going to fill the gaps between them: boards, batts or even wet-blown cellulose. The insulation is then inserted – absolutely no gaps – and plasterboard fixed to the studs. Next,

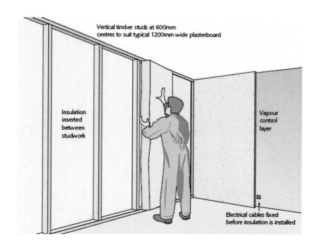

Figure 3.22 *Installing internal insulation with studwork*

Source: © EST

Table 3.5 *Studwork internal wall insulation*

Insulation type	Typical thermal conductivity (W/mK)	Internal wall insulation directly applied						Reveal insulation thickness
		Insulation thickness (mm)						Thickness (mm) to achieve best practice R-value of 0.34m²K/W
		40	60	80	100	120	140	
		U-values achieved						
Phenolic	0.022	0.51	0.39	0.32	0.27	0.24	0.21	8
Polyisocyanurate and polyurethane	0.023	0.52	0.40	0.33	0.28	0.24	0.21	8
Mineral wool (slab)	0.035	0.62	0.49	0.40	0.35	0.30	0.27	12
Expanded polystyrene	0.038	0.64	0.51	0.42	0.36	0.32	0.28	13
Woodfibre	0.044	0.69	0.55	0.46	0.39	0.34	0.31	15

Worse than best practice in refurbishment		Achieves best practice in refurbishment

Source: EST (2006)

Note: Assumptions for Table 3.5: Studwork internal wall insulation
- 12.5mm plasterboard, insulation, 25mm non-ventilated airspace;
- 47mm studs at 600mm centres plus top and bottom rails (Bridging Fraction = 0.118), 220mm brick;
- the U-values quoted are only applicable to the exact construction described.

Contact the manufacturer of the selected insulation to discuss the technical requirements and assess the potential for interstitial condensation. This should be done prior to commencing work.

In these tables 'best practice' is as defined by the Energy Saving Trust in 2006 but the standard was under revision at the time of writing.

an 'intelligent' vapour control layer (VCL) is continuously fitted, by lapping and bonding the membranes together, sealing them back to the floor, internal walls and windows.

In some situations, for example in rented accommodation or where hanging wall units are needed, a more robust structure featuring studs at 400mm centres may be more suitable. Remember, more studwork will reduce thermal performance.

Figure 3.22 shows a wall of vertical timber studs at 600mm centres to suit typical 1200mm wide plasterboard.

Puncture prevention

Home occupiers often want to hang pictures and shelves on walls. Where walls have been drylined and a vapour control layer put in place behind the plasterboard, a single nail puncturing it can ruin it. How can we solve this – and at the same time allow services to penetrate the layer? One solution is to create a services zone separate from the plasterboard, containing less than a third of the total wall insulation and let the services run through. The homeowner can then hang pictures or shelves on this without puncturing the membrane.

Thermal bridges

Insulation with an R-value of below 0.34m²K/W should be turned into window reveals to prevent condensation. However, frame thickness may mean less depth or the use of insulating render. Don't block trickle vents.

Figures 3.23–3.30 *Slate end-of-terrace renovation*

Note: This slate end-of-terrace renovation involved stripping right back, installing a new suspended floor and fixing studwork to the walls. After the damp proof layer, layers of wood fibre board were built up with spacers so that the air could act as further insulation; the gaps were not wide enough for convection currents to form. Foil-backed polystyrene boards were used in the alcoves and reveal, before an airtightness membrane was added, topped with lime plaster.

Source: © Dave Baines

Interstitial condensation

Interstitial condensation, which we examined earlier, presents a special challenge with internal insulation, a high degree of airtightness and (in particular) older solid wall structures. These create a risk of a dew point on the inside face of the masonry. Particularly wet, poorly ventilated, or cold elements may persist after insulating or a permanent damp area may develop, due to the immediate outside conditions or failed ventilation. Direct summer sun can drive water vapour deeper into the walls to condense on the outside of the vapour control layer (VCL). So the vapour permeability of the wall must be improved to let vapour

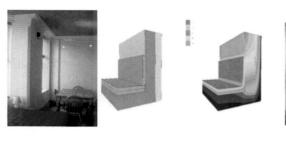

Figure 3.31 *Internal insulation in a Victorian home with period features*

Note: Two layers of 50mm phenolic foam backed plasterboard. Coving added by cutting the foam to form details. Returns also insulated causing change in depth at far wall by the window.

Source: © Penny Poyzer and Gil Schalom

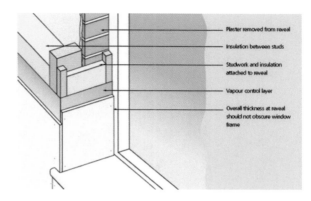

Figure 3.32 *Insulating the reveal to prevent condensation with studwork*

Source: © EST

Figures 3.33 and 3.34 *Gluing expanded polystyrene into a window reveal; the completed reveal and sill*

Source: © Chris Twinn

escape to the outside. This might be achieved with lime mortar joints, but most masonry walling is pointed with less permeable mortar so a solution is holes drilled at intervals through the joints (from the outside) and plugged with lime mortar. The insulation needs some vapour resistance but some systems which employ a VCL outside of the internal insulation rely on the drying out happening into the room.

Some builders don't recommend internal insulation in such cases unless they can construct a frame at least 30mm clear of the masonry wall. (British Gypsum's technical department believes that any air leakage behind thermal plasterboard laminate would probably lead to condensation in the cavity.) Others have never had a problem. One concern is joist ends penetrating the insulation layer and set in a wall. The ends are in danger of becoming dew points and eventually rotting. They are thermal bridges.

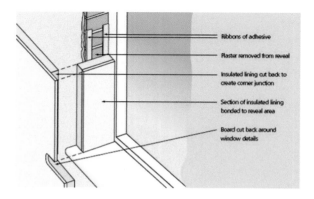

Figure 3.35 *Insulating the reveal with directly applied insulation*

Source: © EST

Figures 3.36 and 3.37 *Internal insulation taken along a solid stone wall of a larder perpendicular to the partition wall to keep heat from the kitchen being transmitted along it. The connecting door is also insulated*

Source: © Andy Warren

Case study 1

The former Highgate Hospital, in Highgate, London, was refurbished, remodelled and transformed into six large luxury homes. The brief was to make it unrecognizable as a hospital, yet blend in with surrounding architecture. A PermaRock insulated render system incorporates mineral wool and EPS insulation to 95mm producing predicted U-values of 0.29W/m²K. Features such as quoins, bands, ashlar grooves and window frame profiles were achieved by cutting into the EPS insulation board, with the white acrylic through-coloured render. Specifier: Cityscape Plc; system designer: Permarock Products Ltd; installer: George Howe Ltd.

Figure 3.38 Highgate Hospital

Source: © PermaRock, an INCA member

If there is any doubt, employ a condensation risk assessment using BS EN 15026 or WUFI (see earlier in this chapter) to calculate the dew point of a building element. There is another standard for this: ISO 21129:2007 'Hygrothermal performance of building materials and products – Determination of water-vapour transmission properties – Box method'.

Case study 2

An estate in Peel Avenue, Wirral, Merseyside, UK, of Wimpey-built 'no-fines' houses: 1940s–1950s mass-produced concrete social housing so-called because of the type of concrete used – concrete with no fine aggregates – has been modernized both internally and externally using external wall insulation. The PermaRock mineral fibre insulation system was installed, with scratch render on the upper floors and dry dash finishes. A predicted U-value of 0.35W/m²K was achieved with 70mm of mineral wool.

Figure 3.39 Peel Avenue, Wirral, Merseyside, UK

Source: © PermaRock, an INCA member

New windows, doors and canopies were added. A much higher level of energy saving could have been achieved with higher U-values specified on the doors, windows and thicker insulation. Designer: Permarock Products Ltd. Installer: E.J. Horrocks Ltd.

Case study 3

Canterbury House, Borehamwood, Hertfordshire, an 18-storey no-fines tower block overclad with Permarock's acrylic through-coloured render in three contrasting colours to provide identity on the elevations, with brick slips at ground floor level. The insulation thickness specified by the Ridgehill Housing Association – 75mm mineral fibre and 20mm phenolic – achieves a predicted U-value of 0.35W/m²K. System designer: PermaRock Products Ltd. Installer: Repex Ltd.

Figure 3.40 Canterbury House, Borehamwood, Herts, UK

Source: © PermaRock, an INCA member

Moisture movement

Not enough research has yet been done on how moisture moves through walls and builds up or dissipates. So much depends on the individual wall, the materials used, their location, construction, external weather conditions and occupancy activities in the room – which may be a bathroom or heated by a gas fire giving off water vapour. The consequences for the health of both the building and its occupants are potentially serious.

Designers and builders need to build with far more awareness of moisture movement. We need to build resilient systems – be that a wall, a ventilation system or the building itself. We need designs that can accommodate things going wrong and can ensure that both structure and the occupants' health are safeguarded. Joseph Little, architect.

Important sources of information are the Fraunhofer Institute for Building Physics and WUFI (Wärme und Feuchte Instationär) calculation software (www. wufi.de).

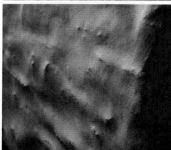

Figures 3.41–3.43 *Lime gives a softer, warmer feel than conventional mortar and plaster (top) as well as dealing with damp problems*

Significant factors are the hygroscopicity and capillary capacity of building materials.

Hygroscopic and capillary properties

Hygroscopicity and capillarity measure the capacity of a material to absorb and desorb water as a gas (water vapour) and liquid respectively, from and to the air, or condensation, as the relative humidity of the air changes. The hygroscopic capacity of a material is related to its equilibrium moisture content and is sometimes measured as the percentage increase in water content in a material when the relative humidity increases from 50 to 85 per cent with a constant temperature of 21°C.

The speed with which a wall surface can absorb moisture is important for avoiding surface condensation. Materials with a combination of vapour permeability and high absorption can quickly moderate humidity variations by storing or releasing significant quantities of water. Lime (and lime plaster) and wood-fibre are good examples of material which, when used internally, will absorb moisture and release it slowly when the internal humidity is lower. They can eliminate condensation, helping to create an internal atmosphere that also feels warmer, not just drier. Lime yields a softer finish and a friendly texture. It is especially appropriate for old buildings to provide softness, breathability and flexibility.

Insulation materials with good hygroscopic qualities include many of those based on plants and animals – wood-fibre, cellulose, hemp, and flax to wool – and timber and unfired earth/clay materials, including calcium silicate board. Mineral wool and plastic-based insulants (EPS, PI/PU) have low hygroscopicity and are unable to absorb and release water vapour.

Breathing walls

Using these materials will create breathing walls which allow moisture to pass from the inside to the outside, driven by the difference in temperature and pressure. Modern breathing walls, using timber frames, wood-fibre boards and natural insulation, are now common. But older buildings of stone construction also breathe and any renovation work should not compromise this or damp problems will ensue.

Figure 3.44 *Applying lime plaster to a breathing (wood fibre board) wall*

Source: © Gavin Killip

Some people confuse airtightness and zero hygroscopicity, in other words, think that an airtight building cannot breathe. A building can be airtight and still 'breathe' because the membrane is permeable. The permeability of the membrane is dependent upon differences of air pressure, humidity and temperature between the outside and the inside. If you are not going to use natural hygroscopic materials like lime plaster then you should use intelligent membranes (see above).

Conservation architects and builders are trained to look at each building differently and to be very aware of the impact of orientation, exposure and the original building materials. It may be appropriate therefore to call in specialist help. Every step of the renovation must allow the wall to dry out, generally in

---

Render types and breathability

Tests conducted by John Straub (2002) revealed these performance characteristics:

- Cement-sand stuccos are relatively vapour impermeable. 38mm thick cement-sand stucco may act as a vapour barrier.
- The addition of lime to a cement stucco mix increases permeance. Adding even a small amount of lime (0.2 parts) may increase the permeance of cement stucco dramatically.
- Earth plasters are generally more permeable than even lime plasters.
- Applying an oil paint to a moderately permeable 1:1:6 stucco will provide a permeance of less than 60 metric perms (1 US perms) and thus meet the code requirements of a vapour barrier.
- Lime washes appear to be somewhat useful for reducing water absorption while not reducing vapour permeance.
- Siloxane appears to have little or no effect on the vapour permeance of cement, cement-lime, lime, and earth plasters while almost eliminating water absorption.
- Sodium silicate did not seem to have much impact on water uptake or vapour permeance.

both directions. Materials should be graded based on their vapour permeability, with the least permeable on the inside and most permeable facing the elements.

In a situation where damp is a real danger, and in historic buildings, insulating plaster is a good solution, but even better are thick clay plasters and hemp-lime biocomposite plaster. This is because the combination of fibrous structure and mineral render surface allow better vapour diffusion than one containing expanded polystyrene. Apply both by building up layers about 35mm thick.

Roof insulation

Roof insulation includes:

- loft insulation;
- internal roof insulation (insulation added between and/or to the underside of the rafters; can be undertaken at any time, but often when an attic conversion is taking place);
- external roof insulation (added between and above rafters when re-roofing work is being undertaken);
- flat roof insulation.

In all cases, before work begins, inspect timbers for damage and repair if necessary.

Wind protection

Whatever the roof design, seriously consider inserting some type of wind protection, space permitting. This can make a significant difference. Research has shown that as the wind speed outside goes up, it causes air circulation within the insulation or sucks warm air through it, particularly at the eaves, corners and ridges, causing far lower U-values than expected. In one experiment (Silerbsein et al, 1991), the U-value of a ventilated compact roof deteriorated by 39 per cent with an external wind speed of 4m/s. In another experiment in Austria, U-values up to $2.5W/m^2K$ were recorded at wind speeds over 7m/s, in other words the U-value worsened by up to 660 per cent – due to cold air entering at eaves level and passing through the insulation into a small attic space and ventilating to the outside.

A barrier to deflect the wind will begin on the building side of the eaves, border the insulation and leave a gap of 3cm between itself and the inside of the roof. It should extend over the top of the insulation, just as an airtightness membrane passes beneath it. These should both remain unbroken throughout, therefore minimize any kinks and bends. Sheeting should be chosen in the largest possible specification to reduce joints. Fit vertically from top to bottom, so that the side lap happens over a stud, where the joint can be filled with mastic and then taped, after which a batten is nailed over it to maximize the longevity of this important physical connection.

Continuous vapour control layer

Fit a continuous vapour control layer on the warm side of the insulation. Usually this is 500 gauge polyethylene, or it might be an intelligent membrane. This should be joined to any vapour control layer in the rising walls, or at least fitted so that this can potentially be done in the future when the walls are renovated. This layer must never be punctured. To accommodate services, create a service zone or route services on the warm side of the layer. Seal any holes that do occur; lap and seal all joints in the layer.

Flexible thermal linings

Flexible thermal lining materials alone will not achieve anything like the standards of insulation required, but might be combined with other measures for difficult areas where wall thickness, available head-room or the risk of mould growth are issues. They may also be a stop-gap where only cosmetic refurbishment was originally planned, for example wallpaper replacement.

Loft insulation

Installing additional loft insulation is a common, basic improvement measure, and relatively straightforward. Aim for a U-value of $0.16W/m^2K$ or better. 400mm of insulation is not considered excessive. Plan the route of the vapour control layer beneath the insulation and wind tightness protection above it, to permit the vital ventilation of the roof timbers so they don't attract damp. The insulation should not block these pathways, especially under the eaves.

Any recessed lights within the ceiling below the insulation must be housed in airtight, fire-proof enclosures – the service zone – and not cause breaks in the vapour control layer and insulation. Cables should be treated as for internal wall insulation.

Quilted or loose-fill insulation is generally used. To minimize thermal bridging and improve airtightness, insert the insulation between and over the ceiling joists. Quilt or cellulose insulation should be about 5–10mm thicker than required, so that a closing board will lightly compress it, but not so much as to crush insulating air cells.

Installation

Add further joists to provide space for the 400mm of insulation where necessary and where a raised

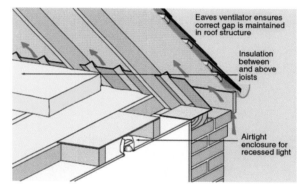

Figure 3.45 *Ceiling level insulation*

Source: © EST

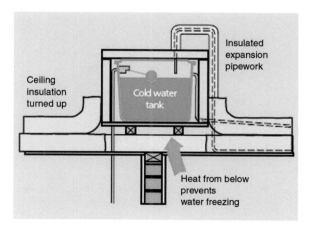

Figure 3.46 *How to insulate around a cold water tank in the loft with ceiling level insulation*

Source: © EST

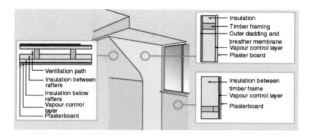

Figure 3.47 *Details for insulation of loft space between and around rafters*

Source: © EST

walkway or storage surface is required. There should be no voids between the insulation and what lies below, or above.

Insulate all cold water tanks and pipes, as the loft space will be colder but do not insulate under tanks (unless they are raised well above the rafters) so they can benefit from heat rising from below. Seal all cracks as well as holes around pipes and cables where they pass through the ceiling to prevent moist air from the house entering the loft and condensing on cold surfaces.

Roof space ventilation

If the roof pitch is less than 15° there should be a 25mm continuous gap around the roofspace at the eaves. If it's over 15° there should be a 10mm continuous gap. Ventilators should be protected by a 3–4mm mesh at the openings, to keep out insects. Low pitched roofs and those with complex geometry may need extra ventilation, as will the ridge of steeply pitched roofs – install ventilated slates.

Table 3.6 *Roof insulation*

Insulation type	Typical thermal conductivity (W/mK)	Ceiling level insulation 100mm joists filled with insulation				
		Additional thickness above joists (mm)				
		50	100	150	175	200
		U-values achieved				
Cellulose	0.035	0.24	0.18	0.14	0.13	0.12
Flax	0.037	0.25	0.19	0.15	0.14	0.13
Sheep's wool and hemp	0.039	0.26	0.20	0.16	0.14	0.13
Mineral wool (blown)	0.043	0.28	0.21	0.17	0.16	0.14
Mineral wool (quilt)	0.044	0.29	0.22	0.18	0.16	0.15
Vermiculite	0.63	0.38	0.30	0.24	0.22	0.20

 Worse than best practice in refurbishment   Achieves best practice in refurbishment

Source: EST (2006)

Note: Assumptions for Table 3.6:
- 12.5mm plasterboard, timber joists (Bridging Fraction = 0.09);
- loft hatch with 50mm insulation;
- the U-values quoted are only applicable to the exact construction described. Contact the manufacturer of the selected insulation to discuss the technical requirements and assess the potential for interstitial condensation. This should be done prior to commencing work.

  In these tables 'best practice' is as defined by the Energy Saving Trust in 2006 but the standard was under revision at the time of writing.

Internal roof insulation

This is the approach for attic rooms or loft conversions – it is not the same as insulating between studs in a vertical wall (drylining). Take care not to obstruct cross ventilation.

Aim for a U-value of 0.16W/m²K (for stud walls and dormer cheeks a worse U-value of 0.3W/m²K might be the aim). This may require large insulation thicknesses (for example over 60mm below the rafters), which can affect internal space and headroom. If there isn't the space it may be more practical to aim for a U-value of 0.20W/m²K. Detailing for dormer windows and more is available on the Energy Saving Trust website (publication CE120, EST, 2004).

On the inside roof, fix foil-faced laminated insulating plasterboard over the existing ceiling, or plasterboard over quilt insulation (more difficult) or over interlocking foil-faced boards. The ventilation path above the insulation should be at least 50mm deep. Rafter dimensions vary considerably; some 19th-century homes have only 75mm which doesn't leave enough room as you have to add insulation to the underside of the rafters. Gaps between slabs are the enemy – press it firmly together. Use caulking or firmly applied tape and mechanically clamped joints between two solid plates, for example between a stud and plasterboard.

At the base of the sloping ceilings, install purpose-made eaves vents that provide the equivalent of a 25mm continuous gap, as well as ventilation at the roof's ridge in order to cross ventilate the roofspace and prevent condensation. Insulate and draught seal the loft hatch, or fit a proprietary insulated access hatch (see Chapter 1).

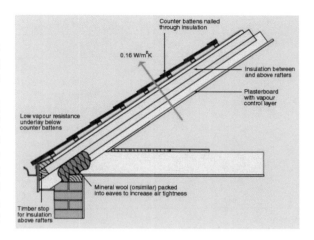

Figure 3.48 *Insulation between and above rafters*
Source: © EST

External roof insulation

Insulating between and above rafters is only done when the roof tiling is being renewed. Aim for a U-value of 0.16W/m²K, which again may require large insulation depths (over 60mm above rafters), and raising the height of the roof. This would need planning permission and consideration of the relationship with any adjacent properties. If renovating an entire terrace, this could be part of a strategy which includes a complete new building envelope across the entire terrace. If the roof cannot be raised to this level, a reduced U-value of 0.20W/m²K might be aimed for, or a combination of this and below-rafter insulation.

Specify foil-faced insulation boards with interlocking edge joints. Increased insulation thicknesses will affect the choice of fixings through the counter battens, insulation and rafters. A wind-tightness layer should pass above the insulation boards and beneath the ventilation gap. Seal the joints between boards with self-adhesive aluminium tape. Any service penetrations in the

Table 3.7 *Insulating between and below roof rafters*

Insulation type	Typical thermal conductivity (W/mK)	Rafter level insulation and below											
		100mm rafter (50mm insulation between rafter and 50mm ventilated cavity)				125mm rafter (75mm insulation between rafter and 50mm ventilated cavity)				150mm rafter (75mm insulation between rafter and 50mm ventilated cavity)			
		Additional insulation above rafters (mm)				Additional insulation above rafters (mm)				Additional insulation above rafters (mm)			
		40	60	80*	100*	40	60	80*	100*	40	60	80*	100*
		U-values achieved				U-values achieved				U-values achieved			
Phenolic	0.022	0.26	0.21	0.18	0.15	0.21	0.18	0.15	0.14	0.18	0.15	0.14	0.12
Polyisocyanurate and polyurethane	0.023	0.27	0.22	0.18	0.16	0.22	0.18	0.16	0.14	0.19	0.16	0.14	0.13
Extruded polystyrene	0.030	0.34	0.27	0.23	0.20	0.27	0.23	0.20	0.18	0.23	0.20	0.18	0.16
Mineral wool (slab)	0.035	0.38	0.31	0.27	0.23	0.31	0.26	0.23	0.20	0.26	0.23	0.20	0.18
Expanded polystyrene	0.038	0.41	0.34	0.29	0.25	0.33	0.28	0.25	0.22	0.28	0.24	0.22	0.20
Cellular glass	0.042	0.44	0.37	0.31	0.27	0.36	0.31	0.27	0.24	0.30	0.27	0.24	0.21

☐ Worse than best practice in refurbishment   ☐ Best practice in some difficult situations   ☐ Achieves best practice in refurbishment

Source: EST (2006)

Note: * insulation this thick may reduce internal space and headroom.

Assumptions for Table 3.7: Insulating between and below roof rafters:
- 12.5mm plasterboard, insulation with 4 fixings per m² (fixings of 7.5mm² with 17W/mK);
- insulation between rafters, 50mm ventilated cavity (Bridging Fraction = 0.08);
- sarking felt, 25mm cavity, 15mm clay tiles;
- the U-values quoted are only applicable to the exact construction described. Contact the manufacturer of the selected insulation to discuss the technical requirements and assess the potential for interstitial condensation. This should be done prior to commencing work. In these tables 'best practice' is as defined by the Energy Saving Trust in 2006 but the standard was under revision at the time of writing.

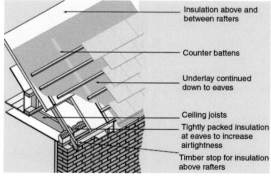

Insulation above and between rafters

Counter battens

Underlay continued down to eaves

Ceiling joists

Tightly packed insulation at eaves to increase airtightness

Timber stop for insulation above rafters

Figure 3.49 *External roof insulation*

Source: © EST

vapour control layer should also be sealed, though they should be avoided if at all possible. Fill the gap between wall and roof insulation at the eaves to reduce air leakage and continue the vapour control layer to connect with any coming up the walls. Use a low vapour resistance underlay or intelligent membrane so that moisture does not get trapped in the roof timbers. Batten and counter batten the roof so that the underlay drains moisture away to the gutter. Special proprietary fixings can be used to install the counter battens above the insulation. If a cavity is created behind the plasterboard for services it is important that this is sealed airtightly and insulated.

Table 3.8 *Insulation between and above roof rafters*

Insulation type	Typical thermal conductivity (W/mK)	Rafter level insulation and below											
		100mm rafter (25mm service cavity and 75mm between rafter)				125mm rafter (25mm service cavity and 100mm between rafter)				150mm rafter (25mm service cavity and 125mm between rafter)			
		Additional insulation above rafters (mm)				Additional insulation above rafters (mm)				Additional insulation above rafters (mm)			
		40	60	80*	100*	40	60	80*	100*	40	60	80*	100*
		U-values achieved				U-values achieved				U-values achieved			
Phenolic	0.022	0.21	0.17	0.15	0.13	0.18	0.15	0.13	0.12	0.15	0.14	0.12	0.11
Polyisocyanurate and polyurethane	0.023	0.21	0.18	0.16	0.14	0.18	0.16	0.14	0.13	0.16	0.14	0.13	0.11
Extruded polystyrene	0.030	0.26	0.22	0.20	0.17	0.22	0.20	0.17	0.16	0.20	0.17	0.16	0.14
Mineral wool (slab)	0.035	0.30	0.25	0.22	0.20	0.25	0.22	0.20	0.18	0.22	0.20	0.18	0.16
Expanded polystyrene	0.038	0.32	0.27	0.24	0.21	0.27	0.24	0.21	0.19	0.24	0.21	0.19	0.170
Woodfibre	0.040	0.33	0.28	0.25	0.22	0.28	0.25	0.22	0.20	0.25	0.22	0.20	0.18
Cellular glass	0.042	0.34	0.30	0.26	0.23	0.29	0.26	0.23	0.21	0.25	0.23	0.21	0.19

☐ Worse than best practice in refurbishment   ☐ Best practice in some difficult situations   ☐ Achieves best practice in refurbishment

Source: EST (2006)

Note: * insulation this thick requires careful consideration in properties such as terraced housing where the roof tiling is continuous across neighbouring properties.

Assumptions for Table 3.9: Insulating between and above roof rafters:
• 12.5mm plasterboard, 25mm unventilated space cavity, insulation between rafters (Bridging Fraction = 0.08);
• insulation with 7 fixings per m² (fixings 7.5mm² and 17W/mK);
• underlay, 25mm cavity, 15mm clay tiles;
• the U-values quoted are only applicable to the exact construction described. Contact the manufacturer of the selected insulation to discuss the technical requirements and assess the potential for interstitial condensation. This should be done prior to commencing work. In these tables 'best practice' is as defined by the Energy Saving Trust in 2006 but the standard was under revision at the time of writing.

Flat roof insulation

Aim for a U-value of 0.25W/m²K or better, but if a flat roof is converted to a pitched roof, it should be insulated to the same standard as a conventional pitched roof (0.16W/m²K). The insulation should be located between the roof deck and the weatherproof membrane in a warm roof deck construction, but above the weatherproof membrane in an inverted warm deck construction. The latter type of construction is less reliable as poor installation can lead to condensation on the underside of the waterproof membrane, which may lead to rot internally. It is most economic to add insulation when replacing the existing roof covering.

Careful detailing at the edge and parapet areas of flat roofs is vital for reliability and durability. The correct specification and installation methods for

Table 3.9 *Roof insulation specifications: Warm deck roofs*

Insulation type	Typical thermal conductivity (W/mK)	Flat roof insulation – warm deck Insulation thickness (mm)					
		60	80	100	120	140	160
		U-values achieved*					
Polyisocyanurate and polyurethane	0.023	0.32	0.26	0.21	0.18	0.16	0.14
Expanded polysytrene and mineral wool (slab)	0.038	0.45	0.36	0.30	0.26	0.23	0.20
Cellular glass	0.042	0.51	0.42	0.35	0.30	0.27	0.24

☐ Worse than best practice	☐ Achieves best practice

Source: EST (2006)

Note: * Concrete roof structures will typically have slightly higher U-values than those indicated.
Assumptions for Table 3.10: Warm deck roofs:
• timber roof: 12.5mm plaster board, 150mm timber roof space with no insulation, 20mm timber decking insulation, 6mm felt weather cover;
• concrete roof: 12.5mm plasterboard, 22mm batters, 150mm concrete deck insulation, 6mm felt weather cover;
• the U-values quoted are only applicable to the exact construction described. Contact the manufacturer of the selected insulation to discuss the technical requirements and assess the potential for interstitial condensation. This should be done prior to commencing work. In these tables 'best practice' is as defined by the Energy Saving Trust in 2006 but the standard was under revision at the time of writing.

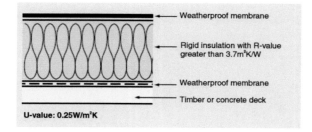

Figure 3.50 *Warm deck construction*
Source: © EST

Figure 3.51 *Inverted warm deck construction*
Source: © EST

these can be found in BRE (2002) and Great Britain Department for Transport, Local Government and the Regions et al (2001).

Dormer bungalows

These present particular problems. The warm roof area runs parallel to a crawl space around the perimeter that is ventilated through the eaves. When the wind picks up, it produces positive pressure on the windward side and negative pressure on the opposite. The air enters the crawl space, hits the wall and is directed into the floor void underneath the bedrooms. From there it can go anywhere. The effectiveness of any insulation in the floor void is dramatically reduced and draughts can penetrate throughout the house. Installing a wind tightness layer and a vapour control layer solves this problem.

Floor insulation

Heat loss through exposed floors can be reduced by up to 60 per cent but much depends on their size and shape, the type of floor and the conductivity of the ground below it. Heat loss is greatest around the edges. For this reason losses differ between a mid-terrace and an end-of-terrace dwelling. Specifying a common U-value for both would result in different insulation thicknesses and finished floor levels, which is usually not practical, and so in this case it is easier to specify an R-value than a U-value. To prevent thermal bridging care should be taken where a concrete frame, floor slabs or edge beams are exposed. The details shown in Figure 3.52 represent options for eliminating thermal bridging. In some situations this isn't feasible, in which case the minimum recommendations are shown.

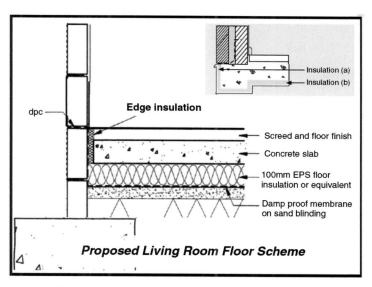

Figure 3.52 *Insulating under concrete ground floor (Edwardian house renovation) and (inset) exposed concrete floor (e.g. above driveway or garage)*

Source: © Parity Projects; inset © EST

Solid concrete floors

Aim for an R-value of 2.5m²K/W; this will generally achieve a U-value between 0.20 and 0.25W/m²K.

Ideally, a concrete floor with no insulation and damp-proof membrane beneath it should be taken up and the whole job started afresh. Where this is not possible, the only choice is to install insulation and a new deck on top, but the higher floor is likely to cause problems at stairs and door thresholds, with skirting boards and electrical points.

You need a minimum 60mm layer of phenolic, polyisocyanurate or polyurethane foam insulant; 200mm would be perfect. If the screed or ground floor slab is being replaced, or a new floor being installed, then insulation can be added above or below the concrete slab. If above, the room will warm up more quickly when the heating is put on. The damp proof membrane should be above the slab. Moisture-resistant flooring grade board should be used, with room for expansion around the edges.

Inserting the insulation below the slab is a good idea in a warm south-facing room or where underfloor heating is to be installed. In both cases the concrete slab on top helps absorb heat and limits overheating and the insulation below prevents it being wasted by heating the ground. An up-stand of insulation (R-value of 0.75m²K/W) the same height as the slab should be inserted around the perimeter of the room encircling the concrete. Joints between the insulation boards should be taped with water-resistant tape to stop concrete seepage. The vapour control layer is commonly incorporated between rigid urethane foam insulation and the floor screed, to prevent contamination of the insulation by

Table 3.10 *Concrete floors*

Insulation type	Typical thermal conductivity (W/mK)	Insulation above and below concrete floor						Up-stand insulation thickness
		Insulation thickness (mm)						Thickness (mm) to achieve best practice R-value of 0.75m²K/W
		40	60	80	100	120	140	
		U-values achieved						
Phenolic	0.022	0.30	0.23	0.19	0.16	0.14	0.13	18
Polisocyanurate and polyurethane	0.023	0.31	0.24	0.20	0.17	0.15	0.13	18
Extruded polystyrene	0.029	0.35	0.28	0.23	0.20	0.18	0.16	23
Expanded polystyrene and mineral wool board	0.038	0.39	0.32	0.28	0.24	0.21	0.19	29
Cellular glass	0.042	0.42	0.34	0.29	0.26	0.23	0.21	32

☐ Particularly suitable for existing floor slabs   ☐ Worse than best practice in refurbishment   ☐ Achieves best practice in refurbishment

Note: Assumptions for Table 3.10:

Source: EST (2006)

- insulation above: 19mm chipboard surface, no edge insulation, 250mm walls (concrete slab excluded from calculation as recommended in BRE 443 Conventions for U-value calculations);
- insulation below: 75mm screed, 150mm dense concrete slab, no edge insulation, 250mm walls;
- these figures are based on a dwelling with a floor perimeter/area ratio of 0.6. This represents a typical period end-terrace with a rear extension. This type of structure has a relatively poor layout in terms of thermal performance;
- the U-values quoted are only applicable to the exact construction described. Contact the manufacturer of the selected insulation to discuss the technical requirements and assess the potential for interstitial condensation. This should be done prior to commencing work. In these tables 'best practice' is as defined by the Energy Saving Trust in 2006 but the standard was under revision at the time of writing.

the screed and minimize cracking should movement occur below the screed. It is brought up the sides of the walls at the edges of the insulation again and behind the skirting boards to connect with the vapour control layer in the walls.

Underfloor heating should be seriously considered as an energy efficient form of space heating at this stage (see Chapter 6).

Suspended timber floors

Aim for an R-value of 3.5m²K/W; this will generally achieve a U-value between 0.20 and 0.25W/m²K.

Use mineral wool or rigid insulating boards. It should fill the space between the joists and be the full depth of the joist. If there is a cellar or basement, insulation under the ground floor might be installed from below. Fit the insulation tight up to the underside of the floor but not over-compressed. The floor may need a fire resistance of up to an hour if over the basement. Do not install a vapour control layer – it can trap spilt water. Ensure the under-floor void is well ventilated.

Figure 3.53 *100mm sheep's wool insulation underneath a suspended timber floor, covered with airtight membrane and 60mm fibre board – fully breathable*

Source: © Penny Poyzer and Gil Schalom

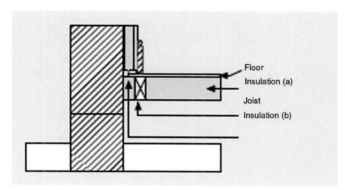

Floor
Insulation (a)
Joist
Insulation (b)

Figure 3.54 *Timber ground floor junction. Specify floor insulation as well as dry-lining to minimize thermal bridging, and insulate between the last joist and the wall, including a vapour check on the warm side of the insulation*

Source: © EST

Table 3.11 *Timber floors*

Insulation type	Typical thermal conductivity (W/mK)	Suspended timber floor insulation Joist depths				
		100mm	125mm	150mm	175mm	200mm
		U-values achieved when fully filled				
Phenolic	0.022	0.24	0.21	0.188	0.16	0.15
Polyisocyanurate and polyurethane	0.023	0.25	0.21	0.19	0.17	0.15
Cellulose	0.035	0.29	0.25	0.22	0.20	0.18
Flax	0.037	0.30	0.26	0.23	0.21	0.19
Expanded polystyrene	0.038	0.30	0.26	0.23	0.21	0.19
Sheep's wool and hemp	0.039	0.31	0.27	0.24	0.21	0.19
Mineral wool (quilt) and woodfibre	0.044	0.32	0.28	0.25	0.22	0.20
Vermiculite	0.063	0.37	0.33	0.30	0.27	0.25

☐ Worse than best practice in refurbishment   ☐ Achieves best practice in refurbishment

Note: Assumptions for Table 3.11:

Source: EST (2006)

• 50mm timber (Bridging fraction = 0.14), 225mm depth of underfloor below ground, 300mm floor height above ground, 250mm edge walls, no edge insulation;

• these figures are based on a dwelling with a floor perimeter/area ratio of 0.6. This represents a typical period end-terrace with a rear extension. This type of structure has a relatively poor layout in terms of thermal performance;

• the U-values quoted are only applicable to the exact construction described. Contact the manufacturer of the selected insulation to discuss the technical requirements and assess the potential for interstitial condensation. This should be done prior to commencing work. In these tables 'best practice' is as defined by the Energy Saving Trust in 2006 but the standard was under revision at the time of writing.

Where there is no access from below, you have to take up the floorboards. Suspended floors can suffer draughts entering with joists at the walls, around radiator pipes and under the skirting boards. Seal these using your complete armoury as appropriate of membranes, expanding foam and mastic.

Conclusion

Using the above methods will make a huge difference to most dwellings' energy performance. Exactly how much is still open to question. This is because many of the calculations that will be used will often be based upon manufacturers' own estimates of the U-values of their products, obtained under ideal or laboratory conditions. Together with uncertainty over local conditions, the quality of the installation and other factors this means that in practice actual performance may only be half as good as expected. This is what has been discovered in the few installations which have been monitored. So whereas we might expect there to have been, say, a 60 per cent reduction in carbon emissions, it might in reality only have been 30 per cent. And that is not even accounting for the fact that two dwellings can have the same theoretical specification yet varying carbon footprints depending on the behaviour of the occupants. For example, a large family with school-age children will have a different pattern of heating and cooling than a dwelling housing a night shift worker, or a homeworker, because they will switch on the heating at different times.

But what if the dwelling is so well insulated and airtight that it needs very little heating? Then the effect of different lifestyle and occupancy patterns is smoothed out. The design of something approaching a Passivhaus style renovation entails the use of design software which takes into account more factors. We can therefore be more confident that the extra investment required and the attention to detail during the installation work, is likely to be paid off. This is what we will look at next.

References

ATTMA (Air Tightness Testing and Measurement Association) (2007) 'Measuring air permeability of building envelopes technical standard 1', ATTMA, www.attma.org, last accessed February 2007

Bednar, T. and Deseyve, C. (2005) 'Increased thermal losses caused by ventilation through compact pitched roof constructions – in situ measurements', study presented at Seventh Nordic Symposium on Building Physics, Reykjavik

BRE (2000) 'BRE good building guide 44: Part 2: Insulating masonry cavity walls – principle risks and guidance', Stirling, C., BRE Publications, Bath

BRE (2002) 'Thermal insulation: Avoiding risks', BRE Report BR262, BRE, Stirling, C., BRE Publications, Bath

BSI (1992) BS8104: 1992 'Code of practice for assessing exposure of walls to wind-driven rain', BSI, London

Energy Saving Trust (2004) 'CE120 – Energy efficiency best practice in housing: Energy Efficient loft extensions', EST, London

Energy Saving Trust (2006) 'CE184 – Practical refurbishment of solid-walled houses', EST, London

Energy Saving Trust (2007) 'CE83 GPG155 – Energy efficient refurbishment of existing dwellings', EST, London

Energy Saving Trust (2008) 'CE252 – Cavity wall insulation in existing dwellings: A guide for specifiers and advisors', EST, London

Great Britain Department for Transport, Local Government and the Regions, and Department for Environment, Food and Rural Affairs (2001) 'Robust details – Limiting thermal bridging and air leakage: Robust construction details for dwellings and similar buildings', Her Majesty's Stationery Office, London

Her Majesty's Stationery Office (2006) 'The building regulations 2000: Approved document C: Site preparation and resistance to contaminants and moisture', HMSO, London

Kunzel, H. M. (1998) 'Effect of interior and exterior insulation on the hygrothermal behavior of exposed walls', *Materials and Structures*, vol 31, pp99–103

Little, J. (2009a) 'An independent analysis of the thermal characteristics of Irish concrete hollow blocks and hollow block wall upgrades and a discussion on hollow block design', self-published

Little, J. (2009b) 'Breaking the mould II: An analysis of single-leaf insulation upgrades', *Construct Ireland*, vol 4, issue 7

Silerbsein, A., Arquis, E. and McCaa, D. J. (1991) 'Forced convection effects in fibrous insulation', American Society for Testing and Materials, West Conshohocken, PA

Straub, John (2002) 'Moisture properties of plaster and stucco for strawbale buildings', report for Canada Mortgage and Housing Corporation, www.ecobuildnetwork.org/pdfs/Straube_Moisture_Tests.pdf, last accessed March 2010

4

Going All the Way: Towards Passivhaus

If you're going to go ahead with a complete building makeover, then – given that such an effort will only take place once every half century, or once in a building's lifetime – it makes financial sense to be as ambitious as possible in reducing its carbon load. It may cost 15 per cent more, but after 10 years or so you'll start seeing the benefit and getting a significant return on investment.

At the moment, this standard is represented by something approximating the Passivhaus target. Whether or not you deliberately strive for it, you'll need to pay strenuous attention to the initial modelling of heat flow through the building's skin, to the drawing of construction details to guarantee a seamless envelope and to scrutinizing installation to ensure they are implemented to perfection.

EST's Enhanced Construction Details

One set of details helpful for designers and architects is the Energy Saving Trust's Enhanced Construction Details (ECDs). These illustrate solutions to minimize heat losses at the junctions between building elements such as lintels, sills, wall-to-floor junctions and ceiling-to-gable-wall junction, and provide in-depth, practical guidance. It's said that these design principles can improve the performance of these non-repeating thermal bridges by over 85 per cent.

They are available free on the EST website at http://tinyurl.com/cmawks. Designed to help the construction industry achieve performance standards that exceed those set out in the UK's Part L1A of the Building Regulations, they help all developers and builders to achieve the equivalent of the energy requirements in the UK's Code for Sustainable Homes.

By using the complete set of three ECDs and ensuring that all remaining details achieve the Accredited Construction Details standards, designers and builders will be able to use a reduced thermal bridging U-value of 0.04W/m²K. The heat loss of a dwelling due to all thermal bridges is the sum of the k or psi-value for all details multiplied by their length. The introduction document for the ECDs specifies default k (psi)-values for each element and gives other ways to calculate it. Solutions are also given for when only some of the elements achieve this level, enabling a

Figure 4.1 *When joist ends are built into the masonry, it's easy to see how there is still potential for heat losses from thermal bridging or uncontrolled air leakage, even if proprietary systems are used to achieve airtightness; for example, where blocks are inaccurately cut to fit between the joists and gaps are carelessly filled with mortar*

Source: Photo from Stamford Brook report on airtightness – courtesy of Malcolm Bell, Leeds Metropolitan University, reproduced in EST (2008)

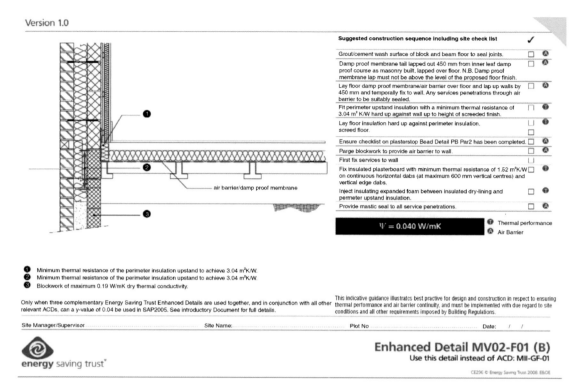

Figure 4.2 *Example from the EST Enhanced Construction Details*

Note: Available free on the EST website at http://tinyurl.com/cmawks.

Source: © EST

Table 4.1 *EST Enhanced Construction Details are available for the following construction types*

Construction type	Type code	Brief description
Cavity masonry	MV01	100mm block inner leaf internally plastered. 150mm fully filled insulated cavity. Brick outer leaf.
	MV02	100mm block inner leaf, internally lined with laminated plasterboard on horizontal continuous dabs on parge coat. 100mm fully filled insulated cavity. Brick outer leaf.
	MV03	100mm block inner leaf, internally lined with laminated plasterboard on horizontal continuous dabs on parge coat. 100mm partially filled insulated cavity. Brick outer leaf.
Timber frame	TF01	140mm fully filled timber frame, sheeted externally, air barrier/vapour control layer and insulated lining internally. Service void and plasterboard. Clear cavity with brick outer leaf.
	TF02	140mm fully filled timber frame, sheeted both sides, air barrier/vapour control layer. Service void and plasterboard. Partially filled insulated cavity with brick outer leaf.
Light steel frame	SF01	70mm fully filled light steel frame, air barrier/vapour control layer. Service void and plasterboard. Partially filled insulated cavity with brick outer leaf.
Ceiling	–	Attic trusses with insulation laid above, between and below, air barrier/vapour control layer. Service void and plasterboard.
Beam & block	F01	Beam and block floor with insulation and air barrier above, with screeded finish.
Solid slab	F02	100mm concrete slab on insulation on damp proof membrane/air barrier.
Suspended timber	F03	Floor decking on insulation on air barrier on sheeting on suspended timber floor joists off joist hangers.

Table 4.2 *k-values for the EST Enhanced Construction Details*

Wall type	Lintel	Gable	Slab on ground	Beam and block	Suspended timber
MV01	0.010	0.057	0.075	0.074	0.048
MV02	0.007	0.049	0.037	0.048	0.032
MV03	0.004	0.040	0.043	0.047	0.029
TF01	0.024	0.045	–	0.034	0.016
TF02	0.025	0.050	–	0.037	0.021
SF01	–0.010	0.068	–	0.070	–

calculation still to be made. The details are robust but the calculations will never be as accurate as those made using PHPP, described below.

These are aggregated to deliver the following ranges for individual building elements, provided all parts meet the requirements:

- Roof: 0.13–0.09 W/m²K;
- Walls: 0.25–0.16 W/m²K;
- Floors: 0.18–0.12 W/m²K.

The details suggest lapping the vapour control layer, foil, or a taped joint behind a plaster stop bead for long-term durability. Some typical enlarged lap details are included within the set of ECDs.

Strategies for ensuring airtightness

Figures 4.3 *and* **4.4** *The airtightness layer should be firmly fixed so that it will last for years*

Note: The paper tape on the left is unlikely to be as permanent as the battening fixed to the studs on the right.

Figure 4.5 *Halfway through the process of fitting and maintaining the membrane in and around the window reveal, connecting securely to the wall and floor*

Source: © Russell Smith

Figures 4.6 *and* **4.7** *The black membrane on the left goes underneath the plaster to connect to the floor layer and the skirting board will be fitted on top of it. On the right, a membrane comes from beneath the floor and the skirting board is ready to fix on to it*

Source: © Author and Chris Twinn

Figures 4.8 *and* **4.9** *While it is better to have a secure letterbox outside of the building envelope, this one has been built into the wall in a specially insulated and draughtproofed box; inside and outside view*

Figures 4.10 *and* **4.11** *The services in this 1930s house are in a draughtproofed cupboard under the stairs that is outside of the insulated envelope. Services that penetrate the envelope have sleeves and tapes to secure all gaps*

Source: © Chris Twinn

Passivhaus standard

What is the Passivhaus standard and is it really applicable to refurbishment? The standard emerged in 1988 from work by Professors Bo Adamson of Lund University, Sweden, and Wolfgang Feist of the Institut für Wohnen und Umwelt (Institute for Housing and the Environment). It (see www.passiv.de) addresses thermal bridging and airtightness and all energy use within the dwelling. Hundreds of new dwellings have been built to this standard now and it is rapidly gaining credence internationally because of the simplicity and flexibility of its approach compared, say, to national Building Regulations.

It requires that the space heat requirement must not exceed 15kWh/(m²/a) – less than one-fifth of the energy requirement mandated by most building regulations currently in force. Total Primary Energy Use (appliances, lighting, ventilation, pumps, DHW (domestic hot water)) must also not exceed 120kWh/(m²/a) (38,039Btu/ft²/yr) – less than half the average consumption of European new housing. Building fabric U-values must be less than 0.15W/m²K, so they overlap slightly with the EST's standards above.

U-values for windows and doors generally need to be less than 0.8W/m²K (4755Btu/ft²/yr) (for both the frame and glazing) with solar heat-gain coefficients around 50 per cent. BRE, a statutory body in the UK promoting Passivhaus, provides Solar Heat Gain Coefficients (SHGC – the proportion of solar energy that enters via the window) to help with calculations which can be adjusted for glazing on different facades. This can help either reduce heat loss on sheltered

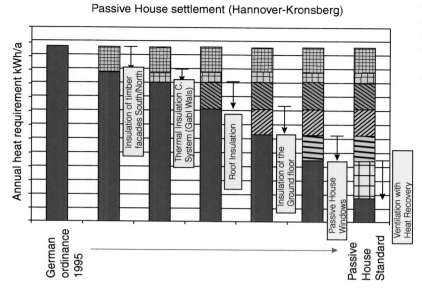

Figure 4.12 *Six steps from average dwelling yearly heating requirements to Passivhaus standard where consumption was reduced by 80 per cent on a terraced row in Germany*

Source: www.passivhaustagung.de

sides/north facing glazing, or reduce the likelihood of overheating when specified in conjunction with other features/strategies (the SHGC of a window usually decreases as the U-value improves). See www.passivhaus.org.uk.

The requirements imply the following features to achieve them:

- Passive preheating of fresh air: brought in through underground ducts that exchange heat with the ground to reach above 5°C (41°F), even on cold winter days;
- MVHR: transfers over 80 per cent of the heat in the ventilated exhaust air to the incoming fresh air;
- hot water supply using renewable energy: solar collectors, biomass, CHP (combined heat and power) or heat pumps powered by renewable electricity;
- Energy-saving household appliances: ultra-low energy lighting, refrigerators, stoves, freezers, washers, dryers and so on.

Additional energy requirements come from renewable energy sources. The Passivhaus Institute claims that 'a passive house is cost-effective when the combined capitalized costs (construction, including design and installed equipment, plus operating costs for 30 years) do not exceed those of an average new home'.

The increased cost of meeting this standard has been calculated for a new build compared to the same house (in a terrace built in 2001) built to normal standards. For the roof it was an extra €10 per square metre. For the external wall an extra €18, for the ground an extra €15, plus the cost of the blower test – about €160. This equated to an extra €8172 or 8 per cent of total costs, an amount entirely justified by the lowered running costs (see www.cepheus.de). In other countries it may well be more.

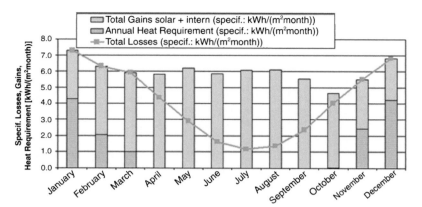

Figure 4.13 *Graph produced by the PHPP software, showing the monthly solar gains, heat losses and heat demand required by a structure*

The Passive House Planning Package (PHPP)

Software is available to help designers model the thermal performance, carbon emissions and energy requirements of a building when developing their plans. The Passivhaus Planning Package (PHPP) has been developed by the PassivHaus Institut, Germany over the last 12 years by comparing its modelling and predictions against the reality in hundreds of passive house constructions. It therefore distils a huge amount of experience and includes tools for calculating:

- U-values of insulation;
- energy balances – solar gain and heat losses;
- ventilation;
- heating and cooling load;
- many other useful tools;
- climate data sets for Eastern Europe, Austria, Switzerland and many European cities; the American version contains data for 40 US cities and imperial units.

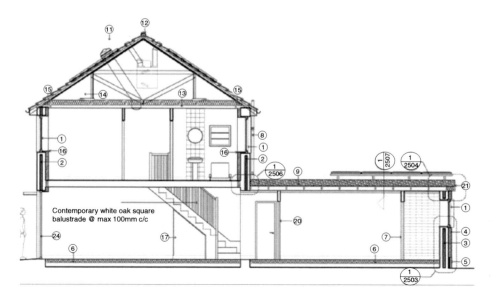

Figure 4.14 *Whole house refurbishment plan for Hyde Housing Association's pilot renovation project*

Source: © Hyde Housing

Users input measurements from their plans, material specifications, measurements and other data and can run the model to see what the consequences are. It can be purchased cheaply from www.passivhaus.org.uk, www.passivehouse.us and www.passivhaustagung.de.

Applying Passivhaus to renovation

PHPP has been shown to work for renovations by using substantial modelling to weigh up the pros and cons of different strategies. The standards allow for a great deal of flexibility and there is a growing body of experience on which designers can draw from a multitude of dwelling types.

Austrian and German research claims that for larger apartment buildings renovations to Passivhaus standard or close cost about €450–600/m². The extra cost compared to a renovation up to national building code is in the range €80–150/m² – around 7 per cent. Another Austrian case study detailed below records extra costs of 16 per cent, offset by 95 per cent savings on heating. The relatively few renovations made in the UK suggest an extra 15–20 per cent may be more realistic, but the difference between the countries is likely to be affected by the maturity of the supply chain; as a national refurbishment programme kicks in, economies of scale drive down prices.

A European project, co-financed by the EC's (European Community's) Intelligent Energy Europe programme, is researching and informing social housing organizations about eco-refit. Six institutions from five countries are involved, including the Faellesbo social housing company and COWI A/S, both in Denmark, the Energieinstitut Vorarlberg research institute of Austria, the ECN Energy Research Centre of the Netherlands, the Asociación de Investigación Industrial de Andalucia of Spain, and Lithuania's Housing Agency. Social housing groups have been selected as they are frequently responsible for a very high number of large, identical buildings. A common definition of 'passive house renovation' or 'high quality renovation' has emerged as one that 'improves the specific demand for heating, and cooling in southern countries to a maximum of 30kWh/m²/a' because in some cases it was shown to be prohibitively expensive to reach 15kWh/m²/a. Even so, many of the projects realized so far have aimed at a specific heating demand of about 25kWh/m²/a. Work is being done to extend the tool to Northern Europe. The online tool can be found at www.energieinstitut.at/Retrofit.

Case studies and options are available in several languages on this website, where it is claimed that 'Depending on the building type, energy savings vary between 80 to 95%. The specific heating demand is typically reduced from between 150 and 280kWh/m²a to less than 30kWh/m²a. In some cases, the Passivhaus standard of 15kWh/m²a is reached.'

About 35 feasible measures are described and although they may differ from country to country due to climatic differences or differences in construction traditions, the main elements are identical. A second part of the tool covers the implementation of Passivhaus retrofit in building typologies for each of the countries involved. The online tool starts by looking at the dwelling types as summarized below.

For each country, between three and nine building types were examined. As well as the five participating countries, nine more national versions of the tool

Table 4.3 Potential improvements by dwelling type with a Passivhaus retrofit

Dwelling type	heating energy demand before	combined energy demand before	cooling energy demand before	heating demand after PH refit	heating energy demand after CSH4 standard refit	combined energy demand after PHR
Terrace, 1970s	175–240kWh/m^{2}a	338kWh/m^{2}a	0kWh/m^{2}a	24kWh/m^{2}a	16kWh/m^{2}a	8kWh/m^{2}a
Compact apartment blocks with balconies:						
1960s large	150–220kWh/m^{2}a	240kWh/m^{2}a	0kWh/m^{2}a	16kWh/m^{2}a	80kWh/m^{2}a	33kWh/m^{2}a
1960s small	200–270kWh/m^{2}a	414kWh/m^{2}a	0kWh/m^{2}a	23kWh/m^{2}a	97kWh/m^{2}a	41kWh/m^{2}a
1970s large, flat roof	135–190kWh/m^{2}a	136kWh/m^{2}a	0kWh/m^{2}a	16kWh/m^{2}a	80kWh/m^{2}a	33kWh/m^{2}a
1970s small	160–220kWh/m^{2}a	198kWh/m^{2}a	0kWh/m^{2}a	15kWh/m^{2}a	96kWh/m^{2}a	29kWh/m^{2}a

Definitions

Dwelling type	No. of floors	No. of dwellings	Enclosed volume	Treated floor area	Ratio of external surface/volume
Terrace, 1970s	2–3	1	350–750m^2	90–180m^2	0.55–0.65
Compact apartment blocks with balconies:					
1960s large	4–6	12–30	3000–8000m^2	1000–2500m^2	0.35–0.45
1960s small	3–4	6–12	1500–3000m^2	500–1000m^2	0.45–0.55
1970s large, flat roof	4–6	12–30	3000–8000m^2	1000–2500m^2	0.35–0.45
1970s small	3–4	6–12	1500–3000m^2	500–1000m^2	0.45–0.55

Definitions

Dwelling type	external wall	roof/attic floor	basement	ceiling	window	airtightness	ventilation	overheating protection
					Building elements			
Terrace, 1970s	1.04W/(m^{2}K)	0.66W/(m^{2}K)	0.81W/(m^{2}K)	2.69W/(m^{2}K)	n50 = 3.0h^{-1}	0.5h^{-1}	(window)	roller blinds
Compact apartment blocks with balconies:								
1960s large	1.03W/(m^{2}K)	0.77W/(m^{2}K)	1.17W/(m^{2}K)	2.7W/(m^{2}K)	n50 = 3.0h^{-1}	0.5h^{-1}	(window)	roller blinds
1960s small	1.61W/(m^{2}K)	0.79W/(m^{2}K)	1.54W/(m^{2}K)	2.66W/(m^{2}K)	n50 = 3.0h^{-1}	0.5h^{-1}	(window)	roller blinds
1970s large, flat roof	0.83W/(m^{2}K)	0.52W/(m^{2}K)	1.04W/(m^{2}K)	2.71W/(m^{2}K)	n50 = 3.0h^{-1}	0.5h^{-1}	(window)	roller blinds
1970s small	0.47W/(m^{2}K)	1.64W/(m^{2}K)	0.97W/(m^{2}K)	2.66W/(m^{2}K)	n50 = 3.0h^{-1}	0.5h^{-1}	(window)	roller blinds

Notes: PH, passivhaus; CSH4, Code for Sustainable Homes Level 4; PHR, Passivhaus refit.

Source: www.energieinstitut.at/Retrofit

exist, including Italy, France, Portugal, Slovenia and the Czech Republic. Work is underway in the UK in several housing associations.

Several problems are presented by smaller buildings. Dwellings don't always conform to the preferred compact shape with a relatively lower surface-to-volume ratio that minimizes the exterior area from which heat can escape, due to extensions, L-shaped constructions, etc. Another is the thermal bridging present where exterior walls meet the foundations or party walls, or chimneys pass though a suspended floor. In one passive house refurbishment, at Pattenbach, Austria, the challenge of getting the insulation envelope under the exterior walls was solved by lifting the house up, which was possible because of its lightweight timber structure! As this is not normally possible, the strategy is to overlap internal and external insulation at the wall/floor junction. At the same time higher U-values for these elements are compensated for by lower U-values for other elements. A further problem will be the location and orientation of the building, which affects how much direct sunshine it can receive throughout the year.

Terraced house renovation

An 1869-constructed Victorian terraced dwelling in Hereford, England, has been converted to Passivhaus standard in this fashion by project manager Andy Simmonds (pictured on the cover). A target for the heating demand of no more than $22kWh/m^2a$ was decided upon together with U-values for floors and walls of 0.12 and 0.09 respectively. Modelling was carried out using PHPP and the thermal modelling program Two-dimensional building Heat transfer Modeling (THERM).

Features include:

- an extension with south facing roof for solar panels. Insulated solar pipe connections to the cylinder from the roof were installed, in anticipation of future completion of the system, since retrofitting the pipes later would have meant increased cost and destroying the work that had just been done;
- external wall insulation using (1) Permarock EPS-Platinum insulated render system (0.030W/mK) adhesively bonded (spread evenly to remove the possibility of air movement behind boards) and mechanically fixed to masonry. Metal and plastic fixings are repeating thermal bridges which were accounted for. (2) Larsen Trusses, with 350mm deep, site-built timber ladder trusses stuffed with installation, sheathed, fixed to the walls and clad in timber sheeting;
- roof raised to accommodate the extra insulation, creating a usable super-insulated A-frame roof from a traditional 'rafters on purlins' roof;
- polyethylene air vapour barrier sealed to the primed brickwork face using self-adhesive polymer bitumen tape;
- floors: (1) a floating floor on existing concrete slab; (2) a solid new insulated reinforced concrete raft in the extension, and (3) a suspended timber ground floor/basement ceiling insulated with three layers of sheep's wool and finished with plasterboard;
- airtightness barrier designated on the external faces of the walls;

Figure 4.15 *THERM is a program developed at Lawrence Berkeley National Laboratory (LBNL) for two-dimensional modelling of heat transfer effects in windows, walls, foundations, roofs, doors, appliances and other products where thermal bridges are of concern*

Note: It permits evaluation of a product's energy efficiency and local temperature patterns, condensation, moisture damage and structural integrity. It can produce graphic visualizations like the one to the left of cross sections, isotherms, colour infrared heat transfer cross-sections and more.

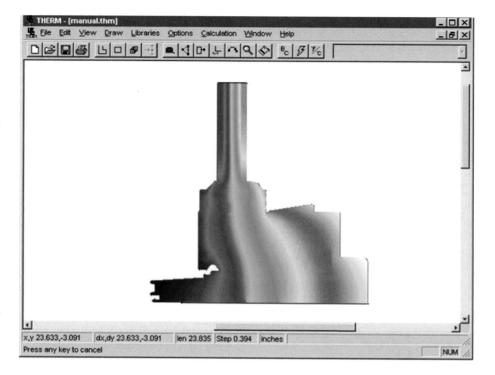

- 25mm gap between the house and neighbouring property filled with expanding polyurethane foam. In the PHPP tool, party walls are not accounted for because it is assumed that the next door will be the same temperature. This cannot be relied upon in refurbishment and instead allowance must be made for heat loss under normal circumstances through this wall;
- Paul Thermos 200 MHVR ventilation system with heat exchanger and an imaginative positioning of the ducts.

The optimum detailing and approaches for Passivhaus-type refurbishment are still being developed. Time will tell which methods for different building types are most successful in preserving airtightness. Whether a renovation can achieve this standard depends to a certain extent upon its existing orientation and location to take advantage of the sun's heat, or 'solar gain', but this is not a crucial factor.

The CarbonLite programme

More advanced detailing than the Energy Saving Trust's is available to members of the Association of Energy Conscious Builders (AECB) under its 'CarbonLite' programme. This is designed 'to help all those involved in the commissioning, design, delivery and use of low energy and CO_2 buildings'. It is a step-by-step guide with three increasingly more challenging standards: Step One/Silver, Step Two/Passivhaus and Step Three/Gold. The standards are expressed in terms of energy use and CO_2 emissions per square metre and year – measured in kWh and tonnes respectively.

There are two versions of the standards:

- a performance only version, expressed in energy and CO_2 emissions, with limits on U values and air leakage; and
- prescriptive standards, which suggest ways of obtaining the targets.

VALUE CARBON ANALYSIS OF THE 24 ECO IMPROVEMENT MEASURES AT 70A AUBERT PARK

Improvements ranked as 'Value Carbon' (best to worst) — Cumulative cost and effects of the improvements

		£ installed cost	Kg saved pa	% CO₂ saved pa	kWh saved pa	fuel bill saving pa	EPC (initially E)
Lighting	Low energy lighting throughout						D
Draught proof	Windows & seating cracks/gaps					£50	D
Draught proof	Ventilate chimney to basement	£1000		10%			C
Hall	Aerogel insulate 9" solid external wall				2000		C
Boiler	Baxi microCHP (inc 10yr maintenance)		1750			£200*	C
WC	Aerogel insulate 9" solid external wall	£7000		50%			C
Bathroom	Aerogel insulate 9" solid external wall						C
Kitchen	Aerogel insulate 9" solid external wall		2100		8000		C
Living room	Vacuum glazing of sash windows					£275	B
Living room	Aerogel insulate 13" solid external wall	£9000		60%	9000		B
Living room	Aerogel insulate wall to common entrance hall					£300	B
Hall	New door to garden, dbl glzd & draught stripped	£10,000				B	
Bedroom	Aerogel insulate 13" solid external wall						B
Living room	Warmcel insulate under suspended floor	£13,000	2500	65%			B
Bedroom	Warmcel insulate under suspended floor						B
Hall	Warmcel insulate under suspended floor						B
Hall	Magic Wallpaper insulate partition to neighbour						B
MVHR	Heat recovery ventilation (inc 10yr maintenance)	£22,500	2670	70%	11,000	£350	B
Living room	Aerog. insulate rtum party wall (thermal bridge)						B
Bedroom	Aerog. insulate rtum party wall (thermal bridge)						B
Hall	Aerogel insulate bedroom wall (thermal bridge)	£24,000					B
Bathroom	Aerogel insulate party wall (thermal bridge)						B
Measure & calc	BRE assess, sensors/datalog, before/after AP & thermal image tests	£29,000					B
Rain harvest	Rain water harvesting system						B
WC low flush	2/4 litre pan, fed by rain water	£30,000	2670	70%	11,000	£350	B

Additional supplementary improvements — Cost & effect of individual improvements

		£installed	cost kg saved pa	% saved pa	kWh saved pa	fuel bill saving pa
White goods	Replacing an E rated washer with an A rated washer	£354	97	3%	230	£30
White goods	Replacing an E rated fridge with an A rated fridge	£472	76	2%	180	£23
Draught seating	Reducing the Air Permeability (AP) by 1 point	£300	12	0.4%	82	£3
Changing habits	Tenants reducing their room temp by 1C	£0	130	3%	670	£20
Changing habits	Tenants reducing their hot water use by 10%	£0	33	1%	170	£5

24 eco improvement measures were made to this 'difficult to treat' Victorian social housing ground-floor flat

	Before tonnes pa	After tonnes pa	Saving tonnes pa	Saving %age
Carbon pa	3.8	1.1	2.7	70%
Capital cost		£22k		£8/kg pa
Tenants' fuel bill pa	£97	£630		35%
Dwelling EPC rating	E	B		

Figure 4.16 *Value carbon analysis of the 24 ECO improvement measures at 70A Aubert Park*

Note: Social housing contractor United House renovated a one-bedroom ground-floor Victorian terraced flat at Aubert Park, London, with the above measures which included a micro combined heat and power unit, aerogel insulation to external and party walls, vacuum glazing in existing sash windows and mechanical ventilation with heat recovery. It cost £22,000, producing a 70 per cent CO_2 saving and was monitored by BRE. Alistair Sivill, technical director, said that other measures yielded no extra carbon saving but cost £8000. These included gravity-fed rainwater collection (tank high up in bathroom) for toilet flushing. Sivill says they did not have a target figure but sought to get the maximum carbon saving for the cost. Project engineer Daniel Johncock said they got the airtightness down from 10 to 7.5ACH. 'The aerogel was hard to cut, there were dust issues, we tried to direct fix it to the masonry but the drill bit chewed it up so we had to fit timber battens, to which we fixed a 10mm concrete facing and 30mm aerogel. The cellulose insulation worked perfectly however. The plaster was the airtightness layer. It was the labour element that put the cost up'.

Source: United House Group interview

They take no account of materials or their embodied energy (which they reckon accounts for under 4 per cent of a new building's lifetime energy use). Dwellings must have a guidebook to explain to users how/why the building differs from many others and how to operate it. The standards are intended mostly for new build, but work is underway to apply and extend them to refurbishments.

The Silver Standard is on a par with the Canadian R-2000 Standard, the German Low Energy Standard and the Swiss MINERGIE Standard. It would probably be met or exceeded by the UK's top 20–50 housing projects, if these were judged by their measured energy performance. Silver uses the best widely-available technology achieving results just below Passivhaus standard. Step Two or Passivhaus Standard requires further improvement in levels of insulation and airtightness, advanced windows, solar water heating system and the most efficient electrical appliances. Step Three or Gold is thermally the same as Step Two, except for additional savings in space and water heating, cooking, lights and more energy efficient electrical appliances/equipment and a requirement for more electricity-producing renewables. It has three principles that underscore what we've examined so far:

- a continuous air barrier;
- continuous insulation;
- minimal thermal bridges.

The heat loss calculations are based on assumptions and methodologies spelt out in CarbonLite Programme 'Volume Two: Principles and methodologies for calculating and minimising heat loss and CO_2 emissions from buildings'. The detailing is downloadable to members of the AECB, but less specific information is freely available via GreenSpec (www.greenspec.co.uk), a web-based specification tool, which discusses some of the systems, products and strategies. GreenSpec is an evolving tool based on experience of how manufacturers' claims live up to reality.

Non-airtight strategies

There are many older buildings, particularly with solid walls, for which Passivhaus is not necessarily the best approach, or which will never reach anything like 80 per cent reduction. Despite the central role airtightness has to play in low energy buildings, extreme levels of airtightness aren't favoured by all in the green building community. Some green builders prefer to avoid super airtight standards and the energy demand of mechanical ventilation heat recovery (MVHR) systems, while still building well-insulated structures that are naturally ventilated – using the 'passive stack' method – and fuelled by low or zero carbon sources. The passive stack method utilizes the innate property that hot air rises to circulate air within a building. This topic will be considered more fully in Chapter 6.

The future

Whether renovation projects can be rolled out on a mass scale, or go beyond Passivhaus to reach Gold Standard is yet to be discovered. But we can expect that it will, because this is the future of low carbon refurbishment for many reasons, not least of which is the increasing prevalence of governmental legislation and targets that will drive the demand and the markets. Reaching an 80 per cent reduction in carbon use, in particular through demand control, is the only way forward – and for many types of construction the Passivhaus philosophy and aspiration makes much sense.

5
Windows and Doors

In a low-carbon building, windows are effectively gaps in the insulation envelope. They let in solar energy for light and heat and allow heat to leave unless we stop it.

Savings from installing new windows and doors are not as high as for most forms of insulation, but if they are to be replaced then let's do it with the best performing units available. If they are not going to be replaced – or can't be for any reason as with a listed or historic building – then consider secondary glazing as this can also really improve thermal performance.

Doors

Replacement doors, whether containing glazing or not, should have insulated cores, in other words, a layer of insulation – typically polyurethane – between the two outer surfaces, whether they're constructed from PVC or timber to minimize thermal bridging. Doors are available which will achieve U-values of lower than $0.6 W/m^2 K$. They should be well sealed into the frame (see Chapter 1) and use ironmongery that secures them as firmly as possible to eliminate all draughts.

In an airtight, ventilation-controlled building it is important not to leave doors open unnecessarily. It's therefore worth considering fitting them with a mechanism to close them automatically. Adding porches and conservatories to existing building entrances helps to buffer the effect of heat leaving or entering the building when the doors are opened, provided that they maintain the wind and/or airtight layer around the building and are insulated to the same value.

Features of high-performance windows and doors

Double or triple glazing: triple is preferred. The gap between panes should be 16mm or more if no gas filling is used. Provide good sound insulation.

Low-e coating: a special coating on the inside of the inner pane to reflect radiant heat back into the room.

Gas filling: an inert gas between panes: argon, krypton or xenon minimizes the conduction of heat. Xenon is most effective, but argon is cheapest.

Insulated frames: to avoid thermal bridging.

Draught-stripping: compression seals around the frame.

With all glazing, allow for safe cleaning and escape through the window in case of fire.

Windows

Windows must be used to minimize the need for artificial lighting and to capture within the building a sizeable proportion of the sun's heat required to keep a comfortable temperature without overheating. The choice of glazing, shading, thermal mass and other factors can help achieve this.

Modern windows are rated by national bodies and come with a declaratory label. In the UK this is the British Fenestration Rating Council (BFRC). Choose windows with the highest possible rating on the label. 'C' is the minimum level for an eco-home (which the Energy Saving Trust says has a payback of five or six years). This label displays the following information:

1 the rating level: A, B, C, etc.;
2 the energy rating, e.g. −3kWh/(m²)/yr (= a loss of three kilowatt hours per square metre per year);
3 the U-value, e.g. 1.4W/(m²K);
4 the effective heat loss due to air penetration as L, e.g. 0.01W/(m²K);
5 the solar heat gain G-value, e.g. 0.43 (see below).

The BFRC is shortly to produce new labels which take into account the life-cycle impact of different framing types. If the building is being renovated to Passivhaus or Carbonlite standards, the U-value is calculated differently. It includes the U-value for the whole of the window, including the frame, plus the thermal bridge dependent on the installation detail of the window or door in the external wall. For details, consult the PHPP Manual.

It is possible to specify windows made with up to 33 per cent of recycled glass.

Solar gain

The heating effect of the sun in a building is called solar gain. It varies with the strength of the sun, its angle and the effectiveness of the glazing to transmit or reflect its energy. We want to maximize solar gain within the building in the winter (to reduce space heating demand) and to control it in summer (to minimize cooling requirements and solar glare). The composition and coating on each face of the glazing can be manipulated to optimize the greenhouse effect, while windows' size, position and shading can be used to optimize solar gain.

Using windows to control solar gain

Variables that may be taken into account when choosing them include:

- thickness;
- number of panes;

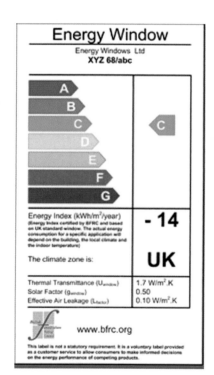

Figure 5.1 *Example of an energy label for a window from the BFRC*

Note: The ratings are (in kWh/(m²)/yr):
A: 0
B: 0 to −10
C: −10 to −20
D: −20 to −30
E: −30 to −50
F: −50 to −70
G: −70 or worse

Source: www.bfrc.org

- coatings on the glass;
- cavity size or fill;
- nature of the spacer bar;
- sealant used;
- frame type;
- frame materials;
- fixing method.

Solar heat and light control

A dwelling with too much equator- or west-facing glass can result in excessive winter, spring, or autumn day heating, too much glare and excessive heat at certain times of the year. Although the sun is at the same altitude six weeks before and after the solstice, the heating and cooling requirements before and after the solstice are significantly different. Modelling must account for this, using Two-dimensional building Heat transfer Modeling THERM software and PHPP. Insulation data giving the annual variability of solar energy for a location is available from national weather centres or government renewable energy agencies.

Latitude-specific fixed window overhangs are frequently used to shade, but are bypassed at times when the sun is low. One permanent and fixed solution is to specify a solar control coating on the inside of the first pane of glass which can be precisely calibrated to reflect any proportion of the sun's radiation back out and prevent it from entering the room. It might be particularly appropriate in an equator- or west-facing conservatory which tends to overheat. The glass can be installed in the roof and reflect, say, 70 per cent of the heat.

Figure 5.2 *Solar shading for south facing French windows on a refurbishment in Nottingham (Lacemaker's House)*

Note: For a more natural look, a trellis covered with vines would do just as well.

Operable shading and insulation devices

Variable solutions include shading control mechanisms, such as:

- interior: window quilts, bifold interior insulation shutters, manual or motorized interior insulated drapes and shutters;
- exterior: shutters, roll-down shade screens, or retractable awnings.

These can help control daily/hourly variations. There are even automated systems that monitor temperature, sunlight, time of day and room occupancy and control motorized window-shading-and-insulation devices. Take care that the energy cost, including the embodied energy of manufacture and installation, is not greater than that saved by reducing the cooling demand.

Shading coefficients quantify the solar energy transmittance through windows. In Europe this coefficient is called the 'G-value' while in North America it is 'solar heat gain coefficient' (SHGC). G-values and SHGC values range from 0 to 1 (a lower value

Figure 5.3 *Interior shutters to keep out solar gain*

Figure 5.4 *Triple-glazed, coated window with insulated frame and spacers to avoid thermal bridging*

Source: © NorDan, supplied with permission

represents less solar gain). Shading coefficient values are the sum of the primary solar transmittance (T-value) – the proportion of the total solar insulation entering through the glazing, plus the secondary transmittance – the proportion absorbed in the window (or shading device).

For advanced refurbishment designs, the software program THERM can help you determine total window product U-values and Solar Heat Gain Coefficients, but it should be used in combination with PHPP because PHPP alone is not sufficient for professional refurbishments. PHPP requires information on all areas, depths, angles and dimensions, including those of the frame, reveal and glazing and any shading outside whether it is from buildings across the road, or trees, etc. All this is potentially significant, because for example a timber window frame may account for 30 per cent of the window area and if a quarter of the wall is glazed, then that is 7.5 per cent of the wall area. Similarly, shading and the reveal angle and depth will considerably affect the amount of solar gain. Modelling with PHPP can help explore this.

Low-emittance coatings

Having regulated the amount of solar heat we want to let in, we want to keep it there. A low-emittance (low-e) coating on the inside pane allows short wavelength radiation inside through the pane, but longer wavelength (warm, infra-red) radiation is reflected back into the building. (Emittance refers to the ability of a material's surface to emit radiant energy.)

Other coatings

A self-cleaning coating can even be added to the exterior face of a window pane – particularly useful in inaccessible places such as the conservatory roof or skylight. These use ultraviolet light to attack and break down organic materials and rain to wash them off.

Manufacturers supply a huge range of coatings: some can permit only 6 per cent of light to enter the building, or 8 per cent of heat. Panes specifically designed for eco-homes have extra clear outer layers, letting up to 80 per cent of light and 71 per cent of the sun's heat in.

Secondary glazing

Secondary glazing holds glass in frames of timber, aluminium or plastic, but flexible plastic glazing can also be used. Economical and permanent, it also provides effective sound insulation if the panes are 150mm or more apart. Avoid condensation by draught-proofing the inner pane. The frames are compression fitted for easy removal to clean the window or escape in case of fire.

Figure 5.5 *Secondary glazing on a sash window, also showing angled reveal to maximize light coming into the room and insulation being fitted to minimize thermal bridging*

Windows and lighting

Windows admit heat and daylight differently at different times of the year and day depending on the angle of incidence. If this is within 20° of the perpendicular it will effectively pass through it; at over 35° the majority of the energy will bounce off. Software is available to calculate cooling-and-heating degree days and energy performance, using regional climatic conditions available from local weather services.

Mostly, with renovation, windows are already in a fixed position, but there are ways to improve the amount of light available from an existing window, such as:

Figures 5.6 and 5.7 *Lacemaker's House in Nottingham could not have windows on one side for planning reasons. This glass floor seen from above and below transmits light to the lower levels from a skylight in the roof*

- by painting the reveal, lintel, window sill and opposite walls a light colour to reflect more light;
- it may be possible to slant the sides of reveal to increase the amount of light entering the room;
- by positioning mirrors in the reveal and opposite the window to reflect more light into the room.

Light shelves

In some places (e.g. high windows in communal areas in blocks of flats and modern dwellings) installing light shelves may help to save electricity used for lighting. These reflect daylight deep into a room from horizontal overhangs above eye-level. High-reflectance surfaces reflect light onto the ceiling and up to four times the distance between the floor and the top of the window into a room. Usually made of an extruded aluminium chassis system and aluminium composite panel surfaces, they are generally used in continental, not tropical or desert climates, due to the intense heat gain.

Light tubes

Light tubes or sun pipes can transport daylight from roofs to rooms that do not have direct access to good natural light. Compared to conventional skylights, they offer better heat insulation and more flexibility for use in inner rooms, but no visual sight of the outside. They assist with seasonal affective disorder experienced in rooms with no natural light. As they penetrate the airtightness barrier just like windows, care must be taken when fitting.

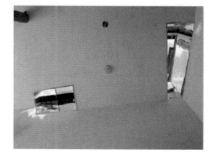

Figure 5.8 *Also in Lacemaker's House, Nottingham these 'light steals' also transmit light to the lower level from windows higher up*

Figure 5.9 *Angled reveal and light coloured paint maximizes the light filling the room*

Heat loss paths around a typical window opening – traditional construction

Figures 5.10 and 5.11 *Sources of draughts around windows; fitting a double glazed low-e hardwood timber frame window prior to sealing and insulating reveal*

PVC or timber for frames and doors?

For years polyvinyl chloride or PVC products have been opposed by environmentalists, principally because of the health-damaging dioxins and furans released as by-products of their manufacture and at the end-of-life when they are incinerated or landfilled. Vinyl chloride is a known human carcinogen. But the PVC industry has been arguing that it is now more environmentally sound because of improvements in manufacturing and procedures being put in place to recycle PVC3 products at the end of their lives. Is it therefore as ecological as timber?

Both products have similar thermal properties and in use timber frames need more maintenance than PVC. However, in February 2007, the Technical and Scientific Advisory Committee of the US Green Building Council (USGBC) published a report for the Leadership in Energy and Environmental Design (LEED) Green Building Rating system which concludes that the 'risk of dioxin emissions puts PVC consistently among the worst materials for human health impacts' (see www.usgbc.org/ShowFile. aspx?DocumentID=2372 and www.pharosproject.net). In other words, since its disposal is unlikely to result in recycling, the dioxins emitted during its decay in landfill pose a threat to human health.

It is claimed that PVC can last up to 35 years but if it cracks the whole frame has to be replaced. Hinges and fastenings can also cause the PVC to crack. Wood effectively is a carbon store inside a building, is more forgiving and parts of a window frame can be replaced without the need to replace the whole frame.

Aluminium frames are definitely to be avoided because of this metal's thermal conductivity. A low carbon building will therefore favour timber wherever possible.

Fitting windows and doors

Correct fitting is important to maintain the integrity of the thermal envelope and to prevent draughts and thermal bridging. In solid walls, insulation in the reveal should meet up with the wall insulation. When this is not possible, spray foam can be used to fill the gap around the window frame once it is in place. Where space inside the reveal is at a premium, thinner slab insulation can be used, or the old plaster can be hacked off and replaced with new plaster with which has been mixed granular insulation such as perlite, vermiculite or polystyrene balls, or a hygroscopic plaster such as lime.

Where large-scale renovation is being rolled out in a block of flats or a terrace, it makes economic sense to replace the windows at the same time as installing external wall insulation or cladding, since the

Figures 5.12 and 5.13: *Examples of secure, draught-proof fittings*

scaffolding is in place, the thermal upgrade will not be compromised by inferior windows and a perfect fit can be obtained.

With cavity walls, proprietary pre-insulated cavity closers are available that prevent thermal bridging. These avoid the need for separate strips of insulation within the cavity or for internal insulated linings that partially mask the frame. This allows much greater versatility in positioning window and door frames within the depth of the reveal. Lintels and sills must be insulated as well to prevent thermal bridging as they may cross the cavity. For detailing see the Energy Saving Trust's Enhanced Construction Details (ECDs) available online.

All of these measures will help to reduce both the heating and cooling bills and the electricity bills for artificial lighting.

6

Ventilation, Cooling and Heating

In a low carbon dwelling the over-riding issue is the control of the internal climate and air quality to minimize the use of energy for heating or cooling and promote health. Non-energy efficient homes rely on natural air infiltration to provide ventilation, but this can increase the amount of energy used to heat them. As insulation standards improve, ventilation heat losses increase proportionately as a percentage of total heat loss. In well-insulated dwellings, these account for around a third of the total heat loss. Conversely, in hot periods, we invest in energy-guzzling fans and air conditioners. Adequate ventilation also removes internal pollutants such as allergens, NO_x (nitrogen oxide), VOCs and carbon monoxide and controls humidity so the air inside is clean and neither too dry nor too damp.

In an airtight and well-insulated building the mantra is 'build tight – ventilate right': minimize the amount of uncontrolled air leakage, then install a controllable system to provide the necessary level of ventilation both where and when it is needed. There are several options for tackling internal climate and air quality:

- conventional extractor fans in wet rooms;
- mechanical ventilation with heat recovery in wet rooms only;
- whole house passive stack ventilation;
- whole house mechanical ventilation with heat recovery;
- whole house passive stack ventilation with incoming air pre-warmed underground using a heat pump;
- the same using an air source heat pump.

In general the first and last options are not recommended for best practice. Conventional extractor fans lose the heat in the outgoing air, but are better than nothing. Without provision for incoming air they also lower the pressure in a building, which can cause the spillage of combustion products from open-flued appliances. Air source heat pumps are generally not as efficient as is often claimed, especially when they are mostly required to supply heat in the coldest months. They are not recommended when the electricity source for the pump is not renewable, in which case even fossil gas is better, carbon-wise, for heating purposes. But more about this later.

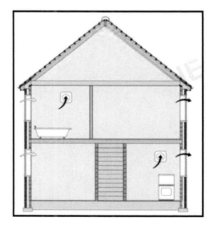

Figure 6.1 *Ventilation with conventional extractor fans in wet rooms*

Source: EST (2006)

As a building approaches Passivhaus standard and obtains much of its heat requirements from solar gain, occupants' body heat and appliances such as cookers, fridges and computers, then often much remaining heat requirement can be met by heat recovery from outgoing ventilated air. Similarly, the standard protects from overheating. This is why we will look at ventilation first before looking at various cooling and heating strategies.

Ventilation

The requirements for health are:

- extract ventilation to the outside for all kitchens, bathrooms and sanitary rooms – intermittent or continuous;
- purge ventilation in every habitable room capable of extracting a minimum of four air changes per hour per room directly to outside;
- equivalent ventilator areas depending on the size of the building.

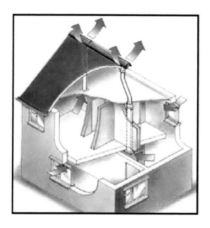

Intermittent extract fans and background ventilators

This system uses intermittent fans mounted in a window, ceiling or external wall, operating under manual or automatic control. If it is mounted in a ceiling, the extract should be ducted to the outside. Replacement dry air is provided via background ventilators (e.g. trickle ventilators) and air leakage. The background ventilators should be large enough to ventilate the whole house continuously. A gap below the internal doors allows air to pass freely around the dwelling.

These are a stop-gap solution only for non-airtight homes. At high levels of airtightness it is difficult to achieve sufficient ventilation with the fans switched off.

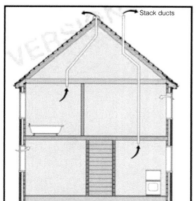

Passive stack ventilation

This process relies on warm air entering the lowest parts of the dwelling and being drawn through ducts by relative differences in pressure caused by the rising heat, to vent into the atmosphere at the apex of the roof. So ducting must be installed, leading from key rooms in the house into the loft space. It is easiest to install in a whole building renovation but can be fitted anyway in most circumstances.

Replacement air is drawn into the property through trickle ventilators in the habitable rooms, especially those (like bathrooms and kitchens) with high humidity. Interior doors must not be draught-proofed, to allow air to circulate. Passive stack ventilation saves electricity because it doesn't use a pump. However, neither does it reclaim the heat from the lost air. Heat recovery is difficult to implement using passive stack because the pressure loss is usually too high in conventional heat exchangers compared with

Figures 6.2 and 6.3 *The path of air in principle in passive stack ventilation*

Source: EST (2006)

Figures 6.4–6.6 *Output, intake, sensor and an insulated heat exchange unit in a bathroom single room ventilation with heat recovery system*

the stack pressure. To minimize heat loss, humidity-sensitive duct inlet grilles should be installed to ensure that the system only works when needed.

If you think that passive stack alone will not provide sufficient reliable draw, a boost facility using an extract fan activated by a humidity sensor or switch can be added. The unit should ideally have multiple trickle speed settings so it can be adjusted for the size of the property and the current conditions.

Duct tips

- ducts can be located in the corners of hallways and landings;
- flexible ducting increases flow resistance, so minimize the length used, pull it fairly taut and keep duct runs straight, with as few bends and kinks as possible;
- avoid angles flatter than 45°;
- there should be no leaks, e.g. where ducting connects to grilles;
- insulate them where they pass through uninsulated spaces to avoid condensation.

Single room intermittent heat recovery ventilation (SRHRV)

Here, a room – typically a bathroom or kitchen – has outlet and inlet grilles in the outside walls, preferably some distance apart so the inlet is not sucking in expelled air. Situate the grilles for the incoming and extracted air inside the room in different places for the same reason. Ducts from each lead to the heat exchanger unit, which may lie beneath a panel in the floor for easy access to clean. The final part of the system consists of humidistat sensors (e.g. above the shower and toilet), which operate the fans when the humidity reaches a certain level. The system therefore only consumes energy when necessary.

This is not appropriate for very airtight buildings because the other rooms may not benefit from sufficient ventilation.

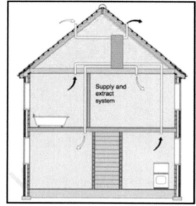

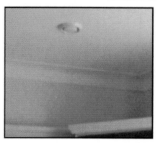

Figures 6.7 and 6.8 *Intake vent in living room – whole house system*

Source: © Chris Twinn

Whole house mechanical ventilation with heat recovery

You can have whole house mechanical ventilation with or without heat recovery. Ducts typically extract air from the wet rooms. A low-wattage pump pushes the heated, clean, incoming air down another duct(s) into a lower room.

They're more expensive with heat recovery, not only because of the cost of the heat recovery unit, but also the return ducting. It's only worth installing if a blower test on the renovated property gives a result of $<5m^3/h/m^2$, otherwise you won't get the energy saving benefits. But if you install it, it will save money, with an efficiency in heat recovery of up to 90 per cent, and reduce condensation and cold draughts. They're also normally supplied with filters to purify the incoming air and optional pollen bag filters for allergen-protection. (There is a trade-off between the effectiveness of the filter and the energy required to pump the air, which experiences more resistance as a result. Larger surface area filters offer less resistance.)

Different types of systems (e.g. crossflow, rotary wheel, counterflow) vary in efficiency and price. Units should be well soundproofed and specified to maximize the amount of heat extracted without obstructing the flow of air too much. Models cater for different building volumes.

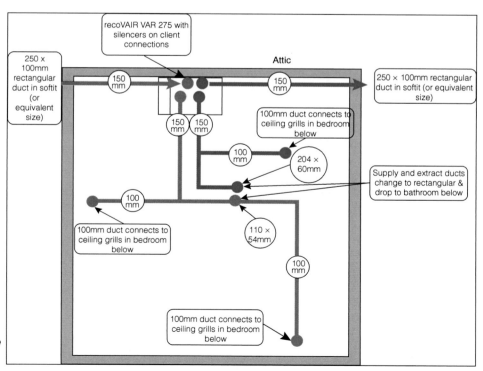

Figure 6.9 *Layout in the attic for a whole house system in a refurbishment for a three-bedroomed house*

Source: © Hyde Housing

Advanced systems can reverse the heat transfer effect in summer, providing cooling – air conditioning – very efficiently.

Figure 6.10 *Insulated heat exchange unit in an attic – whole house system*

Source: © Chris Twinn

Heat recovery units

A well-designed heat recovery system should minimize specific fan power (the power consumption divided by the air flow, in watts per litre per second (W/l/s)) and maximize heat exchange efficiency (the proportion of waste heat usefully recovered). For example, it would have a specific fan power of 1W/l/s or less when running at each of its settings and a heat recovery efficiency of 85 per cent. Automatic controls (e.g. timer, humidity sensor, occupancy/usage sensor, detection of moisture/pollutant release) can minimize energy costs.

You can find European standards for performance testing of residential ventilation products and guidance at www.est.org.uk/housingbuildings/standards.

Passive cooling

Air-conditioning and cooling energy demand is already great in many places during the summer. We have seen how a well-insulated airtight building, window shades, shutters and glass coatings can keep heat out as well as in. But even so, some buildings may overheat at times. Fortunately there are a number of strategies which do not use carbon-fuelled energy available to tackle this problem:

- night ventilation;
- heat pump;
- phase change materials;
- plaster, plasterboards integrated with phase change material;
- water features;
- indoor plants.

Night ventilation

The thermal storage capacity of the building's mass can be used to reduce its temperature peaks. Day-warmed thermal mass is cooled by night-time passive stack ventilation through the roof, when outdoor temperatures are – at least in central Europe – mostly under 21°C and room temperatures are higher. Incoming replacement air is drawn from ground floor inlets opened at night. These vented wall and/or window openings must be equipped with weather, burglar and insect-protection and automatically controlled flaps.

The larger the thermal mass of a building, the more even the room temperature. (Thermal mass equals density × specific heat capacity.) Ideally night ventilation should take place from 10pm to 10am with an air change rate of over two building volumes per hour, and the daily total cooling load of the building should not be higher than 150Wh/m². Thermal modelling software can calculate the exact level of ventilation feasible.

If daytime solar gains are reduced to a minimum, night ventilation can perform well. Wind also generates pressure differences between air inlet and outlet openings. The building must have good passive stack ventilation design. If free ventilation is not feasible then mechanical ventilation will have greater efficiency if it takes place only at night.

Phase Change Materials

Phase Change Materials (PCM) can be used to store and release energy. All substances store energy when their temperature changes, but when a phase change occurs in a substance (melting or evaporating, condensing or solidifying), the energy stored and released is greater. Furthermore, heat storage and recovery occur isothermally, which makes them ideal for space heating/cooling applications.

With an appropriately sized air conditioning system integrated with PCM it may be possible to cool a building without electricity. It would utilize the temperature difference between night and day of the air outside. In the daytime, incoming external air is cooled by the PCM-storage module, which absorbs and stores its heat by changing its phase state (e.g. solid to liquid). At night-time the substance reverts back, releasing its heat by being cooled by the now cooler external air. Running costs would be close to zero.

For example, an air-conditioning device is available that is integrated with a heat exchanger and uses a phase change material based on expanded natural graphite, for heating or cooling a space. The melting point of this particular PCM package is 20°C and its heat capacity is 30Wh/kg. Its rated air flow is around 160m³/h. For cooling loads of up to 50W per square metre of floor area, a ballpark figure for the mass of the material required is 5.5kg per square metre. Thermal modelling will help you size the system correctly.

Plasterboard integrated with PCM

This new product utilizes small plastic capsules with a core of wax – a phase change material – inserted into the plaster or plasterboard during fabrication. The melting temperature of the wax can be defined during manufacturing. If the room temperature rises above this melting point (around 21°C to 26°C), the wax melts, absorbing as it does so the surplus room heat. Conversely, when the room temperature falls, the wax sets, yielding heat to the internal atmosphere. This system works well with appropriate temperature differences between day and night and may be used in combination with night ventilation to ensure the wax solidifies at night, otherwise it will not work during the day. The wax capsules are delivered from the manufacturer as liquid dispersion or powder. During manufacturing it is added to plaster, plasterboards, spackle or chipboards.

Some energy-conscious householders use ordinary wax the same way, stored in suitable receptacles (e.g. plastic bottles) in the direct sunlight behind south-facing windows inside the building.

Water surfaces

Selective positioning of water surfaces in buildings can make a worthwhile contribution to space cooling due to the evaporating heat of water – another type of phase change. Indoor pools can be a pleasant addition to an indoor space but do require maintenance. The cooling power is dependent on the volume of evaporating water, air temperature, velocity and humidity.

Indoor plants

A similar effect is generated from the leaf-surfaces of indoor plants. Indoor plants are also known to remove pollutants such as particulates, dust and unhealthy gases from the air, expelling oxygen and moderating the indoor humidity and temperature. They also buffer sound, muting ambient noise. By close planting, a cooling power of $16W/m^2$ due to evaporating power can result, according to Preisack et al (2002), who have researched the relative benefits of different plants, some are far more beneficial than others.

Heat pumps for cooling

Most water-to-air and air-air heat pumps are reversible, so if a heat pump is to be installed (see the section on heating below) this is another possible advantage – except, of course, it would be better if the home could be cooled without using electricity.

A valve can change the direction of the refrigerant flow to cool the building. Even with water-to-water heat pumps designed for heating only, a limited amount of 'passive' summer cooling can be provided by direct use of the ground loop, for example by by-passing the heat pump and circulating fluid from the ground coil through a fan convector. This system is valuable in areas where the climate induces large seasonal temperature differences between summer and winter as well as between day and night.

Heating

It is possible for all heating needs to be met by the above means (plus the occupants' body heat, solar gain and appliances such as cookers, fridges and PCs) if the home is sufficiently airtight and insulated. However not all homes will reach this standard.

Degree days

To determine how much energy is required for heating a building, it can be useful to use heating degree days. These are derived from daily temperature observations and the heating requirements for a given structure at a specific location. In conjunction with the expected U-value for a building they provide a rough way to estimate the amount of energy required to heat the building over a given period.

A heating degree day is worked out relative to a base temperature; in the UK the convention is to use 15.5°C (the heating requirement). To find it out for a given day, take the average temperature on any given day and subtract it from the base temperature. If the result is above zero, that is the number of heating degree days on that day. If the result is below or equal to zero, it is ignored. These numbers for each day are added up over a year to find the total number of degrees of heating required for all the days.

For example, a location on one day might have a maximum temperature of 14°C and a mimimum of 5°C, giving an average of 8.5°C. Subtracted from 15.5°C gives 7°C. A month of 30 similar days might accumulate 7 × 30 = 210. A year (including summer temperatures above 15.5°C) might add up to 2000.

The rate at which heat needs to be provided to this hypothetical dwelling is the rate at which it is being lost to the outside. This rate, for one degree temperature difference, is simply the U-value of the dwelling (as calculated by averaging the sum of the U-values of all elements) multiplied by the area of the dwelling's external surface. Multiplying the rate at which a building is losing heat by the time (in hours) over which it is losing heat reveals the amount of heat lost in Wh (or BTU): this is exactly the amount of heat that needs to be provided by the heating sources. (To convert Wh to kWh, divide by 1000.) Therefore if the external area of the dwelling (walls, roof and floor) is A, its average U-value is U and the number of degree days is D then the amount of heat required in kWh to cover the period in question is:

$$A \times U \times D \times 24 \ / \ 1000$$

where the multiplier 24 is needed to get the value in kWh rather than kWdays or simply BTUs in the case of US units. (The same method is used (without dividing by 1000) for US units with the result being in BTUs rather than in kWh.)

For example: if the building surface area is 500m^2, the average U-value is 3.5 and the degree days number 2000 then the annual amount of heat required is:

$$500 \times 3.5 \times 2000 \times 24 \ / \ 1000 = 84,000\text{kWh}$$

There are other ways of working out how much heating capacity you need, for example the peak load requirement. More information for the UK, together with free data, can be found at www.vesma.com/ddd.

The same method can be used for calculating the amount of energy required to cool a building, for the days in which the outside temperature is greater than the preferred inside temperature.

This method is not foolproof, since there are other factors involved such as the heat given off by appliances and people, wind factors, exterior shading and so on. Also, heat requirements are not linear with temperature and super insulated buildings can have a lower target point.

Degree days are available worldwide for cooling and heating calculations at www.degreedays.net.

Selecting the heating source

Home heating may be supplied by any number of means, but which sources give off the lowest carbon emissions? An independent survey conducted by the UK

Table 6.1 *Selected results from survey by the UK Energy Efficiency Partnership for Homes*

Space heating system	Water heating system	CO_2 emissions per unit area (kgCO$_2$/m²/yr)
Semi-detached houses:		
Biomass community heating with biomass CHP	Same	4.15
Biomass community heating	Same	7.11
Wood boiler	Same	10.02
Wood boiler	Same + SWH	10.09
GSHP with heating underfloor (timber)	Same + SWH	20.83
Gas boiler	Same + SWH	21.98
Gas boiler with MVHR	Same	22.92
GSHP with underfloor (timber) heating	Same	23.07
Gas boiler	Same	24.28
Gas boiler with underfloor (timber) heating	Same	24.28
GSHP	Same	26.22
Oil boiler	Same + SWH	26.45
ASHP with underfloor (timber) heating	Same	27.42
Oil boiler	Same	29.61
Electric panels	Electric + SWH	42.32
Electric underfloor (concrete)	Electric	56
Flats:		
Biomass community heating with biomass CHP	Same	4.61
Biomass community heating	Same	7.6
Gas community heating with gas CHP	Same	23.42
Gas boiler	Same	25.21
GSHP with heating underfloor (timber)	Same	25.21
Electric underfloor (concrete)	Electric	54.96

Note: GSHP, ground source heat pump; ASHP, air source heat pump; SWH, solar water heating.

Source: Heating Strategy Group of the Energy Efficiency Partnership for Homes (2006)

Energy Efficiency Partnership for Homes which looked at the carbon impact of different domestic heating and hot water systems in both houses and flats concluded that the following performed best, all other things being equal:

- community heating and CHP, fuelled wholly or mainly by biomass;
- wood burning boilers;

- ground source heat pumps with low temperature heat distribution/emitters (e.g. underfloor heating);
- solar water heating panels in conjunction with boiler systems.

Figure 6.11 *This silvered tube takes hot air rising through the floor from a woodchip boiler in the kitchen directly below into the bedroom above, a simple but highly effective feature*

In the house, 59 per cent of the total heating demand was for space heating and 41 per cent for water heating. As homes become more insulated and airtight, the water heating factor will proportionately rise. In a flat or apartment the space heating demand will be lower too. Fewer options for heating are available for flats as they have neither roof area nor ground space for ground source heat pumps, photovoltaic panels, wind turbines or oil boilers.

The conclusions throw up interesting results. Results for the flat are broadly similar to those for the semi-detached house. Biomass combined heat and power (CHP) with biomass community or district heating gives probably the best result attainable, though it is not likely to be common for economic and practical reasons. Biomass CHP is more often installed with gas or oil community heating, to enable rapid response to changing demand.

Wood is assumed to be almost carbon neutral, since it is normally replaced with new trees. A wood-burning boiler gives the best result of the heating systems for individual homes, if used for space and water heating throughout the year. In this case the fuel is wood pellets, which can be semi-auto-fed on demand but are relatively expensive; wood chips or logs are cheaper. Many solid fuel appliances are designed for wood or coal, but if coal is burned there will be considerable CO_2 emissions.

Interestingly, a wood-burning boiler with solar water heating gives a worse result than a wood-burning boiler alone because of the pump's electrical power requirements and the need to use the boiler year round. The solar water heating system comprised a $4m^2$ flat collector plate with typical efficiency characteristics (n0 = 0.8, a1 = 4.0), facing south-east at 30 degree pitch and a 100-litre tank.

Heat pumps come out around as effective as gas boilers because of their electricity use.

Boiler sizing

Figure 6.12 *Oversized wood pellet boiler for a new virtually Passivhaus standard dwelling*

Replacement boilers are rarely sized correctly. Oversized boilers cost more and generally operate less efficiently, resulting in higher running costs and increased carbon emissions. You can use a free worksheet to help you size gas, oil and LPG boilers. It involves adding up the heat losses through all external walls, window areas, roofs, floors and ceilings, based on their U-values and location. The losses are calculated in watts per square metre times the total surface areas. Ventilation losses are then added, plus 2kW if the boiler is to be used for water heating. If a combination boiler is also using solar water heated water, a minimum output figure should be subtracted from the outcome. The worksheet is downloadable from www.est.org.uk in publication CE54 (EST, 2003).

One of its assumptions is a design internal temperature of 21°C. This may be considered too high – some people feel comfortable at 18°C, which can save between 5 and 10 per cent on heating costs depending on the climate and building's leakiness.

If fitting a gas boiler, choose the most efficient, A-rated condensing model. A condensing boiler captures much more usable heat from its fuel than a non-condensing variant by utilising a larger, or sometimes dual, heat exchanger. There are two types: regular and combination. Regular models heat water through a hot water cylinder. Combination models give on-demand hot water without the need for a cylinder. For the UK, the SEDBUK (Seasonal Efficiency of Domestic Boilers in the UK) efficiency of most current and obsolete boilers can be found at www.boilers.org.uk.

If a tank or cylinder is used, it should have as much insulation around it and all the pipework as possible.

Solar water heating

Solar water heating should be installed wherever possible and appropriate. Energy paybacks are short. The carbon load of hot water is both the largest part by far of the entire carbon load of water used in homes, and the largest part of the total heat demand of the building as it approaches Passivhaus standards. The solar heat is transported in pipes from the panels and most commonly used to pre-heat water used in a cylinder or tank. Therefore solar water heating can't be used with a combi-boiler. This topic is examined in more detail in the next chapter on water use.

Controls

Controls for the boiler and hot water cylinder should be upgraded, with a boiler interlock: an arrangement of controls (room thermostats, programmable room thermostats, cylinder thermostats, programmers and time switches) that ensure the boiler doesn't fire when there is no demand for heat.

Programmable room thermostats allow rooms to be independently managed. There should be additional timing capability for hot water. Fit TRVs (thermostatic radiator valves) on all radiators in rooms with no room thermostat. TRVs have an air temperature sensor used to control the heat output from the radiator by adjusting water flow.

An automatic bypass valve controls water flow in accordance with the water pressure across it and is used to maintain a minimum flow rate through the boiler and to limit circulation pressure when alternative water paths are closed. More advanced controls, such as weather compensation, may be considered. Large properties must be divided into zones not exceeding 150m² floor area so that the operation of the heating in each zone can be timed and temperature controlled independently.

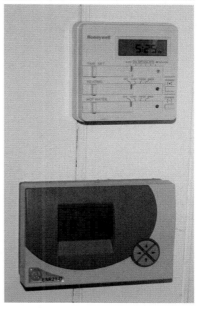

Figures 6.13 and 6.14 *Regular room thermostat and boiler controls for an integrated biomass/electric/solar water heating system*

Figure 6.15 *Individual radiator thermostat*

Figure 6.16 *Buffer tank in a woodchip boiler system*

Buffer tanks

Buffer tanks are large, highly insulated, hot water cylinders used to store hot water when it's not immediately required. They are used with a solar water heating system, heat pump, wood pellet or other boiler to allow the boiler to run for long periods without stopping and starting. They also help a heating system to respond quickly to changing heat loads and provide more heat, for short periods, than the boiler could alone. The tank sits between the boiler and the heating and hot water system acting as a buffer between the two to allow the use of a variety of sophisticated controllers.

Buffer tanks come in sizes ranging from 500 to 3000 litre capacity and can include a number of temperature sensors. Some include coils for solar panels and for the direct supply of domestic hot water. Use if there's space.

Radiant heating

Large areas of heating surface, such as floors or skirting board radiators, give off radiant rather than convected warmth. They give the same overall comfort to conventional radiators but at a lower temperature, making them more efficient. But if the heat source is a gas boiler which also produces the hot water at a higher temperature than the 35–40°C needed for radiant heaters, then there's no advantage to using this form of heating. Nor should the heating be electric, because of its high carbon emissions.

Underfloor heating

If you're installing a new floor, consider underfloor heating. It can be beneath tiles or timber, but timber gives a faster response. Traditional installations consist of flexible piping fastened on to the insulation in a spiral or snaking pattern, with usually about 30cm gaps between the lines. Rooms or sections are divided into zones with separate controls for each – thermostats and valves.

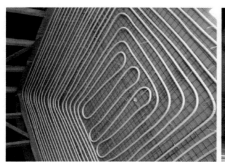

Figures 6.17–6.19 *Two layouts for underfloor heating pipes, the left one to be fed by a ground source heat pump; right, pouring concrete on the pipes*

Note the airtightness of the centre room.

Source: © John Cantor (left) and Russell Smith

Modern underfloor heating systems have faster response times than they used to. Ensure floorboards are bone dry before installation to avoid warping.

Skirting board radiators

These can be a cheap and easy installation option for retrofits and as easy to maintain as traditional radiator-led central heating. Besides giving the same comfort at lower temperatures, their other advantage is that they do not take up wall space. They come in heights equivalent to most skirting boards and circumnavigate the room. They use a pipe circuit similar to conventional radiator systems.

Heat pumps

Heat pumps can take heat from the ground, air or a nearby body of water if it's available. All of them basically work like a fridge, except backwards or inside out (if a fridge was inside out, heat, instead of being extracted from inside the fridge and pumped out the back of it, would be pumped from the outside of the fridge into it).

Typically, in an air-source heat pump, air flows over two refrigerant-filled heat exchangers, similar to those in a fridge, one outdoor and one indoor. In the heating mode, liquid refrigerant within the outside coil extracts heat from the outside air, making the refrigerant evaporate into a gas. It is then pumped to the indoor coil, which reverses the process. The refrigerant condenses back into a liquid and returns to begin the cycle again. As the volume of air outside is much greater, the amount of heat in it, when transferred to a smaller volume, results in a higher temperature. Be sure to choose a system with a refrigerant that has zero ozone-depleting potential and low or zero global warming potential, such as isobutene (R600a) or propane (as long as precautions are taken against its flammability).

Ground source heat pumps work the same way, but the element containing the coolant is buried in the ground and so takes the heat from there.

How efficient are heat pumps?

Heat pumps are judged by their coefficient of performance (CoP). This is the ratio of the amount of heat produced divided by the electricity consumption of the pump. So for example a heat pump with a CoP of 3 (or 3:1) will produce three times as much heat energy as the electrical energy it consumes. The higher the CoP the better the performance.

You can maximize the CoP by choosing a heating distribution system requiring a lower final water temperature – radiant heating like underfloor or skirting board heating rather than domestic hot water and radiators – and by choosing a heat source with a high average temperature (e.g. the ground rather than air). The final efficiency will be significantly better for underfloor heating covered by solid screed (tiled and so on) finishes than timber and/or carpets.

Ground source heat pumps

These require a network of underground coils or loops to extract heat from the ground. A hole must be dug and the collecting coil buried – usually a closed

Benefits of heat pumps

Other benefits of heat pumps over conventional boilers include:

- no combustion or explosive gases in the building;
- no need for flues or ventilation;
- no local pollution (although noise from the outside fan may be a problem if air-source);
- long life expectancy;
- low maintenance costs;
- the payback period can be as short as 4–5 years and save up to 75 per cent of conventional heating costs.

Figures 6.20–6.22 *Two trenches for different ground source collectors for a heat pump, both connected to a similar exchanger like the one, right, connected to a buffer tank*

Source: © John Cantor

circuit loop of 20–40mm high-density polyethylene piping filled with a mixture of water and glycol anti-freeze. Holes take two forms: the commonest is a series of horizontal trenches (wet ground is better than dry), or one or more vertical boreholes. The system also includes a heat exchanger, pump and delivery pipes passing under an exterior wall (typically a French window or other door) to the destination.

The coil needs to have good contact with the ground. As the depth increases the maximum and minimum soil temperatures begin to lag behind the surface temperature. At a depth of about 1.5m the lag is about one month. Below 10m the ground temperature remains effectively constant at around the annual average air temperature. Sizing is complex and specialized software is required, available, amongst other places, via the website of The International Ground Source Heat Pump Association (IGSHPA, www.igshpa.okstate.edu).

Ground-source heat pumps are more expensive but the payback is reduced, financially and carbon-wise, if a hole is being dug anyway, for example for an extension's foundations. However they have a long life expectancy (typically 20–25 years for the heat pump equipment itself and up to 50 years for the ground coil) and are a great idea if the opportunity's there.

A ground source heat pump where the ground is well above freezing (10°C) outputting to radiant heating (underfloor or skirting) would be ideal, especially if it is replacing electric heating. It will yield significant carbon savings. But if it is replacing a modern gas-condensing boiler, which can have over 95 per cent efficiency, the carbon savings are much less.

Air-source heat pumps

These are less efficient than ground-source heat pumps but have a lower installation cost.

Air-source heat pumps extract heat from the outside air, even in the coldest months. However, the colder it is, the less efficient they become and the more warmth you need. In mild weather, the CoP may be around 4, but at temperatures below around 8°C (17°F) an air-source heat pump can achieve a COP of 2.5 – below the magic 3 level at which carbon savings are realized. The average COP over seasonal variation is typically 2.5–2.8, but obviously this depends how cold it gets in the winter. As soon as it drops below freezing, the CoP plummets. Of course, it will never reach 1, but it will be much less carbon-efficient than gas or biomass.

Further questions have been raised about the power used by the pump to de-ice itself. Professor David Strong, chief executive of Inbuilt, has observed that 'ice build-up on the evaporator of an air-source heat pump is a serious problem, with icing typically occurring whenever outdoor air temperatures fall below about 5°C (this can be as high as 7°C with some systems). In these situations CoPs fall to less than one (i.e. worse than direct acting electric heating).' Results of tests from Germany's Fraunhofer Institute show that this performance drop is merely a blip, and that below 2–3°C this ice becomes lighter and the COP returns to decreasing linearly. The automatic defrosting typically happens every 1–2 hours and takes about 10 minutes, during which time heating stops unless there's built-in heat storage in the system. Moreover, most systems don't use coolant reversing for defrosting, which causes this blip. Instead they utilize heated gas bypassing the condensing unit or direct use of superheated refrigerant within the evaporator.

Preliminary results from the research being conducted by the Fraunhofer Institute are shown. Notice that the outdoor temperature is rarely very cold. The average annual CoP was 2.99. For ground source it was 3.72, which is significantly better.

Are they noisy? The exterior pump – around 1.2m × 0.7m × 1m tall – generates around 50dB at full fan speed at one metre distance. This is similar to that of an air conditioning unit. The heat exchanger unit, inside – fridge-sized, around 1.8m tall – is about 42dB at one metre distance, similar to a large refrigerator. The units are usually placed at a distance from the dwelling.

Figures 6.23–6.25
Chris Twinn's system includes introducing preheated air from the conservatory and a heat exchanger in the ground. The centre picture shows an air intake in a garden for a similar system

Source: © Chris Twinn and author

Carbon displacement of heat pumps	
CoP	**Net kgCO$_2$ reduced/kWh of heat supplied**
3.2	0.031
3.5	0.060
4	0.081

Based on a factor of 0.591kgCO$_2$/kWh in the UK SAP 2009, taken from Tom Naughton, xCO$_2$.

Whole house passive stack ventilation with incoming air pre-warmed using a heat exchanger

Heat pumps can transfer their heat to air or water. If to air, it is sucked in from outside, warmed in the heat exchanger and directed through vents in the ground floor. This only works efficiently in a superinsulated airtight structure around Passivhaus standard. The air is drawn through and up the building by pressure differences as for passive stack above.

An advantage of air destination heat pumps is that air into which the heat is passed usually needs a lower temperature than water heating for the same level of comfort, resulting in a higher CoP and increased heat output. Therefore ground source to air would be even more efficient than to radiant heating in a Passivhaus level refurbishment.

Borderline efficiency

Once the CoP drops to 3 or less, if the electricity supplying it is not from a renewable source and if it is replacing electrical heating, then there is no carbon saving from using the heat pump, since generation and distribution inefficiencies account for two-thirds of the energy in the original carbon fuel. It can be seen from the table below how most of the time air source heat pumps will not achieve a CoP which saves carbon emissions – it will happen only if the air is at or above zero degrees and the target temperature is 35°C.

A ground source heat pump will perform better. This is because during the heating season (winter) the outside air temperature is often much lower than the ground temperature (at a depth at which heat is extracted by a ground-source heat pump). Hot water and heating *can* be provided 365 days a year; the hot water can be at 55°C; *but* the CoP will be low, though not as low as 1 – that of a gas or immersion water heater. In other words, it will be more cost-efficient but not as carbon efficient.

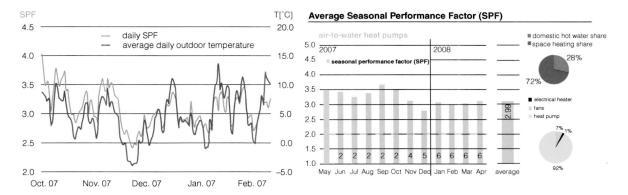

Figures 6.26 and 6.27 *Results of study of performance of air-to-water heat pumps*

Note: SPF = CoP.

Source: © Fraunhofer Institute, Germany

Heat pump manufacturers' own estimates of their CoPs should be treated with caution because real operating conditions will not necessarily reflect the test conditions. The standard used to test and quote for most packaged heat pumps is BS EN 14511. This specifies test conditions of 7°C outdoor (source) air temperature for air-source heat pumps and a return and flow temperature of 40°C and 45°C respectively.

If the heated water is for radiators, they should be larger than the usual kind, with no TRVs and large bore pipes. A buffer tank is recommended, so that, say, a wood stove or gas boiler can provide back-up. A coil much larger than normal in a DHW tank would be used in the tank to give the heat a chance to transfer.

Wood fuel heating

Wood is virtually a carbon-neutral fuel, requiring fossil fuels only in its transportation, processing and planting. A local, sustainably managed source is therefore required. The carbon emitted when it is burnt is replaced by the carbon

Table 6.2 *Heat pump CoP variation with different output temperatures and uses*

Pump type and source	Typical use case	CoP variation with output temperature				
		35°C	45°C	55°C	65°C	75°C
		(e.g. heated screed floor) (e.g. heated timber floor)				(radiator or DHW)
High Efficiency air source heat pump (ASHP)	Air at –20°C	2.2	2.0	—	—	—
Two Stage ASHP air at –20°C	Low source temp.	2.4	2.2	1.9	—	—
High Efficiency ASHP air at 0°C	Low output temp.	3.8	2.8	2.2	2.0	—
Ground source heat pump (GSHP)	Water at 0°C	5.0	3.7	2.9	2.4	—
GSHP ground at 10°C	Low output temp.	7.2	5.0	3.7	2.9	2.4

Source: Figures from Natural Resources Canada (2002), Figure 29 and Tian and Liang (2006), Figure 5

Table 6.3 *Common temperatures for different heating distribution systems (more energy is required to reach higher temperatures)*

Distribution system	Delivery temperature °C
Underfloor heating	30–45
Low temperature radiators	45–55
Conventional radiators	60–90
Air	30–50

absorbed as it grows. Of all heating fuels, coal emits the most carbon dioxide per kWh of heat (0.963kg), followed by oil (0.881kg), then natural gas (0.569kg) (US Department of Energy and Environmental Protection Agency, 1999).

A biomass heating system can be incorporated into any central heating or hot water system, but is especially suited to older, less airtight homes and not generally recommended for radiant heat emitters like underfloor heating in domestic properties – wood pellet systems can be an exception. A buffer tank makes an ideal companion (see above).

Wood fuel (biomass) comes as raw logs, woodchips, briquettes or pellets. Logs may be burnt in stoves and all four may be burnt in boilers. Avoid traditional open fires as 80 per cent of the heat disappears up the chimney. Stoves, like boilers, may have back burners to heat water for space heating and hot water.

Fresh (unseasoned) wood has almost no calorific value; typical two year seasoned logs have a value of 2.5kWh/kg; oven dry wood has a value of just over 5kWh/kg; pellets and briquettes 4.7kWh/kg; and chips 3.6kWh/kg (source: Glasu). Space must be available for storing the fuel; for example, three months' supply of wood pellets for a large house can occupy two cubic metres.

To produce 20MWh of heat the following approximate weights and volumes would be required:

	Tonnes	Volume (m²)
Logs–hardwood @ 30% mc	6	12.5 (stacked)
Logs–softwood @ 30% mc	6	15 (stacked)
Chips @ 30% mc	6	20 (trailer)
Pellets or briquettes	4	7 (bagged)

A small house heated by wood alone would use about 7 tonnes a year; assuming land produces 70 tonnes per acre, then to be self-sufficient in wood fuel would require about 1.5 acres per year. The carbon benefit also depends on the distance the fuel has travelled (sometimes hard to check with pellets).

Airtight homes will require an adequate external air supply. Exempted appliances are required for residences in smoke control zones.

Logs must be supplied seasoned (cut over a year previously) and with as low a moisture content as possible – typically 20–30 per cent to produce the best heat and least smoke. Hardwood is denser and burns for longer.

Wood pellets and briquettes are produced from sawdust and waste wood and have a more reliable moisture content (8–10 per cent). They contain more energy per kilogram and take up a third less space than logs and chips, particularly if the briquettes have a square cross section. Finding a local supplier is becoming easier.

Wood chips are derived from forest or garden waste and more commonly used in larger contexts than individual homes, such as district heating systems or care homes.

It's important to note the potential health-reducing impact of biomass-burning boilers. They can emit pollutants such as nitrogen dioxide (NO_2), particulates (PM) and sulphur dioxide (SO_2), depending on the boiler, fuel quality and the installation of any smoke cleaning equipment. Even a well-maintained biomass boiler will pollute more than a similar gas system, although less than an equivalent coal or oil fired boiler.

Figures 6.28 and 6.29 *Woodchips and woodchip boiler for a multi-occupancy dwelling*

Stoves

Modern stoves have efficiencies of up to 90 per cent, meaning that only 10 per cent of the heat in the fuel is lost. They contain sophisticated systems to achieve the optimum burn and recycle combustion gases. Stoves either burn logs or pellets and larger versions have back boilers to supply central heating and hot water, in which case a maximum efficiency of 80 per cent is to be expected.

Stoves can easily be oversized. This is despite the fact that modern stoves come with temperature controls such as fans, because the burn must occur within a limited range (around 650°C/1200°F) to be efficient and avoid wasted fuel and toxic products such as carbon monoxide from incomplete combustion.

Ceramic and masonry stoves

A well-insulated, airtight small-to-medium sized home can be heated by a single, usually ceramic, stove in one ground floor central room extremely efficiently, if ventilation is supplied for replacement incoming air and to draw the heated air through the other rooms. These stoves are the most efficient because the ceramic or masonry (brick) material has a high thermal mass and absorbs the heat of a properly combusted 'burn' to release it slowly, for up to 24 hours, after the fuel has disappeared.

Superinsulated, airtight homes can be heated through this method by the equivalent of a mere three or four logs a day, in cold weather. The burn must be efficient so that flue gas temperatures remain sufficiently high to prevent tar and acid building up.

Ceramic stoves are available in Europe. They are more expensive but pay for themselves in the fuel saved. Masonry stoves are commonly hand-built and individually designed in North America, where they are also used for cooking – ovens and hobs are incorporated in the designs, obviating the need for a separate cooking appliance.

Figure 6.30 *12kW wood pellet boiler*

Ranges

Ranges are another form of stove but are primarily designed for cooking. Most are gas or oil-fired – not appropriate for a low-carbon home, especially as they are often kept running continuously. Wood-burning ranges are available. Some have back boilers for space and water heating, drastically increasing the fuel demand. Although it may seem attractive to use the same appliance for cooking, space and water heating, it will not make efficient use of the fuel in all but the smallest of non-airtight homes.

Log boilers

These produce space and water heating. They require loading by hand, on average once a day. They need to be in a dedicated boiler/utility room and are available in versions of 5–50kW. They can be an ideal solution for the dedicated householder. Care should be taken to make sure pellets do not disintegrate easily when blown in; the dust produced has been known to jam the auger.

Pellet boilers

These space and water heaters have a hopper or (large models) a silo for automatic feeding, which mean they can only need feeding once a week. They also sit in a dedicated boiler/utility room and come in versions of 5–50kW. They use electricity and can have up to three motors, including an augur motor, convection fan and combustion blower, plus a microprocessor, maybe electronic ignition, and a back-up power supply. So check their electricity consumption before buying.

Combination boilers

These can burn a variety of biomass: logs, chips, even sawdust. Only appropriate for a dwelling with its own fuel supply.

Solar water heating with biomass and gas

Wherever possible, install solar water heating for the hot water supply. But as the sun alone will not provide sufficient heat for water all year round, systems invariably incorporate tanks which hold coils – heat exchangers – from both the panels' circuit and either a gas boiler or a biomass stove/boiler. Sometimes there is an electric immersion backup; these typically consume 3kW and because non-renewable electricity emits three times more carbon dioxide than gas, are not recommended for a low carbon home unless the electricity is renewably sourced.

A typical system will have the bottom coil connected to the solar system and the top coil to either the gas back-up boiler, or the biomass boiler. If there is enough solar energy, in the summer the back-up boiler will not be required. If there isn't, the back-up is used to top up the heat demand.

A buffer tank is recommended if there is space and the dwelling needs this amount of hot water. This will store the sun-heated water until needed and/or to contribute to space heating. (In cooler climates like the UK, solar water heating alone can't do this as there is not enough solar heat generated in winter.)

Micro-CHP

Micro-CHP – combined heat and power – is a nascent technology of small units for individual homes, typically the size of a fridge. They run on natural gas to produce up to about 10kW of power. The current crop of models are based on the Stirling engine, Organic Rankine Cycle (ORC) or internal combustion engine. The first two have high thermal efficiency and output but low electrical efficiency (10 per cent) – and this is a sticking point. Electricity output is around 1.1kW, enough to maintain back-up power in the event of a power cut or boil a kettle. A 1kW$_e$ (1kW electrical power) model from Honda called Ecowill has sold well in Japan.

A 2007 trial by the UK's Carbon Trust concluded that micro-CHP can cut electricity bills and overall CO_2 emissions by 15–20 per cent when they're the lead boiler in larger contexts like care homes, district schemes, apartment blocks and leisure centres. The best individual home for them therefore is a medium-to-large, moderately well-insulated one, maybe with solid walls, solid floors and no loft space, that is hard to insulate well and has a relatively large heat demand. Here, micro-CHP units can potentially deliver carbon savings of 5–10 per cent – fewer than a condensing boiler, since capacity is likely to be best matched to demand, for both heat and power. Payback can be around five years. But they offer limited benefits for smaller and newer dwellings.

The key to success is matching the thermal output to the building's pattern of use so that they operate not intermittently but for many hours at a time, making the value of electricity generated pay for the marginal investment in as little as three years in a typical family home. It therefore works best with a buffer storage tank to save the surplus heat for later.

Grid connection for electricity export is going to be crucial to micro-CHP's widespread acceptance. On average, half of all electricity generated by a typical 1kW$_e$ micro-CHP device is exported to the grid as it's not needed at the time. Reliability is also a key issue – service agreements will be essential. So homeowners shouldn't yet trade in their condensing boilers, which have about the same overall heating efficiency – 90 per cent – without also producing electricity, but they might keep an eye on developments.

Superinsulated homes will have to wait until the next generation of machines, based on fuel cells. These generally come in two types – proton exchange membrane fuel cells (PEMFCs) and solid oxide fuel cells (SOFCs). They have a heat to power ratio that is approximately equal so for example they could produce 5kW of heat and 5kW of electricity.

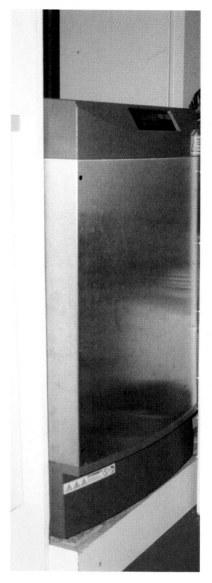

Figure 6.31 *Domestic combined heat and power unit installed in a kitchen – the same size as a small fridge*

District heating

District heating systems are ideal if a whole street, area or block of flats is to be renovated. Economies of scale make this form of heat and power delivery the cheapest on a per-household basis, and by far the most carbon-efficient, if low carbon fuel sources are specified.

A district heating scheme in Southampton, England, serves many residential developments from gas-fired CHP and geothermal energy, saving 11,000 tonnes of carbon a year and benefiting residents with a service price 5 per cent less than the market rate. Systems are most efficient when servicing both homes and businesses or premises used during the day, as the two heat loads throughout a 24 hour period suit the continuous running required of a large plant. District CHP plants may utilize fuel sources from waste to biomass, as well as geothermal where it is available. They work best where buildings are close together. A not-for-profit energy service company is usually formed to manage the system.

References

EST (Energy Saving Trust) (2003) 'Energy efficiency best practice in housing: whole house boiler sizing method for houses and flats', produced by BRE on behalf of the EST, London

EST (2006) 'GPG268 –Energy efficient ventilation in dwellings', EST, London

EST (2008) 'Domestic heating systems ranked by carbon emissions (version 2)', Prepared for the Energy Saving Trust by Bruce Young and John Henderson (BRE) pub. Energy Efficiency Partnership for Homes, London

Heating Strategy Group of the Energy Efficiency Partnership for Homes (2006) 'Domestic heating systems ranked by carbon emissions (version 2)', prepared for the Energy Saving Trust by Bruce Young and John Henderson (BRE), pub. Energy Efficiency Partnership for Homes, 2008

Natural Resources Canada (2002) 'Commercial earth energy systems: A buyer's guide', CANMET Energy Technology Centre – Varennes and by CANETA Research and by TECHNOSIM Consulting Group, for the Renewable and Electrical Energy Division, Energy Resources Branch, Natural Resources Canada, © Her Majesty the Queen in Right of Canada

Preisack, E. B., Holzer, P. and Rodleitner, H. (2002) 'Raum-klimatisierung mit Hilfe von Pflanzen', Programmlinie Haus der Zukunft des bm:vit, Neubau Biohof Achleitner, GebŠude aus Stroh & Lehm, p42

Tian, C. and Liang, Nan (2006) 'State of the art of air-source heat pump for cold regions', *Renewable Energy Resources and a Greener Future*, vol VIII

US Department of Energy & Environmental Protection Agency (2000) 'Carbon dioxide emissions from the generation of electric power in the United States', www.eia.doe.gov/cneaf/electricity/page/co2_report/co2report.html, accessed February 2010

7

Water Management

The environmental impact of water management in dwellings breaks down into three areas:

- the carbon impact of water use;
- water conservation;
- the risk of flooding.

The latter two issues are more location dependent – some areas get too much rain and others too little, and some will be more prone to flooding than others. But in examining water supply from the angle of carbon budgeting, some rather surprising facts precipitate.

Domestic water use in a non-conserving household is around 150 litres per person per day and, as we shall see, this water contains 2.2kg of carbon dioxide equivalent global warming gases in its embodied energy – through sourcing, transportation, heating – a not insignificant amount (UK average). Greywater recycling and roof collection of rainwater for use in the home or garden are frequently recommended for eco-homes. However, new research is emerging to demonstrate that including these technologies on individual dwellings can be questionable from a carbon-saving point of view. This is particularly true of greywater recycling, which involves storing and filtering water from washing machines and sinks and using it either to flush the toilet or water the garden.

As with electricity and energy use, the single most important aspect

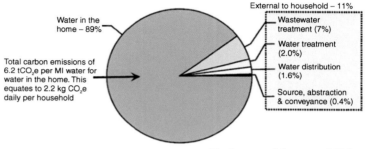

Environment Agency, 2008

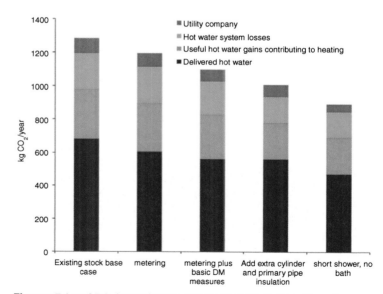

Figures 7.1 and 7.2 *Assessing the carbon impacts of domestic water use*

Note: The two charts attempt to tease out what aspects of the carbon impact of domestic water use happen within the home and which are external to it. The bar chart also looks at what measures in the home have what level of impact.
DM = demand management.

Source: Clarke et al, 2009 and EST/Environment Agency

Figure 7.3 *Water use in a typical existing household expressed in both litres of water used and kilograms of carbon dioxide equivalent global warming gases emitted*

Note: Notice for example how toilet flushing uses a relatively high proportion of water, but a lower proportion of carbon dioxide because of the water is not heated.

Source: Clarke et al, 2009 and EST/Environment Agency

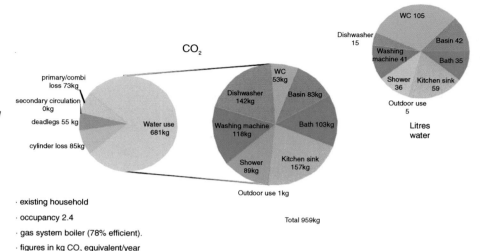

CO₂

primary/combi loss 73kg
secondary circulation 0kg
deadlegs 55 kg
cylinder loss 85kg
Water use 681kg

Dishwasher 142kg
WC 53kg
Basin 83kg
Washing machine 118kg
Bath 103kg
Shower 89kg
Kitchen sink 157kg

Outdoor use 1kg

WC 105
Dishwasher 15
Washing machine 41
Basin 42
Bath 35
Shower 36
Kitchen sink 59
Outdoor use 5

Litres water

· existing household
· occupancy 2.4
· gas system boiler (78% efficient).
· figures in kg CO₂ equivalent/year

Total 959kg

of water use is to minimize it. If the demand is minimized, the energy and financial cost of supplying it is reduced; and we get more from less.

Let's first look at ways to minimize water demand in the home, then reducing flooding risk, and finally greywater recycling and rainwater collection.

Minimizing water use

Any self-respecting low carbon dwelling should have a water meter installed. This very often has the effect of reducing water use – by up to 17 per cent in one survey – when people can see the effect on their bills. Technology can be used to reduce water use, but the greatest impact is caused by people's water-using habits. We'll examine what characterizes water-conscious behaviour as we go.

Check for leaks

Checking for leaks should be done regularly. One way to do this is to take a meter reading last thing at night and again first thing in the morning, in other words when it is not expected that any water should be used. If the reading has changed you may have a leak! Reading the water meter regularly and working out how much average water is used for each individual can yield a benchmark from which to improve.

The AECB has a Water Standard applicable to new homes, the refurbishment of existing dwellings and to non-domestic buildings, to complement its CarbonLite system (see Chapter 5). The Water Standard, aimed at architects, designers, house builders and specifiers, is aimed at reducing hot water use and water use during drought. It is free from www.carbonlite.org.uk/carbonlite/waterstandards.php

---

Source the right contractors

Many plumbers and fitters lack the relevant skills (2008 survey by Waterwise UK) because many of the new water efficiency devices are fairly new and unfamiliar. As the quality of installation is a significant factor in their success, it is important to employ contractors with the relevant training.

Flush success

Toilet flushing is the largest single water use in the home. Flushing with expensively processed drinking water wastes not only water but the carbon emissions involved in its supply. Traditional toilets can flush away as much as 9–11 litres each time. Reducing this amount can be a simple matter of installing a one litre plastic bag full of water in the cistern. Replacing the cistern is the next step.

There are two types of flushing mechanisms which have options for light and heavy flushing:

- the siphon flush is the more traditional type. It does not leak, is fail-safe, robust and familiar. It uses a lever, but its dual flush operation may be less obvious to the user;
- the drop valve is usually button operated and allows low flush volumes (as low as two litres for the low flush and four for the higher) by giving a higher flow rate. A major disadvantage is that the valve will eventually leak – and this is hard to detect. Poor installation or DIY intervention can also cause this. The seals can also leak or break, especially in hard water areas.

The siphon flush has been called 'the greatest water saving device of all time' because it can't fail. Water only goes up and over the inverted U of the siphon when it is lifted. On the other hand, in America and elsewhere, the siphon flush is unknown – there is only the valve – and the American Water Works Association has reported that 'at any one time in the USA one in five of the toilets leak at a rate of over 20,000 US gallons per year' (AWWA, 1993). Unfortunately, siphon flushes are being replaced at a fast rate wherever they exist because it is believed that the dual flush drop valve, ironically, is more water-saving.

The interruptible-flush siphon

The solution is a reduced flush siphon – and there is an interruptible-flush one. (For existing toilets there are conversion kits.) The user presses its lever and when they release it, it stops flushing. So as soon as they see that the waste in the bowl has gone they release the handle and no more water is used. Every other type of device keeps sending water even when the toilet has already been flushed. Flushes can therefore be as low as 1.25 litres.

A further check should be made on the inlet valve to make sure that it does not leak – a common fault responsible for much water loss.

Composting toilets

Composting toilets do not use water, but require users to add a material called 'soak', usually sawdust, after using the toilet. The mixture is composted on site

Figure 7.4 *Spray taps fitted in a bathroom basin*

to provide a sanitary, odourless soil quality enhancer that can be used in the garden. They are not appropriate for most dwellings, but are sometimes chosen for a second, outside toilet, or for locations where water supply or conventional sewage treatment is a problem.

Waterless urinals

Not commonly used in the home, but worth mentioning as they use no water. If there's space, they may be installed for the gentlemen in the dwelling. Urine can even be separately collected for use as a garden fertilizer (dilute first 7:1).

Taps

Taps account for about 20 per cent of domestic water.

Spray taps can save about 80 per cent of this. Some users complain that washing-up bowls or sinks don't fill up quickly enough, in which case a 'Tapmagic' insert can be fitted to most taps with a round outlet hole or standard metric thread. At low flows, Tapmagic delivers a spray suitable for washing hands and rinsing toothbrushes. As the flow is increased it opens to allow full flow.

Water-saving cartridges for single lever mixer taps can also be installed. These operate on a similar principle. An aerator or laminar flow device can prevent splashing.

In-line water filters can be installed for the sink if you don't like the taste of the mains water and used to fill bottles for travelling. Bottled water can be 2000 times more carbon intensive than tap water.

Smooth flowing rules

Basin and bidet taps should be limited to 4–6l/minute and sink taps should be limited to 6–8l/minute. All mixers should have a clear indication of hot and cold with hot tap or lever position to the left.

Flow and pressure regulation

A household with mains-pressure hot water will tend to use more water than one with a gravity system due to the higher flow rates from hot taps and showers. However, with good design you can achieve efficiency savings and better showering with mains pressure hot water by fitting:

- small bore pipes (10mm is the smallest available);
- regulated aerators;
- low water-use showers;
- pressure and flow regulators.

If the mains or header tank pressure is greater than 3.5 bar install pressure regulators to maintain a constant pressure, limit pressures in mains-fed hot

Table 7.1 *Dead leg volumes*

Pipe diameter	10mm plastic	15mm plastic	15mm copper	22mm plastic	22mm copper
Litres per 10m pipe run	0.6	1.1	1.5	2.4	3.1
Max length for 1.5 litre dead leg (m)	25.0	13.0	10.0	6.0	5.0
Max length for 0.85 litre dead leg (m) and for 30 second wait with 1.7 litres per minute spray fitting (m)	14.0	8.0	6.0	3.5	3.0

Source: AECB Water Standards, 'Technical Background Report Version 1.0.0', AECB, 2009

water systems and prevent damage to fittings. They are normally adjustable and maintain a constant flow independent of supply pressure and can be fitted in-pipe or at each tap or shower. An alternative is a showerhead or tap outlet with a built in regulator.

Dead legs

This term refers to the length of pipe between the hot water source and the tap. Taps should be as close to the source as possible to minimize both heat losses along the way and water losses while people run the taps waiting for the hot water to turn up. Use smaller bore pipes to minimize the volume in the pipe – try to aim for no more than 0.85 litres. Table 7.1 will help to work out the maximum such length for the type of pipe used.

All hot water pipes should be properly insulated and sited above cold-water pipes to reduce heat transfer. A radial layout for pipes to outlets from the tank will also help keep heat losses down.

Tips for taps

Finally, some recommendations for occupants:

- A running tap can waste over 6 litres per minute. Turn them off when they're not being used, for example during toothbrushing.
- When using hot water, don't let it disappear straight down the plughole, but fill a bowl or the sink with a tight-fitting plug in.
- Replace washers in dripping taps immediately. They can waste at least 5500 litres of water a year.

Figure 7.5 *Low flow shower head*

Showers and baths

Showers and baths can account for up to 45 per cent of the water used at home. Showers can save water compared to baths, but people tend to take more of them. Showers should ideally take no longer than five minutes. Home renovations often include en suite bathrooms and power showers which don't help save water. Power showers and mains pressure systems are out of bounds.

Energy source

The energy source for the hot water used should be integrated with the rest of the dwelling's hot water system. Is the water for the shower coming from water that is already heated in an insulated tank, or is it heated on demand? If the latter, is it heated by a gas combi boiler or by electricity?

For example, if the dwelling uses solar water heating, a heat pump with a buffer tank, and/or a biomass stove, then the water feeding the shower should come from the tank, using either a gravity feed or a small pump because both these sources of heat are renewable. Gas is a second-best solution, with electricity (unless from a renewable source), the least preferred option.

The problem is that most modern fitted showers now use electric on-demand heaters. Ideally these should be avoided in preference to gas-fired heaters or tank-fed showers fitted over the bath. A report for the Energy Saving Trust (2009) on the carbon impact of water use notes that 'Adding an electric shower over a bath in existing households without showers can potentially save water but increase running costs and CO_2 emissions. A mixer shower (with pump if the existing head from a gravity system isn't sufficient) with flow regulation provides a more carbon effective solution.' (Clarke et al, 2009)

Shower heads

For older houses with electric showers or simple gravity-fed mixer showers, there isn't a lot you can do to save water except install 'water saver shower heads', which can limit the maximum flow rate to below nine litres per minute.

If you have a combi boiler, before spending money on a new shower head measure the flow of the existing one because some combi boilers won't operate at low flows. With the shower on the highest flow rate, fill a bucket for a timed 10 seconds. Measure this volume with a measuring jug or kitchen scales (1 litre = 1kg) and multiply by six to get litres per minute. This will let you determine whether an instantaneous water heater will produce sufficient hot water at, say, six litres per second, before buying a shower that operates at this rate. Table 7.2 shows typical flow rates of different types of showers.

A three-minute shower with the flow adjusted to a comfortable five litres per minute uses only 15 litres of water, while ten minutes at 15 litres per minute will

Table 7.2 *Typical flow rates of different types of showers*

	4 litre/min	7.2kW electric	9.8 kW electric	6 l/min water saver	9.5 l/min water saver	Power shower
Flow litre/min	4 l/min	3.5 l/min 30°C temp rise	4.7 l/min 30°C temp rise	6 l/min reg'd flow	9.5 l/min reg'd flow	Typically 12+ l/minute
Water use for 5 min shower	20	17.5	23.5	30	47.5	60+
As a % of 70 litre bath	29	25	39	43	68	86+
Kg CO_2 gas boiler	0.07–0.27	0.34 direct electric	0.45 direct electric	0.27–0.4	0.42–0.63	0.53–0.8+

Source: UK Environment Agency, www.environment-agency.gov.uk/homeandleisure/drought/38531.aspx

use ten times as much water and energy without getting you any cleaner! In the US there is a maximum permissible flow rate of 9.5 litres per minute. Installing a shower timer can increase awareness of the amount of time spent in the shower.

'Water-saver' showerheads work by creating finer drops or by incorporating air into the flow. This requires a pressure of at least one bar; perfectly fine with mains supply and pumped systems but not usually with gravity-fed systems. They operate at a flow rate of between four and nine litres per minute. Flow rates can go as low as 3.2 litres per minute without users feeling robbed of a good shower experience.

Thermostatic mixers should be incorporated. These have a calibrated dial, so the temperature can be set from experience. The flow is adjusted with a separate control so that reducing the flow is simple.

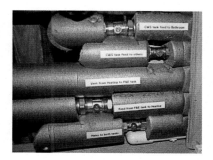

Figure 7.6 *Properly insulated hot water pipes, labelled according to source and destination in a domestic heating system using multiple boilers*

Source: © Chris Twinn

Baths

Baths vary with how much water they use according to their volume or shape. Tapered or peanut-shaped baths create the optimum space for water-saving bathing. You can usually find out the volume of a bath in the promotional literature, but some calculate it to the height of the centre of the overflow and others subtract the volume of an adult (about 70 litres), so it is important to compare like with like. Very few modern baths hold less than 130 litres, which is about 60 litres with a submerged adult. 180 litres should be considered the maximum.

Appliances

Washing machines

Most new washing machines now use less than 50 litres per 6kg wash, with some using as little as 35 litres. National energy and water saving public service websites commonly have lists of the most efficient models around.

Most now have only a cold water inlet and heat the water themselves using electricity. This is unfortunate unless the electricity source is renewable, since it's better to use water that has already been heated by solar thermal panels, biomass or gas. They used to be available with hot and cold water inputs which combined them to the right temperature. Perhaps they will return in the future now that attention has been drawn to the problem. Models which use mains water to condense moisture can increase water consumption to 100–170 litres per wash.

Tips for washing machines

- choose a machine that is A++ rated and with a low water consumption;
- most washes produce a good result at 30°C;
- use only with a full load – many can take 6kg nowadays;
- where possible, dry clothes in the air, not in a washer-dryer.

Dishwashers

The most water and energy-efficient dishwashers can use as little as 12 litres to wash 12 place settings. Leaving aside the question of the embodied energy contained within the manufacturing, delivery and disposal of the machine, it is still debatable whether or not they save energy and water compared to manual dishwashing. Nevertheless, they are a fact of life in many households. Choosing the most efficient model, using it only when full and not pre-rinsing utensils will all help to save resources and money.

Outside use

Depending on whether the property has a garden or the owners possess vehicles, a sizeable proportion of water may be used outside. The exact percentage can be at its highest in the hot season when water supply generally is at its lowest. Therefore it needs to be used carefully and efficiently, to best effect.

Water efficient gardens

Features of water efficient garden management include:

- drought-tolerant plants, e.g. thyme, oregano, crocus, tulips, grasses, geraniums, poppies, cyclamen, daffodils, lavender, juniper;
- mulches on the soil, e.g. bark, gravel;
- organic matter regularly added to the soil that can retain water, such as compost, grass cuttings and manure;
- remembering that lawns can survive droughts;
- watering plants only in the evening or early morning to avoid wastage by evaporation;
- watering using rainwater collected in butts from downpipes from the roof guttering;
- using cooled wastewater from the kitchen, baths and showers (greywater);
- on slopes, using earth banks to retain water;
- if using a hosepipe, using a lance or trigger device to control the flow and direct the water gently to where needed, frequently but lightly and not directly on the soil.

Flood prevention

In times of heavy downpours, water running off impervious surfaces puts tremendous strain on storm water drainage systems and can cause floods and contamination of streams and rivers with heavy metals, hydrocarbons and dust. For this reason it's vital not to cover outside areas with Tarmac, impervious paving or concrete.

Sustainable urban drainage systems (SUDS) are used to prevent run-off and flooding and, in sophisticated schemes, as a method of collecting and cleaning storm water. They come in several

Figure 7.7 *Sustainable drainage system being installed outside a terraced house*

Note: Includes an attenuation tank for surplus rain water to give slow release into the ground and existing tarmac replaced with porous grass reinforcement mesh and new raised beds made of old oak railway sleepers .

Source: © Penney Poyzer and Gil Schalom

forms, from simple permeable paving slabs or gravel on a permeable membrane, to polypropylene matrices through which grass can grow, but which provide a stable surface for vehicles to park on. Sometimes detention ponds are used which can provide an attractive habitat and increase local biodiversity.

Sophisticated systems harvest the water running off from a driveway and purify it in a sump using the action of naturally-occurring bacteria and sunlight so that it can be released later when the majority of the floodwater has subsided or can be used for watering gardens and so on. Since these involve major works utilizing heavy plant they are unlikely to be used except in local regeneration schemes and the opportunity should usefully be taken at the same time to install ground source heat pumps.

Figure 7.8 *Another example of sustainable drainage: Sunken soakaway along the wall of the house and a permeable, gravel-like surface*

Source: © Chris Twinn

Reducing the carbon impact of water use

Water may be composed chemically of hydrogen and oxygen atoms, but it also contains carbon – not literally, but through the way we use it. 89 per cent of the carbon dioxide emissions associated with the water consumed in the average home – around 2.2kg CO_2 a day – arise from its use in the home ('Quantifying the energy and carbon effects of water saving', Clarke et al, 2009). The remaining 11 per cent is the responsibility of the water companies: arising from wastewater treatment, water treatment, distribution, sourcing, abstraction and conveyance, as shown in Figure 7.1. A slightly different picture is given by consultant Cath Hassell (personal communication), who quotes an industry average of 0.7kg CO_2 per litre of mains water being due to the activities of the water companies, which would push the total carbon cost of domestic water use even higher.

Figures 7.1–7.3 at the start of the chapter show that larger users of carbon are the kitchen sink, the dishwasher and washing machine, followed by the bath, shower, losses from the hot water cylinder, washing basin and losses from the inefficiency of the gas combi boiler, where fitted. These figures assume that gas is used to heat the water. In fact it makes a great deal of difference what the heat source is. Assuming an average household with 2.4 persons, the total annual CO_2 emissions for each way of heating water – even with basic conservation methods installed and a degree of user awareness – are as follows (UK averages):

- electric: 1715kg;
- gas: 925kg;
- biomass: 434kg.

If solar heating is factored in, emissions will be lower. However the constant factor in each case is the emissions from the appliances which use electricity to heat the water: washing machines, dishwashers and, perhaps, showers. This is why a low carbon home should include appliances which can take heated water from another source, if the electricity source is not renewable.

Figure 7.2 (p127) shows the cumulative effect of different changes made in a refurbishment to the carbon impact of water use. The dwelling assumed has a 78 per cent efficient gas boiler, 120 litre cylinder with 25mm of foam insulation. Installing a water meter is assumed to yield 12 per cent savings (Herrington, 2007). Installing a water efficient shower head, tap inserts and an improved cistern yields further benefits. Simple energy efficiency measures like insulating the cylinder and pipes help, noted in the fourth column of Figure 7.2, while consumer behaviour helps further. This reaches the limit of how much can be saved without changing the fuel supply.

Heat gains and losses from water and plumbing

In a superinsulated building heat flows that used to be considered inconsequential become significant. Energy used to heat up water can heat the home as the water cools from:

- baths – if left to cool;
- showers;
- poorly insulated tanks;
- washing machine and dishwasher;
- pipes, e.g. from the boiler to the storage tank or from the tank to the appliances, sinks and shower.

Surprisingly, heat can even be lost as cold water in a toilet absorbs heat from the room and is flushed away. This heat gain has been measured as in excess of 4°C. According to a report for the Energy Saving Trust, this 'is of a similar magnitude to the CO_2 emissions from water supply and wastewater treatment needed to supply water for WC flushing. We calculate it to be around 20kg CO_2 per year for a family of 4, so it is not a "significant" heat loss in all but the best insulated buildings.' Therefore in a superinsulated building, even cisterns can be insulated – which would also prevent condensation on their outer surface.

Heating water using the sun

To reduce the carbon impact of water use, we should try to heat it using renewable sources of energy. The most widely available of these sources is above us – the sun. Up to half of UK dwellings could in principle benefit from its free energy because solar thermal systems can be extremely tolerant of factors such as orientation and cloudy weather. It is a highly proven technology with widespread use, and very different from solar electricity. In sunny hot periods it can supply all of a home's hot water requirements. The rest of the time it supplies a proportion of them, and auxiliary energy sources are switched in to heat the water to the required level.

It would not be possible for the majority of homes to be heated using biomass, notwithstanding the potential air quality impacts of doing so. There are no such problems with solar water heating, which therefore, wherever possible, should be an essential component of a carbon-reducing refit.

The energy performance of a system is influenced chiefly by:

- the amount of solar radiation hitting the collectors;
- the collector type (panels or evacuated tubes);

- their area;
- their efficiency;
- the orientation (azimuth);
- the slope;
- the end-use water temperature and volume required.

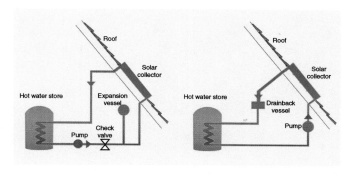

Solar collectors absorb the heat from the sun and transmit it to a fluid, typically water with antifreeze, which circulates into a heat exchanger which can either be separate from (a buffer tank) or the same as the hot water tank. A buffer tank feeds the main hot water tank, otherwise the solar coil feeds into the bottom of a larger hot water cylinder. In either case, the heat

Figure 7.9 Two common primary system layouts: fully filled and drainback

Note: Essential safety equipment and other best practice omitted for clarity.

Source: EST (2006)

transfer fluid heated by the sun is not the water that is consumed; this circulates endlessly, in the same way as the refrigerant in a heat pump or refrigerator. As with heat pumps, the fluid should be zero ozone-depleting and of minimal global warming impact, such as isobutane (R600a) or propane.

System layouts

There are two basic system layouts:

- fully filled systems require a check valve to prevent heated water thermosiphoning out at night to cool down and an expansion vessel 'after' it in the flow, for when the fluid heats and expands;

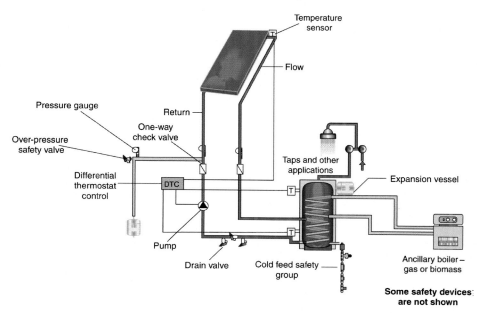

Figure 7.10 *Schematic diagram of a standard solar water heating system for cooler latitudes with a fully filled pumped collector (only one panel shown), storage tank with two coils – the top one being for the ancillary boiler*

Source: Laughton (2010)

Figure 7.11 *Flat plate solar water heating collector that has been working well for almost 20 years*

Note: The slate tiles on the walls of this home in Wales, incidentally, had to be removed for repair, and now cover external wall insulation.

Figures 7.12 and 7.13 *Modern evacuated tube collectors being installed on a flat roof in London*

Note: Note small pump powered by a photovoltaic electricity. The heat collecting fins inside the tubes can be angled to face the sun and so do not need a south facing tilted roof.

Source: © Russell Smith

- drainback systems which contain air in the loop and a drainback vessel for the hot water when the pump is switched off. A temperature 'interlock' should be included so it cannot transfer heat outside the insulated building.

Both systems utilize a pump since most building designs do not permit thermosiphoning, where no pump is needed. All systems require highly robust components because of the extreme weather and temperature conditions they need to endure over the lifetime – 15 to 20 years – of the installation. They also need safety, monitoring and control equipment.

System efficiency

The system layouts above can use either of two types of solar collector:

- insulated, glazed collectors, which contain usually copper pipes containing the transfer fluid loop;
- evacuated (vacuum-filled) collectors, which contain conductive elements that conduct the heat to a phase change fluid that then releases it into the heat exchanger.

Systems will typically deliver 35–45 per cent of the solar energy arriving at the collector. The evacuated panels are usually the more efficient and thus require less surface area, but are more expensive. They are often employed in places where space is at a premium.

The system losses are in the glazing, reflections and re-emittance (<40 per cent) in the panels, and in the pump, pipes, tank, etc. (20 per cent). This efficiency level is factored into the system sizing dependent on the amount of solar energy available at the location and the heat demand.

The electrical input power of the pump should preferably use no higher than two per cent of the peak thermal power of the collector. By using a differential thermostatic control (DTC) pump controller, it is possible to modulate pump speed in relation to temperature and minimize losses, producing greater efficiency.

System sizing

How much solar energy is available at a given site? The measure of solar radiation energy received on a given surface area in a given time varies according to the latitude, time of year and climate and is called the solar isolation. It is commonly expressed in watts per square meter (W/m^2) or kilowatt-hours per square metre per day ($kWh/(m^2/day)$). If it is known how many kilowatt-hours of hot water heating energy is required, the efficiency of the system and the amount of solar insolation received by the site, then the total surface area of collecting required can be worked out. Most national governments or their agencies supply insolation data for given locations, which show how much solar energy is available throughout the year.

A rough guide for a home is one square metre plus an additional square metre per occupant.

Panel positioning

They are normally installed on a roof. Collectors should ideally face towards the equator, but in practice they can face up to 45 degrees in either direction away from the equator with only a 10 per cent loss of performance which can be accommodated by collector 'oversizing'. Observations should be made year-round to check whether, especially in the winter, nearby objects (trees, buildings) shade the site for a significant proportion of the daytime. Software can model this.

Tank positioning

Extra physical space is required inside the thermal envelope for the storage tank and controls. Tanks should be large enough not to overheat in the summer and small enough not to need too much extra heat in the winter. A rough guide is that pre-heat storage space is equivalent to the number of occupants multiplied by at least $0.05m^3$ plus an amount for controls and insulated pipes. They are not light – rafters must be able to hold a vessel weighing at least 60kg multiplied by the number of occupants.

Community solar water heating

There is increasing interest in large-scale municipal and community heating schemes using solar thermal power. Numerous examples exist across Europe, many of which are on blocks of apartments or flats. A database of projects (now no longer updated) is available at www.solarge.org.

Water re-use

We've minimized the use of water in a dwelling, and found the lowest-carbon means of heating our water. Do we need to do anything else? The simple answer is: very little. But what about preparing for droughts? Shouldn't we try to be more self-sufficient in water? Many modern environmental residential schemes incorporate means of collecting and using rainwater from the roof, or of reusing the water from sinks, baths, showers and appliances to flush toilets and water the garden. In the UK and elsewhere, credits under low carbon building regulations are given for employing these technologies. But what is the evidence for their effectiveness?

Rainwater harvesting systems

It would seem to be a straightforward concept: saving the rainwater that falls on the roof of a building and using it inside

Figures 7.14 and 7.15 *Both these tanks combine feeds from solar panels and a wood pellet boiler with an electric immersion heater*

Note: The second system also includes a buffer tank, seen on the right.

the house will save expensively produced and, in certain parts of the world, increasingly scarce, mains water. Sophisticated systems involve:

- reliable guttering (steel or copper);
- downpipes;
- accessible filtration;
- frost-protected storage away from sunlight at a temperature which prevents bacterial growth;
- a floating intake to draw water from the top of the water so sediment at the bottom is not collected (new water comes into the tank near the bottom);
- a clearly labelled separate system of pipes alongside the existing mains back-up plumbing system to pump and direct the water to where it is going to be used within the house. The water should be oxygenated;
- a rat-proof overflow.

As part of the system design the rainfall in the locality needs to be measured to determine the tank capacity required. The roof area also needs to be measured and factored in. The distribution system should send the water to those applications which have the highest consumption first. Retrofitting rainwater harvesting is even more complicated than designing it into a new building.

Such a comprehensive system can supply much of the water used in a dwelling if there is sufficient storage capacity. However, an analysis (Clarke et al, 2009) shows that the carbon impact of rainwater systems is six times greater than using mains water. Why is this? It's simply a question of scale. Much of the carbon impact of rainwater harvesting systems comes from the energy used to run them in the pumps, but a significant proportion – 35 per cent on average – comes from the embodied energy and installation costs of the infrastructure: the underground tanks, pipes and so on. It is much better in economic and efficiency terms for water supply companies to concentrate their efforts on reducing leakages and making their systems less carbon intensive. This will both save water and carbon much more efficiently.

Simple gravity-fed harvesting systems are an exception. A refurbishment for a social housing terraced home in south London includes a system based around a filtered 318 litre tank located in a void above the stairs. The tank is fed directly from an external downpipe, which requires no pumps. Prior calculations implied that all the water needed for flushing toilets could be supplied from the local annual average rainfall. Such systems are worthwhile in low-rainfall areas where space permits.

Figure 7.16 *The tanks of a rainwater harvesting system installed in the cellar of a Victorian house*

Note: The complex system has been partially abandoned. Simple gravity fed systems like Figure 7.18 are preferable.

Source: © Penney Poyzer and Gil Schalom

Garden use

Another exception is to capture water from downpipes in large butts which can be used in the garden. The plastic butts have taps near the bottom from which watering cans can be filled, or to which hoses or hand pumps can be attached. Unless there is a renewable supply of electricity avoid any system which

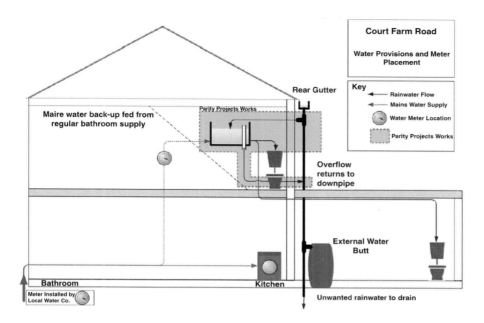

Figure 7.17 *Simple gravity fed system*

Source: © Parity Projects

involves an electric pump. Care should be taken that any overflow is directed to the storm sewer or soakaway.

Greywater recycling

Perhaps reusing the water from sinks, baths and so on might be better? In fact, no research has been done to establish this. Perhaps it depends on how it is used. The simplest greywater system diverts the water directly to a garden. It will need separate plumbing from the toilet, which is still discharged to the mains sewerage system or septic tank. The greywater is then sent via a distribution network of underground pipes into the garden using gravity. If local gradients don't permit this, the temptation to do it anyway using a pump should be resisted. There needs to be a filter, which will have to be cleaned regularly. Common guidelines for safe usage include not storing the greywater for more than 24 hours and ensuring it cannot form unhealthy pools or run-off.

More complex systems utilize a sump pump and surge tanks. They might try to purify or treat the water using ultraviolet light and reuse it by pumping it to toilet

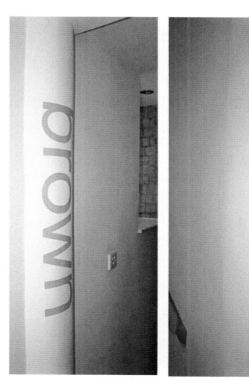

Figures 7.18 and 7.19 *Separate greywater and 'brownwater' – from the toilets – downpipes, labelled for design effect in the hallway of Lacemaker's House, Nottingham*

Note: This system was abandoned after a major disaster caused by a malfunctioning switch on a pump.

Figures 7.20–7.23 *Elements of a water-recycling system: The tank before and after installation at the rear of the house*

Note the insulation – and the complex pipework from the various outlets. The access hatch allows for cleaning of the filter, which has to be done regularly as it blocks easily.

Source: © Author and Chris Twinn

cisterns. This seriously increases the carbon load. In some cases an intelligent control mechanism flushes the collected water if it has been stored too long (it becomes hazardous after 24 hours), avoiding the need for filtration and chemical treatment. This has a carbon load too. In some cases again, where the water is going to be used for toilet flushing, it is kept in a tank, perhaps hidden above the cistern. It also needs a pump and controls.

Conclusion

Water is the stuff of life and life is impossible without it. But nowadays, for many people life is also intolerable without electricity. We have learnt how to minimize water use and where it is most useful to make savings, but what is the minimum amount of electricity we can maintain a modern lifestyle on? This is the subject of the next chapter, together with sourcing those remaining needs from renewable supplies.

References

AECB (2009) 'AECB water standards', Technical Background Report, Version 1.0.0, AECB, London

AWWA (1993) *The Water Conservation Manager's Guide to Residential Retrofit*, Denver, Colorado

Clarke, A., Grant, N. and Thornton, J. (2009) 'Quantifying the energy and carbon effects of water saving', Environment Agency/Energy Saving Trust, London

Herrington, P. (2007) 'Waste not, want not: Sustainable water tariffs', report by the Centre for Sustainable Energy for WWF-UK, London

Horne, B. and MacDermot, J. (2008) *How to Buy Wood Fuels*, Glasu, Wales

8

Electricity Efficiency and Supply

We've found that if we insulate well and protect from draughts, we need far less energy for heating and cooling. We've also found that to minimize the carbon impact of water we should use it as efficiently as possible. It comes as no surprise then, to find that the low carbon home will minimize electricity use before looking to supply the remaining demand from renewable energy sources.

Some refurbishments and new builds attempt to proclaim themselves as environmentally sound by bolting on a renewable energy feature like a wind turbine or photovoltaic panels to a fairly conventional structure. This is simply a waste of resources.

Energy efficiency: Invisible earnings

The gadgets we use in our homes have been getting more energy efficient over the last 20 years. However, we're still using the same amount of electricity. Why is this? Because we have a lot more of them of course. They have got cheaper, but the price of electricity has not, yet habits like leaving the computer on are hard to break.

There are two ways to save energy and money, not to mention carbon emissions: by designing out wasteful uses of electricity and by making it easier for people to switch things off or turn things down. Only some of these fall within the scope of refurbishment (only governments can ban patio heaters and there will always be some people who want to have their houses blazing with light all day and night). So we will look first at ways to encourage residents to save energy and then at energy-frugal pieces of kit, beginning with lighting.

Volts, amps and watts

Volts x amps = watts (V × A = W), that's the *power* required to operate the appliance (1000 watts = 1 kilowatt).

To get the *energy* consumed by the appliance, you need to multiply the power by the number of hours the appliance is used for. This gives watt-hours. A kilowatt (1000W) used for one hour = 1 kilowatt-hour (kWh), or one unit of electricity, that appears on electricity bills.

If you look at the label of an appliance or an adaptor you can see what its power requirements are: the more volts, amps or watts, the more it needs. These usually give the wattage, but sometimes just the current, in which case multiply that by the voltage to get the watts. Multiplying the watts by the number of hours of use will give the energy consumption in watt-hours. Divide that by 1000 to get the number of kilowatt-hours.

Example: a 500W appliance is on for 3 hours. 500W × 3 hours = 1500Wh = 1.5kWh.

What needs watt?

It's a good idea to know how much power gadgets use. Some typical appliance energy requirements are:

Appliance	Average watts
CFC lightbulb	15
Kettle	2000
Microwave	600–1000
Toaster	800–1500
Induction hobs	1800–3500
Iron	1000
Refrigerator	35
Washing machine	700 (2000 heat, 500 spin, 250 wash)
Clock radio	15
Home security system	100
Vacuum cleaner	300–1100
Electric fire	1000–2000
Laptop	50–75
PC	120
LCD monitor	75
Modem	15
TV - LCD	115
Sky+ on	22
Sky+ on standby	12
DVD player	20
MP3 player charging	5
Mobile phone	1–5
Game console	25–200
Hover mower	1000–2000
Strimmer	300
Jig saw	300
Electric drill	500–1000

Voltage optimization

In some countries large businesses have been benefiting from voltage optimization for years, saving huge sums of money. Now the technology is available for homes. A small box connected to the consumer unit (fuse box) where the power supply enters the property adjusts the incoming voltage to a constant 220V, regardless of the incoming voltage.

The actual savings vary from country to country because the delivered voltage varies. Most electrical equipment manufactured for Europe and the UK is rated at 220V and may operate satisfactorily at voltages down to 200V. By efficiently bringing supply voltages to the lower end of the statutory voltage range, less electricity is used which can generate average carbon and cash savings of around 13 per cent – and equipment is protected from power surges too. It works particularly well with motors – e.g. pumps, as in fridges – and lighting.

What gets monitored gets saved

Seeing what is being used enables the occupier to observe or measure the effect of their behaviour. Estimates of the energy-saving benefit of these features vary from 5–20 per cent depending on user attitudes.

Energy monitors are easy for occupiers or landlords to install. They come in two parts: one part clips on to the cable near the meter; it sends information wirelessly to the other part, a display, which can be positioned in a convenient, obvious place – such as a kitchen counter. This shows in real time how much electricity is being used, how much it costs (per day, week or year), the temperature in the room and the time and date. This often revelatory feedback can immediately demonstrate how much energy is being used and bring it into full consciousness. This is a far cry from getting an electricity bill months after you have used the electricity – especially if the bill is estimated.

Smart meters must be installed by the energy service company. They enable energy companies to monitor electricity use remotely and save money. Depending on the features they may enable more accurate billing, half hourly remote updates and readings and lower prices in return for customers using electricity during off-peak times. Customers can even get feedback on their electricity use channelled via their computers and mobile phones. Because they are slightly delayed, by up to 30 minutes, unlike energy monitors their impact on behaviour change may be slightly less. They must be placed somewhere visible and convenient.

Advanced metering

Further efficiencies using smart meters can be gained by wirelessly connecting electric appliances to them, allowing the appliances to be remote-controlled. This will enable the energy service company to switch on and off appliances which are not time sensitive according to the level of demand elsewhere on the local grid. This benefits district-level CHP or reduces peak loads on the system (meaning less overall generating capacity is needed) without affecting the performance of the appliances.

This is called advanced metering. Already widespread in Italy and Sweden, it is being introduced elsewhere in Europe. Customers receive favourable tariffs in return for surrendering control of their appliances (although they'll hardly notice any effect on performance). In a major refurbishment programme of a block, a housing authority may be able to negotiate the roll-out of advanced metering with the energy service company as part of a bulk energy procurement deal.

Exorcising phantom loads

Standby electricity use is that which is trickling away even when electric products are switched off or not in use. These ghostly energy vampires could be little LED lights, internal or external transformers and chargers, or features such as remote control, memory, clock display and instant-on features.

A survey in 75 houses in Halifax, Canada (Fung et al, 2003), found that the annual average standby energy consumption per household was a staggering 427kWh, equivalent to a constant load of 49W.

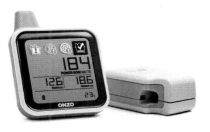

Figures 8.1 and 8.2 *Two electricity monitors, by Onzo (top, with the sensor part that clips on to a cable by the meter) and by British Gas, which gives more detailed information*

An international effort is ongoing to get all standbys reduced to one watt. Meanwhile, aside from persuading everyone to laboriously turn each one off every night, some techno-fixes are available, all of which plug into electric sockets between the appliance and the socket:

- Standby busters: enable easy switching off of whatever is plugged into them via a remote control.
- Timer switches: can be programmed, with manual override, to turn appliances on and off automatically when no one is around to use them.
- IntelliPanels and IntelliPlugs: automatically power up and down peripheral equipment like printers when the desktop computer is switched on and off.

Don't stand for standbys should be the motto.

Lighting

Traditionally, lighting can account for up to 30 per cent of electricity use in a building. It is possible to cut that figure by 90 per cent by using the tricks outlined

Cost (£)

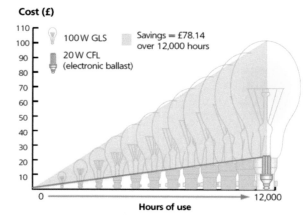

Figure 8.3 *Savings that can be achieved by replacing a 100W incandescent lamp with a 20W CFL, based on an electricity price of 7.9 p/kWh and 1100 hours of use per year*

Note: According to research the average lifespan of the two most often used lamps in the average home.

GLS: General Lighting Service

Source: EST (2005a)

in Chapter 5 on daylighting, together with modern lighting solutions. These mean that all kinds of exciting effects can be created very cheaply.

Old-fashioned tungsten-filament incandescent lights bulbs are being phased out in many places. Compact fluorescent lamps (CFLs) are the main energy-saving alternatives to these, being eight times more efficient and lasting up to 12 times longer, meaning that you can save more than 10 times the cost of the bulb over its lifetime compared to the cost of using incandescent, while using one-eighth of the carbon emissions. There are many new kinds of CFLs coming on to the market and LEDs (light-emitting diodes) are adding to the interior design possibilities. Organic LEDs (OLEDs) are on the horizon.

Lights sold in Europe have to carry EU energy labels. These show the energy efficiency category, how many lumens they emit and their average expected life in hours.

Some lamps contain hazardous substances like mercury. You can now obtain lamps all of whose components are compliant with legislation like the Restriction on the Use of Certain Hazardous

Lights, brightness and power

How much light do you need for a given space?

Light is measured in lumens, and illumination in lux. The lux (symbol: lx) is equal to one lumen (lm) per square metre. A bright office may have about 400 lux of illumination.

Lux tell you how many lumens you need to light a given area. 500 lux directed over ten square metres will be dimmer than the same amount spread over one square metre. A kitchen may be lit by 500 lux from a single fluorescent tube with an output of 1200 lumens, or 12 directed LED fixtures of 100 each.

How do lux relate to watts? They don't. For brightness study the lumens – and get the most for the least watts.

Type	Lumens per watt
Incandescent bulbs	12lm/W
Halogen	10–30lm/W
LEDs	40lm/W
Some fluorescents	60lm/W (LEDs will get there soon)

Figure 8.4 *Channelling daylight*

Note: As we saw in Chapter 5, the demand for electricity for lighting can be reduced in many ways, including by channelling daylight.

Substances in Electrical and Electronic Equipment Regulations 2008 (the 'RoHS Regulations'), which bans new equipment containing more than agreed levels of lead, cadmium, mercury, hexavalent chromium, polybrominated biphenyl (PBB) and polybrominated diphenyl ether (PBDE) flame retardants. It is also possible to recycle all lights at special recycling centres – important because of the hazardous components they contain.

Luminaires can be replaced at any time. A key opportunity, though, is while rewiring – especially where existing pendant fittings are being replaced.

Types of bulb and fitting

CFLs

Compact fluorescents, or CFLs, used to have a bad reputation of being slow to start up, producing a cold light and not working with dimmers. No longer: the latest range includes daylight, cool white and warm comfort light – very similar to standard incandescents – in many styles to match the variety of modern fittings, including downlights, spotlights, dimmable wall lights, mirrors and much more.

Many lights require 'ballasts' and most dimmable ballasts require additional wiring, but some are available which require no additional wiring for changing a centre pendant. For multiple lights a three core and earth cable is required to carry a permanent live and a switch live for control.

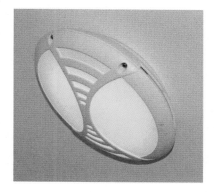

Figure 8.5 *LED cluster behind a frosted cover, fitted in a ceiling recess within the airtight membrane in a near-Passivhaus standard home*

LEDs

The light-emitting diode is a semiconductor which converts electricity into light. They use a tiny amount of electricity and last for over 25,000 hours, compared to CFLs' 10,000 hours and incandescents' 1000. But the light is directed and groupings of LEDs are required to get the equivalent amounts of lux to CFLs. They can be ideal for reading and task lighting, strip lighting and furniture etc, outdoor and landscape lighting, stair and low-level lighting, and backlighting.

The technology is developing fast: white LEDs are now available, prices are reducing and light levels increasing. LED ribbons and

Figure 8.6 *With one cover removed, the cluster of LEDs can be seen in this luminaire*

Figure 8.7 *Programmable switching and a projector can create stylish mood lighting at minimal cost using LEDs*

Source: © Penney Poyzer and Gil Schalom

projections produce astounding mood effects and a huge variety of stylish fittings for every taste and location (except larger area lighting) is available.

Halogens

A halogen is a type of incandescent lamp with a tungsten filament. This means it gives off a lot of heat, which is wasted energy, but is more efficient than old-fashioned incandescents, using 30–50 per cent less energy while lasting perhaps two to three times longer. Because of their smaller size, halogens achieved popularity with directed and mood lighting. Nowadays, the same effect can be achieved with LEDs and CFLs much more efficiently and they should be replaced with these when they wear out.

Intelligent lighting systems

Every now and then people forget to turn the lights off. They can then be on for a few hours and this adds up. There are a couple of ways to deal with this:

- Occupancy sensors, also known as microwave, radar or Doppler sensors, can be used with all lights. These work by sending out high-frequency sound waves and listening for the bounce back. When it is returned at a different frequency it knows there is a moving object around. It then sends a signal to the dimmable ballast to raise the light levels. When no movement is detected after a certain period of time, the light will return to its original level. This type is preferable to infrared motion sensors, which are vulnerable to dust and blocking objects, can be confused by radiators and fires and have a shorter lifespan.
- Adjustable light level sensors make lighting even more intelligent. They can automatically turn a light on and off in response to changing amounts of daylight.
- Timers: there's always the tried and tested method used in apartment block and hotel stairways throughout the world: a switch with a timer built into it.

Gadgets and appliances

Of course, the low carbon dwelling will host the most efficient appliances and gadgets. In some cases it's quite clear what these are, but in others it is not. We'll confine ourselves to just clearing up a few possible areas of confusion and giving a few tips.

Labelling

Energy labels appear on a variety of products, but by no means all of them.

- The EU energy label rates products from A, (the most efficient) to G (the least efficient). For refrigeration the label goes up to

Figure 8.8 *When Chris Twinn refurbished his home, it was wired up so that alongside the light switches by the door in the living room were switches that turned off the entertainment centre too. Making it easy means it's more likely to happen! But don't forget that all wiring needs to be compliant with the wiring regulations.*

A++. It appears by law on all refrigeration appliances, electric tumble dryers, washing machines, washer dryers, dishwashers, electric ovens, air conditioners, lamps and light bulb packaging.

- The Energy Star® voluntary logo appears on office equipment to signify that it uses energy below an agreed level in 'stand-by' mode. Look for it on computers, monitors, printers and fax machines. On some products, such as computers, the Energy Star features have to be enabled to save energy. See www.eu-energystar.org.

- The Energy Efficiency Recommended logo is a certification mark that covers appliances, light bulbs and fittings, gas and oil boilers, heating controls, hot water cylinders, loft insulation, cavity wall insulation and draught-proofing. It is a UK Energy Saving Trust initiative. See: www. saveenergy.co.uk.

- The Energy Technology List is UK-based, but viewable by anybody. It covers a huge variety of plant and machinery. See www.eca.gov.uk. UK companies and organizations buying products on the list are eligible for tax credits. The scheme is run by The Carbon Trust.

It's not always possible to make the best choice however just by looking at the letter on the label. The EU energy label actually states the annual energy consumption in kWh per year, and this is the most important figure to look at. To see why, let's look at refrigerators and fridge freezers.

Refrigerators and fridge freezers

Larger fridges (and they have got a lot larger lately) will inevitably use more energy than smaller ones, so a more useful measure of how much energy they will use is to look at their consumption over time. As an example, compare the following two real models which are both A-rated for energy efficiency:

Model	Fridge volume	Freezer volume	Running cost
A	150 litres	45 litres	£15
B	158 litres	56 litres	£42

As you can see, the difference in volumes between the two supposedly identically efficient models results in one consuming nearly three times as much electricity as the other. This can be checked by looking at the annual energy consumption on the label. The same applies to air conditioners.

It is also important to check whether refrigerators and fridge freezers are ozone and climate friendly. The preferred cooling agent (or refrigerant) is isobutene (R600a) or propane (preferably), which neither affect the ozone layer nor have significant global warming impacts. A common one is HFC-134a. This is better for the ozone layer than CFCs, which are banned, but is classified as a greenhouse gas by the United Nations panel on climate change and so contributes to global warming.

Different types of products contain different information on the EU energy label. The labels on washing machines, dishwashers

Figure 8.9 *Using old-fashioned clothes drying racks can replace the need for tumble driers*

and dryers show the energy consumption per cycle and it is also what you should look at when comparing models.

Cookers

Cooking can be done either with biomass, gas or electricity. Induction hobs are more energy efficient than gas hobs, using up to 90 per cent of the energy produced compared to 55 per cent, making them more economical. However this does not mean they are more carbon efficient, since only 30–35 per cent of the energy in the original fuel used to generate the electricity ends up being used on the hob. This means that cooking with gas is still twice as carbon efficient as an induction hob. However, if electricity has to be used, then induction hobs are a clear winner.

Ovens should always be extremely well insulated. Similar concerns apply to labelling for cookers as mentioned above for fridges.

A word on kettles: since they use electricity, for the reasons described above it is more carbon-efficient if water can be heated by gas or biomass. It is possible to buy kettles that work on gas hobs or wood-stoves. As electric kettles turn themselves off when they have boiled, and these can't, it is important to have one fitted with a whistle!

Other items

Many appliances do not have energy labels yet. We often don't think of looking to see what the power consumption is when we buy gadgets for leisure like games consoles and DVD players. The list ('what needs watt') on p144 is a guide for what to expect as a minimum standard, but the UK Consumers Association does have a calculator on its website that can help, www.which.co.uk.

Intelligent homes?

There is a move in some new homes to install wireless systems that remotely control all elements of power usage and broadband access. Some systems can be retrofitted and include several of the above-mentioned features, such as occupancy sensing, timers, heating controls, energy management and voltage optimization as well as smart metering capability and remote control. It is unclear at present whether these novel innovations are cost-effective, carbon-saving or reliable in the long term.

Having bought down consumption as much as possible, now is the appropriate time to consider how to supply a home's electricity needs on a warming planet.

Renewable electricity

The really great thing about renewable energy is that the fuel source is free. As long as the sun keeps shining, the wind keeps blowing and trees keep growing then it is there, right on your doorstep. No one is going to have to go to war or handle radioactive products or look after waste that will be dangerous for thousands of years just so that you can listen to your favourite music. With solar, wind or hydro energy there is no possibility of price increases. And using this energy will not contribute to global warming.

Renewable electricity on a domestic scale generally comes from the sun, the wind or, to a lesser extent, flowing water. It can be supplied on a community or individual dwelling basis. For example in a community context, in the case of a block of flats, solar panels can be put on the roof or on cladding and can help supply the electricity demands of the whole building. Generally, the most common renewable technologies available in most locations are solar photovoltaic power and wind power. On a community level burning waste or biomass in a boiler can power a generator. Power from flowing water might be available in some places.

How much do you need?

There are several ways of working out the power requirements of a renewable energy system:

- list all your appliances and gadgets, how many watts they use and how many hours a week they will be used and multiply this by 52 to get the annual requirements;
- look at the electricity bills for the whole year, as long as the bills reflect the savings made from following the above efficiency recommendations.

This gives the annual electricity requirement in kilowatt-hours. If the home is connected to the grid, it can supply the extra electricity needed above what is being generated at the time. When more is being generated than is being used, that is sold to the grid. To do this requires a 'net metering arrangement' with the utility company.

How much energy is available? We've already looked at how to find out how much solar power is available in the section on solar water heating. Average figures for wind power are generally available from a central location as well, but there is no substitute for taking measurements on the site, over a year. For larger waste and biomass plants, contractors will have this data.

The final step is to design the entire system and calculate its efficiency in order to work out how much power will be available at the sockets. This includes not only the efficiency of the generator, but other equipment such as controls. One essential piece of kit is an inverter; this converts the direct current produced by the generator into the alternating current required by the mains, but some energy is lost on the way. Often systems are bought in as turnkey 'plug and play' installations – which inevitably costs more but saves time and headaches. Several estimates should be sought from different suppliers.

Combined heat and power (CHP)

On a community scale, a combined heat and power (CHP) facility, powered by natural gas, municipal waste or biomass, can contribute to both heating and electricity requirements. CHP is effective because it takes advantage of the heat produced when generating electricity in power plants (that can burn coal, oil or natural gas), that is normally wasted. This means they can reach efficiencies of up to 89 per cent, compared with 55 per cent for the best conventional plants,

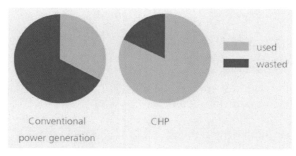

Figure 8.10 *With conventional grid-generated electricity about two-thirds of the energy in the fuel is wasted (blue in the left circle). With combined heat and power, one-eighth or less is wasted (right hand circle), as the heat is captured as well and since it is used locally there are no transmission losses*

Source: EST (2005b)

and so less fuel needs to be consumed to produce the same amount of useful energy. CHP plants are ideal for the community context.

The most appropriate applications of CHP are likely to be on housing estates with a minimum density of 50 dwellings per hectare that already have communal heating from central boiler houses, as the existing heat distribution systems can often be re-used. The local electricity distribution systems will need to be modified and a net metering contract negotiated to sell any surplus electricity to the grid.

Or the system can be sized to match the base heating load, with conventional stand-by boilers meeting the peak thermal load. Here, overall carbon emissions will be slightly higher because less mains electricity is 'displaced'. In the summer there may be a surplus of heat, which would need to be stored as hot water, allowing the plant to be used intermittently.

Renewable gas

In the future, mains gas will become increasingly more sustainable as anaerobic digestion plants will begin feeding the biogas that they produce into the gas network, with which it is completely compatible. Anaerobic digestion takes food, animal or biomass waste and composts it under special conditions to produce the gas, methane. A municipal authority could even construct an anaerobic digestion plant for locally collected waste and burn the output biogas in an adjacent CHP plant for local supply of heat and electricity.

Micro-CHP

This is the same principle on a smaller scale. We discussed this topic in the heating section, because the primary motivation for installing micro-CHP is to provide heat. However, while on it, it can also deliver an electrical supply of around 1kW (fuel cell types will produce more) and more if the units are to supply several dwellings, say in a small block of flats. Most homes which have access to the gas mains can have gas-powered micro-CHP, although it is not mainstream yet in terms of production and availability.

Photovoltaic electricity

This is the type of shiny solar panel which most people think of when it comes to home generated electricity. Expectations have been high for many years that photovoltaics (PV) will achieve mass-market breakthrough. It remains expensive but efficiencies are improving and the price is coming down. The new UK feed-in tariff should make it an attractive option for many building owners with more or less guaranteed pay-back periods and thereafter income from the PV array.

Figures 8.11–8.13 *Photovoltaic roof tiles being installed on a suburban roof and the final appearance*

Note: Two 'Sunny Boy' inverters control the electrical conversion from DC to AC and the exporting of surplus electricity to the grid.

Source: © Chris Twinn

On average in temperate countries, on an equator-facing roof, 20m² of panel will generate 2kW and 100Wp of capacity will give you around 70–75kWh over the year. This is a very rough guide and detailed calculations will need to be made based upon the site and the insulation figures. The economics depends on the energy and funding regime in each country.

Feed-in tariffs

In parts of the world where feed-in tariffs have been introduced by governments, PV panels have become a more familiar sight on roofs. These financial carrots guarantee payment to householders for the electricity they generate way over the market rate in order to encourage them to install renewable technologies and speed up their spread into the mass market. This has been remarkably successful wherever they have been introduced.

To illustrate the difference it can make consider the case of Jerry Clark's house in Cornwall, admittedly one of the sunniest spots in the British Isles. This system comprises eight Sanyo 215W panels with an installed rating of 1.72kWp. This was commissioned in 2008 and during the first year of operation generated 1824kWh, which he says equates to around 1060kWh per year per kWp (kilowatt-peak) installed. Jerry calculates that if he had waited until the feed-in tariff had come in, in April 2010, his payback time would have been roughly halved, to 12 years.

Figure 8.14 *A wireless solar powered burglar alarm means that there's no worry about the connecting cables piercing the airtight membrane of the building, maintenance or the financial and environmental cost of its energy supply*

With micro-CHP

PV electricity generation can make a good partner to CHP (at district or dwelling scale), since it can supplement the latter's electricity production, particularly in the summer when the CHP plant may not be operating because no heating is needed. The electricity can be distributed via the same on-site distribution system and any surplus power from both sources may be sold to the grid via the same net metering contract.

Integrated with roofs or cladding

PV comes in forms for integration into cladding and roofs. You can even buy them disguised as roofing tiles and therefore if a new roof or cladding is being put on a building, that is an ideal time to invest in photovoltaics.

Economies of scale

Photovoltaics can work financially better on larger scales and at greater capacities because the fixed costs of the grid connection, getting the construction crew on-site, the administration and so on, become proportionately less as the size of the installation grows. This brings down the cost of each individual installed watt.

Environmental impacts of photovoltaics

Solar panels use silicon and hence much of the same technology in manufacture as the industry that makes computer chips. Some panels use other potentially toxic materials such as cadmium and gallium. A report, published in January 2009 called 'Towards a just and sustainable solar energy industry' (Silicon Valley Toxics Coalition, 2009), lists all the corrosive and toxic chemicals used in their production including the greenhouse gases sulphur hexafluoride (SF_6) and nitrogen trifluoride (NF_3). The first of these two chemicals is 25,000 times worse than carbon dioxide in its global warming ability. The second is used to clean reactors and etch polysilicon semiconductors and is 17,200 times worse than CO_2; furthermore it emits toxic fumes when burned or reacted and can cause breathing problems. Writing about a report published in May 2009 (van der Meulen and Alsema, 2009) its co-author Erik Alsema says 'The problem of SF_6 or NF_3 emission may occur with some production processes for thin film solar cells, especially with thin film silicon or amorphous silicon'. On this basis, mono and poly or multicrystalline silicon panels should be preferred (the vast majority are anyway) until more information about life cycle impacts becomes available, otherwise the carbon payback of the panels might be longer than their lifetime! (See also Fthenakis and Alsema, 2006).

The Silicon Valley report is of the opinion that there may be no cause for alarm in countries with well-regulated environmental pollution regimes, but increasingly solar panels are being manufactured in China and other parts of the world where it's not clear that such controls exist. The report also draws attention to the problems posed at the end of the panels' lives on how to recycle or dispose of them. This is another subject on which insufficient evidence is currently available.

Wind power

Some dwellings can make use of wind turbines, and indeed generate more than their own electricity needs, but this is only going to be possible in a minority of cases. Sadly, domestic scale wind turbines are generally only effective in rural areas. Lower wind speeds in urban areas coupled with the turbulence caused by nearby buildings mean that the wind speeds required for modern turbines to work efficiently very rarely occur in towns and cities.

This has been established by a substantial monitoring exercise of real micro-wind turbines both on urban rooftops and free standing in rural areas, published in July 2009 by the EST (2009). To operate efficiently turbines do require a tower and no surrounding obstructions in the direction of the prevailing wind. As the report says: 'a properly sited and positioned 6kW rated free standing pole mounted turbine ... would be expected to generate approximately 18,000kWh per annum'. It represents a very quick payback.

The success of a wind turbine is measured by its load factor and the higher the number the better. The performance of free standing turbines in the survey frequently exceeded the manufacturers' quoted annual load factors of 17 per cent; the average was 19 per cent and the best were 30 per cent. By abysmal contrast, 'No urban or suburban building mounted sites generated more than 200kWh or £26 per annum, corresponding to load factors of 3% or less.'

Where micro wind works

Turbines need an uninterrupted wind flow and the higher above the ground the more wind there is. This is why they are commonly mounted on poles 10m or 25m above the ground and in exposed places. The same survey by the Energy Saving Trust estimates that in the UK 1.9 per cent of homes are situated in conditions like this and can make use of wind power. That is 455,650 households.

If all those households installed 6kW wind turbines then the annual generation from them would be in the order of 3459GWh. This is the amount of electricity used by twice that number of homes – approximately 870,000, or nearly 1 per cent of the UK's electricity requirements and over 3 per cent of its domestic demand. They would need to be grid connected – and could generate an income. Even without feed-in tariffs, the payback period is something like six or seven years under these conditions (this depends mainly on annual average wind speeds). Of course turbines can be bought that generate more than 6kW.

Calculating the power

The UK has some of the windiest locations in Europe and not all countries would be expected to have the same proportion. The annual average wind speed needs to be greater than 5m/s and is preferably monitored with an anemometer for 12 months before designing the system, but desktop evaluation can be made first to see if it's worthwhile doing this by looking at figures from the weather monitoring agency in your country. This usually provides information accurate to 1km squares, but because local conditions can vary enormously – for example due to thermal updraughts, local topography or sea breezes – there is nothing like real on-site measurement.

Once the average wind speed is known, then it is useful to examine manufacturers' brochures. These contain power/energy curves like the one illustrated, which allow you to read off how much power/energy you would

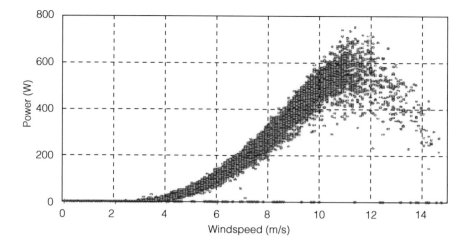

Figure 8.15 *Example of a wind turbine power curve*

Source: EST (2009)

generate from that wind speed. Of course turbines can be bought which generate more than 6kW.

Buyers also need to be aware that they will need to purchase control equipment and inverters that convert the DC electricity to the mains quality AC that their appliances will need. As with photovoltaic systems, it's best to commission experts – and obtain competing quotes first.

Conclusion

We've reached the limit of what can be done on a per dwelling basis to generate electricity. We have discovered exactly what we found with rainwater collection and greywater recycling: there's no point in trying to make each dwelling self-sufficient. It's like trying to be self-sufficient in food. Even with one acre of land per household using intensive permaculture growing and a backbreaking 60-hour week with no holidays you would still struggle to produce enough food to feed a family, at the level of quality at which we are currently used to living. This is just the reality of what a carbon-based economy has gotten us used to: relative luxury and year-round plenty.

Renewable electricity is generally, but not always, more cost efficient when done on a larger scale than on a smaller scale. But there are also advantages in generating electricity close to where it is used – it can eliminate the need for a new power-distribution infrastructure and also avoid losses in power lines over long distances. However, decentralized electricity can probably only ever be a small percentage of the overall power mix. Installing a national renewable energy network is really a job for utilities, energy service companies, governments and municipalities. Schemes at the level of apartment blocks, streets or districts generally make more economic sense.

Meanwhile, probably the best option for the majority of householders is to simply sign up to a proper, certified renewable energy tariff from a reputable electricity supplier that really is investing in new build renewable energy, and spend their money wisely on the cost-effective energy-saving measures.

References

EST (2005a) 'CE56 – Cost benefit of lighting', EST, London

EST (2005b) 'CE102 – New and renewable energy technologies for existing housing', EST, London

EST (2009) 'Location, location, location – The Energy Saving Trust's Field Trial Report on Domestic Wind Turbines', EST, London

Fthenakis, V. and Alsema, E. (2006) 'Photovoltaics energy payback times, greenhouse gas emissions and external costs: 2004–early 2005 status', *Progress in Photovoltaics: Research and Applications*, vol 14, pp275–280

Fung, A. S., Aulenback, A., Ferguson, A. and Ugursa, V. I. (2003) 'Standby power requirements of household appliances in Canada', *Energy and Buildings*, vol 35, issue 2, pp217–228

Silicon Valley Toxics Coalition (2009) 'Towards a just and sustainable solar energy industry', Silicon Valley Toxics Coalition, California

van der Meulen, R. and Alsema, E. (2009) 'Fluoride gas emissions from amorphous and micromorphous silicon solar cell production: Emission estimates and LCA results', Copernicus Institute/Utrecht University, the Netherlands

9

Contextual Issues

A truly sustainable building will concentrate not just on its own energy and water management but also on all the materials used in the renovation and the responsibility that comes with using them. There is also the question of the external environment and its integration with the life of the building. Finally, the ease with which the occupants can live with and maintain their home will contribute greatly to its sustainability.

Supply chain

Different countries are at different stages in the development of a mature market for products used in sustainable renovation and building. More and more materials and products are coming on to the market in terms of installation, windows, plumbing and airtightness. This means that for project managers, sourcing materials that are reliable and economic is a major part of the planning process. It is time-consuming and advice should be sought from professional organizations which often have online forums where questions can be posed and answers may already have been posted.

Amongst the issues to consider in sourcing materials and the integrity of the supply line are: embodied energy, manufacturing impacts, labour conditions, distance of materials, transportation and disposal at end of life. Then there is the issue of building waste management.

Reducing waste when building and renovating

Up to a third of all waste generated in some countries is construction waste and up to a quarter of materials bought for construction are thrown away unused. Latest figures show that Germany recycles over 80 per cent of its construction waste and Denmark over 90 per cent, but other countries are lagging behind.

The waste hierarchy is to prevent, reduce, reuse and recycle, in that order, before considering sending to landfill. You prevent it in the first place by only ordering what is required and by reusing materials from elsewhere. Good project management includes exact calculations of materials that will be used. Just-in-time logistics and having somewhere protected to store materials minimize damage due to poor storage or weather. Sourcing

Figure 9.1 *Exterior patio tiles made from recycled glass: Glasscrete*

Buying recyclable products made from recycled materials creates a market demand for recycling and a virtuous circle

Source: © Spartan Tiles

Figures 9.2 and 9.3 *Reusing materials can stimulate creativity*

In Lacemaker's House, Nottingham, these cardboard tubes from a carpet company would have been landfilled, but here provide attractive, unusual heat and sound insulation, while the old bottles, cut in half, form a distinctive window, projecting aesthetically pleasing patterns.

unwanted, surplus or second-hand materials 'closes the loop' by turning waste back into resources and is not as hard as you think. Potential sources include:

- online builders' surplus recycling exchanges can be used to pass on leftover building supplies or materials and also find fantastic, low cost or free building materials in your area, e.g. www.builderscrap.com;
- Freecycle (www.freecycle.org) permits the advertising and swapping of surplus materials;
- facilities such as industrial symbiosis (e.g. in the UK www.nisp.org.uk) can advise on resource efficiency through 'the commercial trading of materials, energy and water and sharing assets, logistics and expertise' on a municipal scale.

The priority of choice of materials to use should ideally be:

1 second-hand/reusing;
2 recycled materials;
3 renewable or local, new materials;
4 new materials from further away.

The exception is when more distantly sourced materials will save more energy over the lifetime of the building. Reusing materials generally uses far less energy than recycling them, which involves processing and transportation costs. For sourcing new materials, the table below shows the typical embodied energy of many common materials (in practice it can vary widely). This table gives a reasonable indication of the amount of environmental damage caused by a substance, but it should be balanced by the actual amount of the material you use and its environmental benefit. A website, T-zero, is a free tool that provides independent sustainable refurbishment advice, 'with the option of linking directly to the suppliers' (www.tzero.org.uk).

Designing for deconstruction

Using standard sizes for building elements such as windows and doors can prevent future waste. Designing for sustainable deconstruction involves specifying components which can easily be disassembled and recycled at the end of the building's life. Natural materials are usually easier to recycle than plastics or composites. Specific detailing for the easy deconstruction of buildings is becoming increasingly available. A free, downloadable Scottish resource (www.seda2.org/dfd/) contains such detailing and looks at the context and principles before revealing five typical construction details that allow easy deconstruction for recycling or reuse. It means designing assemblies with independent components that can be removed without affecting each other. Some fixings are easier to dissemble than others – from screws at one end of the scale to strong adhesive and rivets at the other. If you specify 'fixing-free'

Embodied energy

Energy requirements for manufacturing and/or producing some building materials by volume and weight:

Material	kWh/tonne	kWh/m³
Fletton bricks	175	300
Non-fletton bricks	860	1462
Engineering bricks	1120	2016
Clay tiles	800	1520
Concrete tiles	300	630
Local stone tiles	200	450
Local slates	200	540
Single layer roof membrane	45,000	47,000
Concrete 1:3:6	275	600
Concrete 1:2:4	360	800
Lightweight blocks	500	600
Autoclaved blocks	1300	800
Natural sand/aggregate	30	45
Crushed granite aggregate	100	150
Lightweight aggregate	500	300
Cement	2200	2860
Sand/cement render	277	400
Plaster/plasterboard	890	900
Steel	13,200	103,000
Copper	15,000	133,000
Aluminium	27,000	75,600
Timber (imported softwood)	1450	754
Timber (local airdried)	200	110
Timber (local greenoak)	200	220
Glass	9200	23,000
Plastics	45,000	47,000
Plastic insulation		1125
Mineral wool		230
Cellulose insulation		133
Woodwool (loose)		900

Source: Pat Borer, Centre for Alternative Technology

zones in structural timber, good lengths of defect-free timber may one day be re-used. If you consider insulation as a separate layer it can be repaired or replaced more easily without disrupting the airtightness.

Natural materials are ultimately biodegradable or combustible (the energy content can be partly reclaimed). Durability of materials is a significant factor: some can perish or crack more easily than others in different conditions. All the different service systems should also be installed in a way that allows them to be accessed, repaired or easily replaced.

Creating a log that describes all you have done during construction and how the building works in terms of maintenance, running, replacement and alterations, will be an invaluable tool for occupants and later deconstruction. It can include photographs and even videos.

Waste handling on site

During construction, skips or bins should be set aside for different types of waste for ease of reuse, sale or recycling – builders and contractors should be encouraged to separate waste into these bins for this purpose. Some materials can be resold or swapped using Freecycle or similar services, to reduce your budget. The Considerate Constructors Scheme (www.ccscheme.org.uk) offers a voluntary code of practice that can be used during construction to help minimize waste, noise and inconvenience to local residents.

The most common types of waste are:

- packaging (plastic and cardboard), particularly of roofing materials and installation;
- insulation materials and plasterboard;
- rubble.

Waste management tools

- 'SWMP Builder' is a free tool available from Envirowise (http://tinyurl.com/yzql94p) to help in waste management in construction by organising all the likely types and quantities of waste arising from the project, stage by stage and offering options for its management
- The SMARTWasteTM System (www.smartwaste.co.uk) is a similar tool developed by the Building Research Establishment (BRE) who developed the SMARTWaste (Site Methodology to Audit, Reduce and Target Waste) system for a step-by-step evaluation of waste and its generation.

Soil

It is very important to protect soil. Soil is a valuable resource, so this means that either it shouldn't have to be imported or covered up by rubble. You should use excavated soil on site, or sell it to a recycling contractor. Remember that some packaging waste, especially cardboard, is compostable and can be disposed of on site. You can bury rubble in a hole or pile and place compostable material on top of it, such as cardboard, wood, sawdust or paper, when landscaping the garden, perhaps placing glass or a rockery over it, or use it as hardcore beneath paths or extensions.

Only as a last resort should materials be sent to landfill.

Other sourcing tips

Life-cycle analysis

Most sourcing issues revolve around life cycle analysis, which is an attempt to quantify the impact of a material or process or service over its lifetime. In the case of complex products, this would have to include all the materials involved in production. It would also include end-of-life disposal, which is not always something we can be confident about, as it lies in the future. Life cycle analysis is an imprecise science, because it depends what is being measured. Are we taking into account acidification, off-gassing, impacts of mining, employment conditions and so on? It is important to make sure we are comparing like with like. Often only rough guides can be given, and these can be wildly inaccurate.

Timber

In certain sectors, however, attempts are made to verify supply chains just as they are made in waste streams where notes are carried along with waste in order to keep track of it. Two of the best known and most successful of these are the FSC (Forest Stewardship Council) and PEFC Council (Programme for the Endorsement of Forest Certification). These are supposed to guarantee that timber comes from a sustainable source. Always make sure your source timber is labelled in this fashion if it is new and is not supplied locally from a source you know – which is preferable because there is less transport impact.

Walls and floors

Masonry is usually highly durable. However, the quality of the mortar and workmanship can affect its lifetime and must be repaired with a sympathetic material. Well-repointed and well-maintained walls will only need attention once every hundred years or so.

Masonry is not completely waterproof and breathes, and in areas facing driving rain may need further protection. Silicon water seal is safe to use in these situations as long as precautions are taken to avoid condensation within as the wall is made vapour-impermeable in both directions.

Lime

If you need a breathing wall, lime mortar is ideal, especially for old and historic buildings. Lime mortar is not a cement mortar with hydrated lime added. It comes premixed, blending fat lime putty with selected aggregates. The colour and texture of the original mortar must be considered unless the brickwork is to be limewashed. Traditional fat lime mortars are used differently from modern mortar. Your supplier will be able to advise you.

Hydraulic lime is produced from limestone containing clay, which means it can set without being exposed to the air (in water). It is ideal in harsh climatic or buried conditions. Hydraulic lime gains strength over time and is flexible, so expansion joints are not required. It is more environmentally friendly than cement and is reclaimable and reusable.

Advantages of lime

- lower firing temperature than cement so less polluting;
- breathable and flexible;
- easier to re-use bonded masonry;
- less cold bridging than cement;
- re-absorbs the CO_2 emitted by its firing as it sets, but the more hydraulic the lime, the less CO_2 is reabsorbed.

Limecrete is a further alternative to concrete and is also breathable. It can be used in solid floors. Glaster is another sustainable product made from lime: a blend of lime and 20 per cent recycled glass aggregate that can be made into plasters, renders and mortars and used as a more benign substitute for conventional materials; for example, for traditional lime plaster made with sand. It may be painted with a vapour-permeable paint or left as it is. Roughcast renders made of coarser glaster are ideal for exterior use. Glaster screeds are used with lime screed floors and compatible with underfloor heating. They can be ordered in mixes of various levels of hydraulic-ness and aggregates. A coat of limewash comes in many different colours and gives a beautiful, soft, warm finish, inside or out.

Finishes and paints

Choosing environmental paints and finishes is about preserving your hard-won healthy internal atmosphere and breathability of the surfaces where appropriate while at the same time protecting materials. Of course you also want it to look good as well! Clay paints and those which use natural oils and pigments are favoured as they are vapour permeable and likely to be less harmfully polluting during manufacture. Some paints fully declare their constituents and origin – so you can have a 'green' wash without the greenwash.

There is evidence that paint finishes which give off volatile organic compounds (VOCs) can affect those with breathing difficulties and allergic responses. Studies used by the American Lung Association suggest an increased prevalence of respiratory problems consistent with higher VOC levels in freshly painted homes. Paints are often labelled on the tins: you can choose paints with low (0.3–7.99 per cent), minimal (up to 0.29 per cent) or no VOCs.

One VOC is formaldehyde, emitted by many materials such as paints, adhesives, wall boards and ceiling tiles. It irritates the mucous membranes.

VOCs can also off-gas from new furnishings and equipment such as photocopy machines. Most products containing natural materials and oils will emit no or low VOCs and certain houseplants are much better at absorbing these gases than others. Non-solvent based brick cleaning agents are also available for exterior use. They don't contain hydrochloric acid and will not harm surrounding grass and plants.

Floor coverings

Natural (rather than synthetic) floor coverings are also available, for example:

- linoleum made completely from natural ingredients without VOCs or other toxic chemicals. It may be installed with solvent free adhesives and one product needs no adhesives;
- wool, flax, sisal and other hard wearing natural substances are available in many types of carpet, rug and floor covering;
- underlays for carpets are available made out of old tyres – recycled rubber.

Drains and ironmongery

Use vitrified clay pipes for drains and steel or copper for gutters and downpipes rather than PVC, for reasons outlined in the section on PVC and windows.

Integration with the environment

A building occupies land which would otherwise naturally harbour a thriving ecosystem of one sort or another. Integration of the built environment with the natural one benefits both the environment and the occupants. For example, plants can:

- provide habitats for species of insects and the birds which feed on them;
- combat the 'heat island' effect whereby urban areas become too hot in summer;
- moderate humidity and air quality;
- absorb carbon dioxide and other pollutants and emit oxygen;
- produce food;
- be attractive;
- improve human well-being.

The use of plants in conservatories and porches provides a pleasant halfway point between the inside and the outside. Outside, plants can be both productive and decorative – for example blossoming fruit and nut trees and bushes, of which there are many varieties. Some herbs and salad vegetables can grow all year round.

Plants and emissions reductions

Leisure time spent in gardens reduces the climate impact of more journeys to further destinations.

Growing food also cuts down the transport and other embodied energy of food we buy in supermarkets. A study cited by the Leopold Centre for Sustainable Agriculture, Iowa State University (2001) says that 'growing just 10% more produce in a regional system would result in an annual savings of 1.2 million to 1.4 million litres of fuel and an annual reduction in carbon dioxide emissions of 3 to 3.5 million kg'. In many parts of the world food is even grown on balconies and window ledges.

One source of these plants is Plants for the Future, which holds a bank of unusual and endangered species of productive and non-productive indigenous and imported plants. These plants are listed on its website www.pfaf.org.

Labour-saving productive gardens

To reduce the labour and climate-harming energy cost of mowing lawns, consider instead having a wildflower meadow area, which will attract plenty of beautiful insects and birds. This only needs to be cut twice a year, and can even be done the old-fashioned way – with a scythe! You can save more hard work by using bark mulch in between the plants, sourced locally perhaps from a recycling company to reduce maintenance. Any compost used must be peat free.

Part of the philosophy accompanying the labour-saving gardening concept is permaculture, which argues that learning from the inter-relatedness of natural ecosystems increases biodiversity and productivity without making it hard work for you. Two examples of this discipline, which overlaps with a related discipline sometimes called bioclimatic architecture, are the use of green roofs and green walls.

Green walls

Imagine shelves holding plants fixed on to an exterior wall of a building. Most popular in France and Mediterranean countries, this is a method of both maximizing the growing capacity of an area of land and altering the cooling and heating character of the building. A Victorian terrace renovation with a south facing front wall in Nottingham is installing green shelves, intended to support a 'library' of strawberry species that fruit at different times of the year. The shelves are made of timber or polypropylene plastic containers, geotextiles, irrigation systems, a growing medium and vegetation.

Gravity-fed irrigation is essential to avoid the need for a pump. Depending on the climate, water could be fed directly as an occasional night-time trickle system from water collected from the roof above or by mains water. Some systems are more complex than others. They should be mounted away from the wall.

Green façades is a fancy phrase for plants climbing either directly up a wall or on specially designed supporting structures. The plant is rooted in the ground.

Green roofs

These are a great addition to any building whose roof is not too steep and whose structure is strong enough to support the weight. Besides the above advantages, they absorb run-off to storm sewers, increase thermal mass and reduce summer overheating. They do not really improve insulation.

Green roofs consist of:

- a timber or aluminium frame;
- a layer of fleece to protect the membrane above it;
- a waterproof membrane (often butyl), which must be robust enough to last for many years; water must be able to run off this into a drainage system;
- a filter sheet that allows water through but not fine particles;
- another fleece layer that holds water, such as geotextile;
- a substrate or growing medium, usually an aggregate such as recycled crushed concrete, bricks, chippings, gravel or clay pellets; sand or soil may be placed on top;
- a few clumps of sedum or whatever plants you want.

Sedums are succulents, which store water and are drought resistant and spread across the ground rather than grow upwards. They attract butterflies and the roof will soon establish its own ecosystem and be colonized by spiders and insects (many of which are becoming rare) which provide a source of food for insectivorous birds. High roofs away from predators can be safe preserves for rare invertebrates and ground-nesting birds.

It is easier to make a green roof on a flat roof than a sloping one. The structure must be strong enough to take the weight. In building circles there is some controversy about the embodied energy of green roofs, but this must be balanced against the embodied energy of whatever would be there as a roof surface instead. On balance it probably doesn't make much difference. Unless punctured, the liner will last longer than otherwise as it is protected from ultraviolet light and extremes of temperature, so will need to be replaced less often.

They require little maintenance, perhaps annual tidying, and are usually only accessed for maintenance.

A study on green roofs in the Greater Manchester area found that they can 'have a dramatic effect on maximum surface temperatures, keeping temperatures below the 1961–1990 current form case for all time periods and emissions scenarios. Roof greening makes the biggest difference...where the building proportion is high and the evaporative fraction is low. Thus, the largest difference was made in the town centres.' Manchester City Council is now considering whether to mandate the use of green roofs as part of planning requirements in line with its low carbon policies. It has a pilot scheme on five buildings in the South Manchester corridor.

Toronto in Canada already has legislation requiring up to 50 per cent green roof coverage on multi-unit residential dwellings over six stories, schools, non-profit housing, commercial and industrial buildings. Larger residential projects must have green roofs on 20–50 per cent of the roof area. But Chicago is leading the way, being the city with the most green roofs in the world: 50,911m^2. Washington DC comes second with 46,548m^2.

Figure 9.4 *One of the UK's largest green roof projects atop Ethelred Estate, in Central London, adjacent to the Thames*

Note: Tenants opted for this sedum roof, part of a major refurbishment of these blocks of flats by Lambeth Council, despite the slightly higher cost, because of the perceived benefits to wildlife and surge flood amelioration.

Source: © Lambeth Council

The Ethelred Estate, Central London, is a residential regeneration project on 10 medium-rise buildings and is the largest green roof refurbishment in the UK at 4000m², It is a sedum roof based on a geo-textile fleece with a nylon-loop substrate matrix.

Reference

Leopold Centre for Sustainable Agriculture, Iowa State University (2001) 'Food, fuel and freeways', available at www.leopold.iastate.edu/pubs/staff/ppp/food_mil.pdf, last accessed February 2010

Index

Made in the USA
Middletown, DE
08 October 2021